LIFE IN THE PAST LANE

VOLUME ONE

A LOOK INTO MEDIA HISTORY THROUGH
THE EYES OF THOSE WHO MADE IT!

BY JASON HILL

LIFE IN THE PAST LANE—VOLUME ONE
©2013 Jason Hill

Published in the USA by:

BEARMANOR MEDIA
P.O. BOX 71426
ALBANY, GEORGIA 31708
www.BearManorMedia.com

ISBN-10: 1-59393-746-6 (alk. paper)
ISBN-13: 978-1-59393-746-1 (alk. paper)

DESIGN AND LAYOUT: VALERIE THOMPSON

TABLE OF CONTENTS

DEDICATION

For NORMAN CORWIN
Who gave me the confidence to put this together.
He was always there for me.

ACKNOWLEDGMENTS

My deepest gratitude goes out to Michaela Nelson for all of her aid in doing the final edit of some difficult material and also for educating a total Luddite on the many uses of a computer.

Additional praise must go to Paula Slade for getting me through some of the technicalities involved in the publishing business.

I must also thank all of the many folks who gave so much of their precious time to allow me to do these interviews. Without them, I would have nothing.

J. H.

FOREWORD/
PROGRAM NOTES

Welcome to my tribute to the wonderful world of the media. There have been many, many volumes written about various forms of those creative arts, but this will be a different approach. Instead of just relating cold facts, I will present the information in the words of some of the marvelous folks who attempted day-by-day and year-by-year to keep us informed and entertained. I will offer, for your reading pleasure, recollections of a variety of people from assorted genres. The strength of this is enhanced by the fact that nearly all of those included are no longer with us and can no longer speak for themselves. There are a few notable exceptions. In the latter part of the 1980s, I wrote and produced a series of broadcasts, which I called *Life in the Past Lane*.

My purpose was to interview, in depth, as many actors, writers, producers, directors, and musicians as I could find—plus one very knowledgeable personal manager—to find out what each might have to say about his or her contributions and feelings toward their facet or facets of show business. Each of these discussions was at least two hours in duration. They were recorded in their entirety and then edited to program length. There were eighty-five shows *in toto*. Out of them, for this first Volume, I have chosen to focus on just a few of them in order to give each his/her due props.

INTRODUCTION/ OVERTURE

The chronological beginning of this story would seem to have to be in the days of the vaudevillians that tramped coast to coast and beyond to entertain audiences large and small. It was a stressful occupation, one which offered mostly minimal financial remuneration. Most fared poorly while others did quite well and moved on to bigger and better things in terms of stage, screen, radio and television.

For now, we will consider just four of them (although there were many examples of careers that sprung from Vaudeville). My choices are four of the most successful products of that revered form of show business, selected, not because of direct access, but rather, because of personal contact with close associates. There will be much more about them in Act II, but for now, we speak only of beginnings. These four are household names: Jack Benny, Mary Livingstone, George Burns and Gracie Allen.

It has often been said, and it was true, that Vaudeville actors brought their spouses into their acts for two reasons. First, it was a good way to keep expenses down and second, maybe even more important, they could keep an eye on each other. In our examples, both reasons applied.

Let us begin with a would-be concert violinist, Benjamin Kubelsky, who began his career playing his fiddle with the pit orchestra at the Barrison Theatre in Waukegan, Illinois at the age of fourteen, while also doubling as an usher. This got him into all sorts of trouble at home as well as at Central High School, where he was a freshman. As it turned out, that would be his last year of formal education, a year he did not complete because the school thought him to be a lost cause. It was something he regretted until his dying day.

When he began his career at the Barrison he was still using his birth name, but as time went by, and for many reasons, his name underwent a gradual transition to the one familiar to us all. First, he was forced to lose Kubelsky by lawyers due to concert violinist Jan Kubelic, who feared for his reputation. He agreed to Ben K. Benny while working an act with Cora Salisbury, a 45-year-old pianist who needed a partner. When Cora left the act, he teamed with Lyman Woods in another piano/violin duo dubbed *From Grand Opera to Ragtime*. They worked all the way up to the Palace Theatre in New York, where they were not well received.

In 1917, he took a hiatus from Vaudeville, joined the Navy and before long found himself entertaining his fellow Servicemen, still with his violin. He was not necessarily a hit—however, before he would let them boo him off the stage, he saved the day ... with his mouth.

This was his first real stand-up act in a style he would develop through the years. Before long, his audience was rolling in the aisles. He had found his identity.

Returning to the Vaudeville stage as a single, *A Few Minutes with Ben Benny*, using his violin less and his words and actions more, he once again ran afoul of lawyers. This time it was Ben Bernie who objected to his name, claiming it was too confusing. For the last time, he changed his moniker, and became Jack Benny.

While all this was going on, another very young man was working his way up the Vaudeville ladder. He began at an even earlier age, dropping out of school in the fourth grade to enter show business full time. Prior to that, he and three friends started singing together as *The Pewee Quartet*, performing in saloons, on ferries, in brothels and on street corners, where they passed the hat for contributions.

He went into Vaudeville, doing whatever it took to keep him going. Somewhere along the way, very early on, two things happened that would remain with him throughout his long life. The first was a permanent name change from Nathan Birnbaum to George Burns. He arrived at the name by drawing from several sources. Two were a pair of major league baseball players named George H. Burns and George J. Burns. Also, his brother was named

George. The final source may be the best reason, if you have a sense of humor. He recalled the Burns Brother's Coal Company where he used to find coal before it was lost. The other trait he picked up at an early age was his lifelong cigar habit, always El Productos.

He worked with limited success as a single and with a series of girl partners until he found Gracie Allen. All of the sudden everything began to fall into place

Gracie had been working while attending Star of the Sea convent school, in an act with her three older sisters called *The Four Colleens.* In 1909, she went into Vaudeville with her sister Bessie who was by then a seasoned performer. In 1922, she met and joined George Burns in his act. The two were soon a big hit. It did not happen right away, but when George noticed that she was getting more laughs doing her straight lines than he was delivering the gags, he turned the formula around. It worked amazingly well, right up until Gracie retired many years later.

Mary Livingstone (birth name: Sadie Marx) was a cousin of the Marx Brothers, who also spent years on the circuits. During those years, they had become acquainted with Jack Benny. In 1919, Zeppo Marx set up a blind date for Jack with young Sadie, who was only fourteen at the time. They did not hit it off. Jack walked out in the middle of dinner, for which he paid dearly. The next evening Sadie and a number of her friends showed up in the front row of the theatre and heckled Jack relentlessly until he almost walked off the stage. No matter what he said or did, they refused to react the way he wanted his audience to.

Move the clock forward a few years and another blind date for Jack and Sadie, whom he did not remember from their first encounter. This time the results were more positive and they began to see each other regularly. At the same time, she was still going out with other men and even got engaged to one of them. Jack tried to tell her she was too young to marry. He also realized he was falling in love with her. He proposed, even though he was afraid of the commitment. They were married in 1927.

Quite by accident, Sadie was forced into her reluctant acting career in the radio days because of the last-minute illness of one of the people on Jack's show. The character she played was named Mary Livingstone–a small part. As time went by, the role grew, so

Sadie legally changed her name, but she never really wanted to be a performer.

That is enough of a foundation—just a teaser for Act II.

ACT I:
SILENTS PLEASE!

Finding someone who could speak with first person authority about the days of silent movies was not an easy task even back in 1987; however, with a little help from some Hollywood friends, I was able to locate a man who admirably filled the bill.

He was a man who first appeared on stage at the tender age of six months. He was in his first movie at the ripe old age of fifteen months. How could this be? The answer lies in the field of genetics.

To begin with, his maternal grandmother starred on the San Francisco stage and also ran a very successful drama school in Oakland. In the next generation, both of his parents were actors in silent films, giving him a natural entre into the medium as he grew up. By age six, he too was deeply involved in the genre. It was an adventurous time in the life of a small boy. It may not have been the most prestigious segment of his long career, but, as he himself said, it was the most fun.

I am referring to True Boardman. Here is what he had to say on February 4, 1987.

****

JASON: True, I'm sure you don't consider those baby days as real acting, but it wasn't too many years later when you were in the *Bronco Billy* movies.

TRUE: That's right. I was a kid in the *Bronco Billy* series. Fortunately, I have a couple of prints of them that

I got from the Library of Congress. A little later came some others called *The Hazards of Helen* starring Helen Gibson. *Hazards of Helen* was in competition with *The Perils of Pauline*. I remember being rescued off a boxcar by Helen Gibson, racing along at the side of the boxcar. Even more exciting was one where they put me in the cab of a big locomotive. The engineer showed me how to push the rod to start it. So I get up there and the camera rolls. I push the rod and the engine starts moving. Well, the script said that a kid was supposed to get it going and it would soon become a runaway headed for the inevitable open bridge where it was going to fall into the raging river down below, losing both train and child. The valiant Helen, hearing of this, jumps on her horse and gallops along to catch up with the train. At the very last moment, she clambers aboard and pulls the rod. The engine stops with the cowcatcher actually hanging over the abyss ready to fall. Obviously, there was a real engineer in the cab but I did get up there and push the rod, toot the whistle and look scared as it rocketed along, kind of fun for a five year old.

JASON: I know of another incident that wasn't so much fun. It had to do with a shotgun.

TRUE: In that scene, I had a sister. She and I were playing Cowboys and Indians. At one point I was supposed to shoot her, you know, bang, bang. I picked up my father's shotgun. As a kid, I thought it wasn't loaded. One thing they neglected to tell me was that, since it was a double-barreled shotgun, it had two triggers. Foolishly, they thought that even one trigger would get the proper reaction, but I pulled both triggers and was knocked on my keester. Of course, everyone on the set was rolling with laughter except my mom. She came running up, grabbed me and said, "What are you doing to my child?" The prop man told her he had only loaded the gun with wadding and, anyhow, I wasn't supposed to pull both triggers. In the end, we all survived.

JASON: One time you had a very different problem with a member of the cast, someone called Snookie.

TRUE: Snookie was a chimp. There was a scene where I was riding beside Snookie on a cart propelled by a goat pushing from the back. In order to stop I was to pull up on a rope, raising the goat's head and making him stop. So, we were shooting the scene, going along, and the director yells out, "OK Trudie, pull back and stop the cart." So I pulled back on the deal. Snookie was sitting right beside me, and when I pulled back, my hand went right to her jaw. She was obviously startled. She grabbed my left hand and opened her huge mouth and simply pushed it against her upper teeth. She didn't really bite me. She just put my hand on her teeth. I was scared. I don't know whether I was crying or not. Then everyone came running over. They were concerned, but only relatively concerned compared to nowadays. If it happened today, they would rush me to a hospital and give me all kinds of shots. I think someone put some iodine on it and I said, "Gee, I'm sorry." I also told Snookie I was sorry. The second time I pulled with less vehemence. As a matter of fact, when we finished the scene—and this is hard to believe—that chimp put her big arms around me as if to say she too was sorry. I treasured the scars on hand for a long time. I'm looking now and I'm afraid they're all gone. After all, it was only sixty years ago. I don't know why they should be gone.

JASON: You know what they say, True, whoever **they** are, that time heals all wounds. Let's move on to something else. You were on the set for several Westerns. Is it true that in some scenes the Cowboys and the Indians were the same people?

TRUE: That really happened. They'd have ten or twelve men, sometimes more. In the morning they were Cowboys and then around noon they'd strip off their cowboy outfits, they'd put on Bolarnemia, a makeup that made their faces red, reddish brown. They'd put on their Indian outfits with feathers and what not. Then get on other horses or sometimes the same ones with their saddles taken off and blankets thrown over and ride through the same material. When it was cut together, they would be in front with the cowboys close behind. There was once–I'm sure it happened more than once because the story is legendary in Hollywood, but I have it on good authority that it happened at least once. The director said to the guys, who were getting three dollars a day, "In this scene when you come into clearing–this is where, if you remember, you shot your guns as Cowboys. Well, now you're the Indians ahead of them. When I shoot off my signal gun, every man who hits the dirt will get five dollars instead of three." Those guys all understood this. They went off out of camera range. When the director shouted for them to ride on in, they came riding in and when they heard the signal shot, twelve of the thirteen guys hit the dirt.

JASON: Now we know why the cowboys were such remarkable marksmen while riding at full tilt. There came a time in your youthful career when you were growing too fast for your own good.

TRUE: I started my last juvenile role when I was twelve,

almost thirteen. It was a wonderful part. It was a
film made by Gene Stratton Porter about a boy
named Michael O'Halloran. It was a very sentimental
yarn about a newsboy who finds a starving little
girl and decides to take care of her. When she gets
well, the script separates them. Irene Rich and Bill
Boyd were the adult stars. It was a marvelous part
for me, a thing I had hoped for since I was born.
They finished the film, but did not arrange a
release date while they were making it. It took
them two years to get it into theatres. It was very
well received and this twelve-year-old boy got some
nice reviews. There was only one problem. By then
that twelve-year-old boy had put on six inches. He
was a gangling teenager. He no longer looked like a
little news kid. So, when the casting directors
would send for me I wasn't the same character.
There weren't many adolescent jobs in those days
so for the first time in my life I was out of the
business. I did just about everything for a few
years from stock boy in a grocery store to elevator
operator to file clerk. I also taught English to
Rudolph Valentino's nephew who had just come
over from Italy.

JASON: Along the way, you got to rub elbows with some
very accomplished actors. One of them was Charles
Chaplin.

TRUE: I was in *Shoulder Arms* with Charlie Chaplin in
1917. They originally made it as a longer film.
The first part of it included his family, a big fat
wife and two pesky kids. Unfortunately, when we
finished it Charlie decided to release it as a four
reeler. Whatever happened to the additional three
reels, we'll never know. I even wrote to the Chaplin
Estate one time hoping to get some stills from it,
but I got no response. I did a film with Mary

Pickford in 1919, *Daddy Long Legs*. They did send me some stills of the sequence I was in so I have some evidence of that. I don't remember much of working with Mary Pickford, but I do remember well working with Charlie Chaplin. He was a rare man. It was a wonderful experience for an eight year old.

JASON: Moving on to your radio days, you began primarily as a writer.

TRUE: No, no, primarily as an actor. I was originally an actor and then for two or three years I was a writer/director. At one point when I was on staff at KHJ, I was a disc jockey. I was director of dramatics. I was a writer. I was an announcer on special programs. I also performed my own poetry program. One time, believe it or not, I wrote twenty-five scripts of one kind or another in a week. Most of those were music continuity scripts, but it did include three half hour dramas as well.

JASON: The only other people I can think of who were that prolific were Arch Oboler and Norman Corwin.

TRUE: Actually, I'm not sure they were doing as many scripts. They were doing what in those days, and probably still are, more prestigious scripts. I know Arch well and am very, very close to and fond of Norman Corwin. In my mind he was the peer of us all, a peer intellectually and in his creative skills. He is a remarkable, wonderful man. Anyone listening, who has not read his book, *Trivializing America*, should pick it up. I strongly recommend it. It is the work of a truly thinking, caring man. It concerns where our country is and where it should be going.

JASON: Let's talk about some of the radio shows you wrote. I know you wrote for *Lux Radio Theatre* and *Screen Guild Theatre*. I think you may have done the first *Screen Guild*.

TRUE: I did the very first one. Interestingly enough, there was recently a story of a man who was convicted of a mercy killing in Florida. While I was still on staff at KHJ, I wrote a script called *The Quality of Mercy*, which was performed by an actor named J. Donald Wilson, a character man. When *Screen Guild* started, I was in on some of the planning. I had been working for Young and Rubicam on *Silver Theatre*. They came to me and asked what they should do. I suggested that they should do *The Quality of Mercy*. Even though it was somewhat rewritten by Norman Riley Raines, it was basically my script. That was the first *Screen Guild* and Paul Muni starred in it.

JASON: Was that before or after *Skippy Hollywood Theatre*?

TRUE: I wrote a couple of originals for *Skippy*, but, truth be told, most of those were reruns of scripts I'd written for other shows. Most of them had been on *Silver Theatre*. I don't mean to put them down. They were just new productions of old scripts.

JASON: Those were produced by a man named MacGregor, who was recording programs as far back as 1922.

TRUE: Some of the shows I had done on *Silver* were lost. They were done again on *Skippy* and there are recordings of them.

JASON: On *Silver Theatre*, weren't you the only writer?

TRUE: I did at least half of them over the first four or five years. There would be times when I would do three weeks in a row but that was rare. Normally I wouldn't do more than two in a row. Other people would come in. Robert Riley Crutcher was one of the people who used to write for that series. Taswell wrote a couple. There were other writers on the show. It wouldn't have been possible to do every week because it was for stars. We had the problem of providing a script that was going to work for a top star.

JASON: I think one of the most important things you did for radio was your part in organizing Armed Forces Radio.

TRUE: You flatter me when you say that. The key man was Tom Lewis with whom I had worked at Young and Rubicam all through the *Silver Theatre* days and other shows. Tom was asked by the war department, after the war had started to set up radio for the troops serving wherever they would be going in the course of the war and, as it turned out, afterword as well. Tom simply called on some of us who were his friends and whom he had worked with, so there was a rich nucleus of seven or eight of us. A nucleus that included Jerry Lawrence and Bob Lee who, as you know, are a couple of renowned, outstanding playwrights.

JASON: Who wrote *Inherit the Wind* and *Mame* and many others. While you were with Armed Forces Radio, you hired a pair of previous guests on this show. One was Elliott Lewis and the other was Howard Duff.

TRUE: I remember giving Elliott his first job. I don't know if he remembers it, but I definitely do. We had been together at City College. I graduated before he did. I was director of dramatics at the station, KHJ. I was doing open auditions. I would have twenty or thirty people come in at one time to audition. There were only two in all those weeks and months that I did this that were truly outstanding. One was Elliott and the other was Jeanette Nolan. Jeanette was one of the two or three really superb actresses to come out of radio. She and Elliott could read three lines, and you knew right there and then that they "had it." It was a magic something. I don't know what "it" is, how you tell, but you can sense it.

JASON: That must be true. Jeanette's list of credits goes on forever, radio, television, movies and whatever else.

TRUE: On *March of Time*, she used to do all kinds of wonderful voices—great dialectician, fine actress.

JASON: You did some Abbott and Costello movies.

TRUE: That was so strange because I wasn't basically a comedy writer, though for one season I wrote a lot of *Maisie*, Ann Sothern's show. Some of the *Silver Theatres* that I wrote, were comedies, for instance, one for Clark Gable called *For Richer, For Richer*. It was in Max Wylie's book as the best comedy of that year. So while I did do some comedy, most of the things I did were dramatic shows. I was interested in seeing *Anastasia* because I did an Anastasia show for Roz Russell or Bette Davis, I've forgotten which. At the time I did a great deal of research into the story, then, because of a comedy script I'd written on *Silver* for Ann Sothern, I got a job at Universal. Just prior to the war, I did three Abbott and Costello's. Not alone! Nobody did an Abbott and Costello alone because John Grant was their great gagman. When you wrote a script, you would turn it in and here and there indicate a three-page comedy scene that you didn't even try to write. You just said, "Here is where they're alone and have no food." So they'd spend fifteen minutes dividing up a pea or something, but you don't know how they're going to do it. In a script, you would allow four minutes for that particular sequence and the dramatic sequence that went with it would be twelve minutes. What would come out were twelve minutes of comedy and four minutes of drama.

JASON: When television arrived, you were pretty busy. You did some stuff for Raymond Burr, *Perry Mason* and *Ironside*. You also did some Westerns, *Bonanza* and *The Virginian*.

TRUE: I wrote a lot of *The Virginian* series, either alone or in collaboration. I did fourteen or fifteen of those. That was interesting too because even though I may have started my career in *Bronco Billy*, I was not a Western writer, but I'll tell you a secret. My stories were not really Westerns. They were just the same kind of stories I was doing for everything else, but they were set in that period with different clothes. Basic stories will always be basic. It doesn't matter what the locale is. I have one pride. In my latter years, I've been a crusader for gun control so I never liked the idea of much violence. In the guild, I sponsored a resolution against excessive violence in both television and films. In doing the Westerns, doing *The Virginian*, you had to figure there you are in times of violence and people are going to be shot. *The Virginian* was a ninety-minute show. I once did an analysis of my scripts and only one and one-quarter people got shot in each one. Considering it was a ninety-minute format, that wasn't bad.

JASON: Not bad for a Western.

TRUE: No, not bad for a Western. I don't know how I managed to shoot a quarter of a person but that's how it worked out.

JASON: What are you doing these days to keep busy? I know you're not retired by any stretch of the imagination.

TRUE: I'm not keeping as busy as I should. After a lifetime in Hollywood, I've moved to Pebble Beach, lured here by my beautiful wife who has a beautiful home here, and the fact that it was time for a change. For a number of years I was chairman of the documentary committee of the Motion Picture Academy down there. I was the interim chairman, even though I was technically the chairman, because Norman Corwin had held that position for years. It was through him that I got on the committee. He was away for four years, during which time I served in his place. One of the things I miss up here is being called for that documentary committee. It was a wonderful job. It was a source of great satisfaction to see all those fine documentaries from all over the world, but I have sort of followed through on that by being involved here. This week we're having the first Monterey Film Festival and I have made my presence known to them as far as my background in documentaries. I have been influential in getting some of the ones they are showing here this week. So I'm still doing some work in that area. The other thing I'm doing is working, slowly, but surely, on an autobiography.

                     ****

Fourteen years after this conversation, True Boardman succumbed to pancreatic cancer on July 28, 2001. In 1993, he was honored with a Valentine Davies Award for lifetime achievement by the Writers Guild of America. It was just one more well deserved tribute after a long career in show business. As anyone in the media will readily tell you, his kind of staying power in one of the most fickle industries is very rare.

There was no end to the directions his writing talent took him. He wrote straight drama, comedies, Westerns, stage plays and even five treatments for *Mr. Magoo*, in which Magoo played several fictional historical characters.

My hat, if I ever wore one, would be off to Mr. True Boardman, a true gentleman of the arts.

ACT II: JACK, GEORGE AND GRACIE

One of the most precious words in our lexicon is friend. Without friends we would experience the lonely existence of a hermit living somewhere in a remote cave. We may live in a huge city or a small town or even on a farm out in the country, but if we do not cultivate at least one good friend, we are no better off than that hermit. Man is not by nature a solitary being. No man is an island. Some friends may be casual, but occasionally there is one who can know our innermost thoughts.

A case in point is the connection between two comedians who fit the description for a long, long time: in fact, fifty-five years. Though their careers often separated them by thousands of miles, in their hearts they were always together. When one died the other was too broken up to give him a proper sendoff at his memorial service.

These two people were Jack Benny and George Burns. Their relationship began in 1919 when they met on the Vaudeville circuit and only ended when Jack passed away in 1974. Each man, in his own way, was unique.

Before going into their sometimes-odd interactions, I will discuss them individually with some help from people who knew them well. In order to do this we must also consider their wives, Gracie Allen and Mary Livingstone.

ACT II:
SCENE ONE
JACK

Jack Benny left behind many people who could attest to his loyalty to them in a variety of ways. We will hear from members of his cast who benefited greatly from his benevolence but first, here is a man you may not know, Irving Fein. Who is Irving Fein you ask? Let's let him tell why he is the most logical person to talk about the Benny legacy.

This is from an interview done on September 27, 1986.

****

IRVING: I was with Jack for twenty-eight years, from early 1947 until he left us all with holes in our hearts on the day after Christmas in 1974. Before '47 I worked, first for Warner Brothers and then a little later for Columbia Pictures in their publicity department. It took me a few years to get to that level, but that's the short version of it. By '47, I had built somewhat of a reputation and I was presented with what would prove to be the opportunity of my life. *The Jack Benny Program* had been at the top of the ratings for a long time, but by '47, they had slipped to number four behind Bob Hope, Edgar Bergen and the *Lux Radio Theatre*. Nobody was happy about it. Since Jack was also a film actor at Columbia, it could be said that we were fellow employees. At that time, I was approached to do some PR work for the show to see if we could get him back on top. Six months later, he was back at number one and my career took off as well. We had a close relationship for the rest of his life. As time progressed, good things happened for me. I became his producer and his manager as well as his agent and his best friend outside of George Burns.

JASON: We'll get back to George a little later, but before we discuss Jack's long and illustrious career, I want to make a statement and get your reaction. During the run of this show, I've had the pleasure of speaking with some of Jack's radio and television co-workers. In the course of conversations with Mel Blanc, Phil Harris, Sheldon Leonard and briefly with Frank Nelson, one point came to the surface over and over. It was that Jack Benny was the sweetest, kindest and all around best person any of them had ever met.

IRVING: And they were absolutely correct. I know from my own experience over those lovely twenty-eight years, we never had any serious disputes. Oh sure, we had some bad moments, but Jack was never one to harbor a grudge. He always worked out any disagreements post haste. Towards the end, he was doing so much charity work that there were times when I had to rein him in. There was nothing he wouldn't do for a friend with a problem, some-times folks he hardly knew. I also want to add that he never thought of himself as the star of his own show, giving the bulk of the credit to his cast.

JASON: And what a cast it was. I mentioned Mel, Phil, Sheldon and Frank, but that was only the beginning. There were so many others. They were Dennis Day, Don Wilson, Bea Benaderet, Artie Auerbach, Verna Felton and, of course, Eddie

Anderson. Here is Phil Harris talking about how he got on Jack's show.

****

JASON: Phil, when Jack Benny came to the airwaves in 1932, he had a different band every year until you came along. He had George Olson, Ted Weems, Frank Black and Don Bester. Then along came Phil Harris. You were with him for eighteen years.

PHIL: I met Jack when I had my own show, my own radio show. I was staying at the Essex House in New York when he and Mary were living there. I met him and we became good friends. His current bandleader at the time, Don Bester, used to complain about him. A couple of times I heard him complain about Jack kidding him about his spats. I was standing next to him one time in the men's room at the hotel and he said "I wish he'd quit talking about my spats." I said to myself, "I wish he'd start talking about anything about me," not knowing I was going to be with him. I was seventy-eight weeks on my own show. Then I had a circuit I was playing for the National Hotel chain. I played New Orleans. I played Galveston. I played Dallas. I played Cincinnati and I played the New Yorker. I was on this tour of my own so I had no worries, but my radio show was discontinued. George Burns called me. I was in New Orleans. He told me he wanted me to work for him. They were big on the air too, as you know. I had a contract so I went to my boss and he said, "Certainly Phil, I'd like you to get it." That was Seymour Weiss. He was the man who owned the Roosevelt. I get out to California and for some reason they booked Wayne King. So now, I'm without a program and without a job. Jack Benny was in town and he invited me to go with him to the Trocadero, one of the top clubs on Sunset. During dinner, he asked me what program I was on. I said, "I haven't got one." He said, "Well, then you're with me." I just happened to be in the right place at the right time.

****

IRVING   Most of the time they all got bigger laughs than Jack, but don't forget, he set them up. Not everyone knows it, but Jack had a terrific sense of humor, sometimes breaking up so bad he'd be screaming with laughter and rolling on the floor at just about anything that struck him funny. Sometimes he was the only one who saw the humor. It took all the control he could muster to keep a straight face at times, although, Mel could destroy that image on many occasions.

JASON: Much proof of that is available on tape. Let's listen to Mel Blanc describe it.

****

When I first came on the Benny show, I was doing just one simple thing. I was the roar of the polar bear standing guard over Jack's infamous vault. Then one day the soundman had trouble doing the old Maxwell in the throes of trying to start. I took over and did it verbally and stayed with it throughout the run of the show. Until then I had done no actual voices so I asked Jack about that. After that, I became professor LeBlanc, his violin teacher, the P.A. announcer at the train station, but the one that always fractured him was a little guy named Sy.

****

JACK:	You came all the way from Tijuana just to play in my orchestra?
MEL:	Si.
JACK:	I see you brought your bass violin with you.
MEL:	Si.
JACK:	And you brought a young lady with you. Is that your sister?
MEL:	Si.
JACK:	What's her name?
MEL:	Sue.
JACK:	Sue?
MEL:	Si.
JACK:	What does Sue do?
MEL:	Sew.
JACK:	Sew?
MEL:	Si.
JACK:	And what's your name?
MEL:	Sy.
JACK:	Sy?
MEL:	Si.

JACK: Now cut that out!

****

MEL: Jack loved it. He used to break up almost every time we did a variation on that theme.

****

IRVING: Then there was Sheldon Leonard–doing the tout with a Brooklyn twang. Jack used to run into him all over the place, occasionally, even at the track.

****

JACK: Mary, let's look over the list of entries for the next race. I want to see if …

SHELDON: Hey bud–bud!

JACK: Me?

SHELDON: Yeah.

JACK: What is it?

SHELDON: You gonna eat here?

JACK: Yeah.

SHELDON: What table?

JACK: Table one.

SHELDON: Uh-uh…Take table nine.

JACK: Look, I'm happy with table one.

SHELDON: Think it over bud. Table one is a card table.

JACK: A card table?

SHELDON: Yeah. If it carries too much weight, the legs will fold.

JACK: Gee, I never thought of that. So you think I should take table nine?

SHELDON: Certainly, look at the breedin'.

JACK: The breeding?

SHELDON: It's by Birdseye out of Grand Rapids.

JACK: Gosh, I didn't think they even knew each other.

SHELDON: Think it over bud. Get wise.

JACK: Wait a minute. This is the first time I ever ran into you at a racetrack. Why don't you give me a tip on a horse?

SHELDON: Who knows about horses? So long, sucker!

****

IRVING: Don't forget Frank Nelson.

****

JACK: Oh mister–mister.

FRANK: Yeeeesssss!

JACK: Why do I always have to run into him? Now look mister, all I want is to buy a magazine.

FRANK: Ok, do you want to read it or tear it in half to show how strong you are?

JACK: I want to read it. I'll take this one here.

FRANK: Weeelllll! *House and Garden*, aren't you lucky. Today only, with every copy, we give away a pocket full of fertilizer.

JACK: Now look, clerk, I can't stand here all day. I'll take this magazine here, a copy of Saturday Evening Post.

FRANK: You want it gift wrapped, I suppose.

JACK: You burn me up you stupid clerk!

FRANK: When you come 'round, I go berserk!

MEL: Train now leaving for Albukerk!

JACK: Now cut that out!

****

JASON: There were many running jokes on the Benny show. Maybe the most enduring one was the fact that he was so cheap. Phil Harris had this to say about that.

****

"No! No! No! Jack was one of the most generous guys in the world. That's why the gag played so well. One time we were on the Chief going back home. I'm walking through the cars and I get a tap on my back. I turn around and Jack is there. We had a manager then, Myrt Blum, who was married to Mary's sister.

Jack says, "Go tell Myrt to give you more money." I said, "Gee whiz, I've finally got a home. I'm off the road. I'm doing great. All I do is say, 'Hello Jack, here comes Rochester.'" He said to go ahead and ask for more money. In the same breath he'd say, "Got a quarter? I want to get a couple of Robert Burns cigars." That's the kind of guy he was. I'll tell you, he was as close as any man ever got to me. He was one of a kind. It really busted me up when he went.

****

IRVING: Let me repeat, he was a man who would give you the shirt off his back or anything else you might need. His image on the air was just the opposite. He had a lock on his refrigerator, a pay phone in his living room, and best of all, he had a mysterious subterranean vault where he kept his money. It was guarded by a vicious polar bear played by Mel Blanc and a man named Ed played by Joe Kearns. When he'd go down there, usually for small bits of cash, it would take forever to get there. He would be greeted, after crossing the drawbridge, by the horrendous clang of alarms and bells. When the racket died down Ed would detain him with a forlorn voice.

****

ED: Halt! Who goes there?

JACK: It's just me Ed.

ED: Oh, hello Mr. Benny.

JACK: Hello Ed, how have you been?

ED: Oh, fine Mr. Benny. Is anything happening up there?

JACK: The war is over, Ed.

ED: Oh, good, did they catch the Kaiser?

****

IRVING: Poor Ed. He got above the ground so seldom, he never heard the news. In this case, he was several wars behind. He did get to go up once on vacation, but he came right back. He couldn't understand cars and airplanes. The vault was one of their best running gags, but to keep it fresh it was only done a few times each season. The cheap thing would go on where ever he would go. It never went away because it worked so well. There was a short skit that most people remember, even though it was done only one time. It was in 1948. Jack was walking over to his next-door neighbors' house, Ron and Benita Coleman, who incidentally, didn't live anywhere near him in the real world. He was accosted by a mugger who put a gun to his back.

****

MUGGER: Don't make a move! This is a stickup! Your money or your life! (*Long pregnant pause*)

MUGGER: Look bud, I said your money or your life! (*Another long pause*)

JACK: I'm thinking it over.

****

IRVING: That short bit brought the house down thanks to

two clever writers, Milt Josephsburg and John Tackaberry. Nothing could happen without good writers but their work would have been ineffectual without Jack's impeccable sense of timing. He could milk more laughs from silence and a straight face than other comedians could wring from a steady stream of gags. One more time, Jack was no miser.

JASON: How about the violin shtick? People always thought he was better at it than he let on. After all, his fiddle was what got him into Vaudeville.

IRVING: That's a tricky question. The answer is yes and no. Yes, he was better than he ever let on, and no, he was not an expert although he did go back to professional training in his later years and became proficient enough to play benefit concerts with nearly every symphonic orchestra of any note all over the U.S.A., Canada, England and even Israel before he died. He liked to say that there was no real difference between Jascha Heifetz and himself. They both held the bow in their right hand and their violin under their chin. He raised nearly six million dollars and to help keep many of those orchestras afloat with his performances.

JASON: There were other running gags. There was the age thing, never wanting to admit to anything over thirty-nine, and the toupee, but there was one that lasted for twenty-five years. It was Jack's feud with Fred Allen, who was a good friend in real life.

IRVING: That all started with a jab at Jack's ability to play the violin. Fred had a ten-year-old virtuoso on his show, Stuart Canin. He played "The Flight of the Bumblebee" flawlessly. At the conclusion Fred said, "Benny should be ashamed of himself." The next week, not to be outdone, Jack said that he too could play "The Bee" perfectly when he was ten. Then Fred brought on a character who claimed to have been a neighbor of Jack's back in Waukegan and swore that Jack had not played well enough back then to even attempt a piece of music like that. Another week went by. Jack had another witness to debunk Fred's charge. He purported that he was Jack's teacher at ten. He said that Jack had indeed played "The Bee" even then. The feud was on. It hadn't been planned but the publicity was great for both of them. The sparks continued to fly endlessly until Fred's sudden death in 1956. They showed up unannounced with regularity on each other's shows as well as at personal appearances elsewhere. Fred made comments like, "Before shoes were invented Benny was a heel," or "When Jack plays the violin it sounds like the strings are still in the cat," or "Jack has no more hair than an elbow." From his side of the court Jack picked up the ball and batted it back. "Listening to Allen is like hearing two Abbotts and no Costello," or "He looks like a short butcher peeking over two pounds of liver," or "Allen is so tight, when he finally spent a five dollar bill, Lincoln's eyes were bloodshot." It never stopped. I could go on and on, but just let me add two more, one from each camp. Jack went to Waukegan for the premiere of one of his movies, *Man About Town*. While he was there, the city planted a tree to commemorate the event. Soon the poor tree died. Hearing of this Fred said, "How could a tree live in Waukegan when the sap is in Hollywood?" After a benefit show Jack quipped, "I was doing this show and there were many important stars, Bob Hope, Bing Crosby and I thought I saw Jane Russell. Then I put on my glasses. It turned out to be Fred Allen. You see, the bags under his eyes are so low ..."

****

Irving Fein will be back. I would like to clear up something that you may have wondered about. We did not talk much about Mary Livingstone. That is because she was a person who did not deserve a man like Jack Benny. Truth be known, she never referred to herself as Mrs. Jack Benny until after he passed away, when she thought it might arouse some sympathy from the Hollywood population. It did not work. She died a lonely woman in 1983, after which her adopted daughter, Joan, admitted that even she did not like her mother very much. She was a selfish person who tried to climb over anyone she thought was standing in her way. She wore the pants in the family, and without Mr. Fein's help, Jack would have died a pauper because Mary spent every penny she could get her hands on. George and Gracie were Jack's nearest and dearest friends, but they only tolerated Mary for Jack's sake. Everything they did, Mary had to try to do bigger and better.

There is much more I could add, but that is enough about a very unpleasant subject.

Jack Benny died from pancreatic cancer on the day after Christmas in 1974. As Phil Harris put it in his own inimitable way, "He was one of a kind."

ACT II:
SCENE TWO
GEORGE AND GRACIE

"A faculty for expressing the amusing or comical," that is the definition of humor in the Random House dictionary of the English language. How does humor present itself? It may come from many sources. Sometimes it can arise from a simple event in our daily lives that just does not seem quite right, sometimes from our own nonsensical actions. Most commonly, we think of humor as something resulting from the words or actions of performers called comedians. It can be one standup comic doing a monologue or, better still, a pair working off each other.

There have been many of those small teams but the pair I put on the top of the mountain is George Burns and Gracie Allen. While George did not really succeed until he met Gracie, it was not too long before they clicked as a duo. Gracie's pretended stupidity played well with audiences, but she would not have been as funny without George to set her up. In truth, both of them were highly intelligent people with enough moxie to make us laugh.

Before we get into the subject, let me present a small sample from their early days in Vaudeville.

****

GEORGE: Gracie, I'm sorry to hear about your missing brother.

GRACIE: Oh, that's too bad George. My brother's missing too.

GEORGE: The only difference between you and me is that I have the power of mind over matter. You have no mind and it doesn't seem to matter.

GRACIE: I bet you say that to all the gals.

GEORGE: Never mind. I would like to know, how is your brother?

GRACIE: My brother? I think they ought to open up all the prisons. It would help posterity.

GEORGE: Wait a minute. That's the wrong answer.

GRACIE: That's the right answer, but you asked me the wrong question. Now look, it costs the government seventy million dollars a year to feed and clothe the prisoners. When they're out, they only steal sixty million dollars a year. That gives the government a ten million dollar profit right there. Don't you think so?

GEORGE: I think so. See you later.

GRACIE: Now take my brother Harry.

GEORGE: You take him.

GRACIE: They got him. He's running Sing-Sing. He eats them out of house and warden. And my brother Willie, there's an appetite for you. Willie goes to San Quentin.

GEORGE: He goes to San Quentin? He takes his books and goes to San Quentin?

GRACIE: Yeah. I'll never forget when my brother got out, how proud my father was. As he left the gate there was my father standing there waving to him.

GEORGE: Your father waved from his cell?

GRACIE: Yeah. He shouted, "Goodbye kid," and my brother shouted back, "Goodbye Pop."

GEORGE: Nice family!

GRACIE: He said to tell Uncle Ed he left his toothbrush in cell twenty-two.

GEORGE: Cell twenty-two?

GRACIE: My father didn't like his first cell. They wouldn't let him gamble. They said it gives the place a bad name.

GEORGE: Listen Gracie, how is it that it's so easy for you to talk and so hard for me to listen.

****

As you can see, their work was still a little rough around the edges in those days. As time went by, they polished and polished until they developed a much smoother delivery.

Now it is time to bring in a couple of people who are well qualified to speak on the subject of George Burns and Gracie Allen. They had recently published a book titled *Say Goodnight, Gracie! The Story of Burns & Allen*. On June 29, 1986, I had the pleasure of talking with Cheryl Blythe and Susan Sackett.

****

JASON: George and Gracie hold a special place in show business history. Since our time is limited, why don't we jump right into their radio days?

SUSAN: When they started doing their radio show, one of the Network executives thought that Gracie would never survive on radio. He said her voice was too squeaky. They almost didn't get on the air at all. Audiences proved him wrong.

JASON: They actually made their radio debut on the BBC in 1930 and when they returned to this country Gracie worked alone until they teamed up on *The Rudy Vallee Show.*

SUSAN: She worked with Rudy on his show and then with Eddie Cantor. George was with her near the end, but not from the start of *Rudy Vallee.* Finally, they had a show of their own.

JASON: George often said that he was a technician and that Gracie was the only one in the family who was a Performer. Do you agree with that?

CHERYL: George is very modest. He never took the credit. Gracie used to say, "He's been entertaining people for years but he never knew it."

JASON: Here's what George had to say on the subject.

****

People believed everything she said. When Gracie read, she read like she believed it. You didn't know she was reading. If you're a good actress, you make it so people don't know you're reading a script. As far as I was concerned, I didn't have anything to do in the script anyway. If I could stand in front of the microphone and keep the pages from rattling, I was a good actor.

****

SUSAN: The audience recognized George as a good actor

on the show, a monologist, a performer. What I
don't think people are aware of is that he supervised
every single aspect of production as well as being a
writer and a performer. What a talent! Nobody to
date has been able to duplicate the comedy timing
George has when he performs. They were both
exceptional performers. George still is. It was a
perfectly matched team. When they came on, he'd
set up the laughs and she'd deliver them. It was an
intricate balance.

JASON: They were an oddly matched couple when it came
to marriage, a Catholic girl and a Jewish boy. It
worked out well for them.

CHERYL: That's right. He went home and announced to his
mother, who was a very orthodox Jewish woman,
that he would be marrying a Catholic girl. Her
reaction was, "That's fine if she'll have you." It
worked out very well. They adopted two children,
both of whom did some work on their show.
Neither Ronnie nor Sandy continued as actors in
later life.

JASON: The transition from radio to television was relatively
painless, but there were a few problems.

SUSAN: Yes there were. The big one was Gracie. She was
absolutely terrified of going on TV. They had done
quite a few motion pictures but she was nervous
about television. Primarily, there was dialogue that
had to be learned. In Vaudeville, for seventeen years,
they did basically the same routine every single
night. Now they'd have to learn thirty minutes of
dialogue every two weeks. The show would be
done live in front of an audience which meant no
scripts and no cue cards. It was a lot of work. She
had most of the lines and they were ridiculous

lines. They weren't just simple things that were logical. They were convoluted and made an illogical kind of logic in the mixed up world of Gracie Allen. In reality, she was not like that person. Most of her work was learning lines.

JASON: And some lines they were. The writers had several basic rules. The first was that Gracie's character did not think she was dumb, she thought she was smart. The second rule was that when you write for Gracie; keep her consistent, which was not easy to do. The final rule was that if it's a logical problem, Gracie would pursue it in an illogical way. Somehow, when all was said and done, it all made some sort of weird sense. Here is an example.

****

GEORGE: So you're taking up painting. What are you going to paint?

GRACIE: Masterpieces. They make the most money. I'll only paint one masterpiece a day. I saw the rock bottom price, one hundred thousand dollars. That's one hundred thousand dollars a day, three hundred and sixty four days a year.

GEORGE: Why not three hundred and sixty five?

GRACIE: I'll need one day to take the money to the bank.

GEORGE: Gracie, before you can paint masterpieces you have to be a master, a genius.

GRACIE: I think geniuses run in my family.

GEORGE: In your family, I don't blame them for running.

GRACIE: My Uncle Charlie used to draw pictures of Lincoln and Washington. They were so good you couldn't tell them from real money. He'd be famous but he gave it up and tried baseball.

GEORGE: Where did he try baseball?

GRACIE: Sing-Sing.

GEORGE: If he was so clever, how did he get caught?

GRACIE: He was so proud of his work he signed his own name.

GEORGE: I'm glad they put him away.

GRACIE: Not for long though. He painted a picture of an open door on the prison wall. While the guards were trying to close it, my uncle walked out the front gate.

GEORGE: Well, if you want to take up painting as a hobby it's all right with me. Maybe it'll keep you busy. You certainly bought enough—hey, what's that little animal in a cage?

GRACIE: Oh George, I'm afraid you don't know much about painting. That's something every artist needs, a weasel.

GEORGE: A weasel?

GRACIE: And did I have trouble finding one. No wonder great painters are so scarce. There aren't enough weasels to go around.

GEORGE: Honey, you don't understand. Painters don't use a weasel, they use an easel.

GRACIE: Oh, a male weasel, huh?

GEORGE: An easel holds a picture while you're painting it.

GRACIE: What a clever little animal, but you could do it. You're strong as a weasel.

****

JASON: They also experienced difficulties going from live to film even though the transition was gradual.

CHERYL: It wasn't that gradual. They had been doing a live show for about two years. At that time, there was no coaxial cable but the shows were still done on kinescope which meant the show would go live in California. At the same time they were broadcasting the show another camera was set up in front of a very high intensity monitor and would film the show from that monitor. Copies were made from that and shipped across the country so that it could air all over.

JASON: Which presented some real quality questions.

CHERYL: Those shows could not be rerun and George realized that the money out of television was going to come from reruns. The only way they could do that was to do the show on film from the start, which was still very new. In fact, *The Burns and Allen Show* was only the third television show ever to go out on film from California. Most were still being done live from New York. He got himself a terrific crew using some of the people who did the original *I Love Lucy*. That started the usual three-camera system, three cameras running simultaneously with an audience in the studio. It's still done that way today. For example, at Paramount Studios, where I work, they do *Cheers* that way. As it happens, the system was pioneered back in the *Lucy* days.

JASON: You wrote a story about the cameraman in charge of the system and how he couldn't get on the set the first day of the shooting.

SUSAN: On that first day of filming, right. They'd made their decision they were going to do their show on film. They'd hired the best cinematographers they could find. The big morning came. They'd been in rehearsal for two weeks and everybody was ready to go. There was no cameraman. They waited and they waited. Finally, the production manager called down to the front gate thinking that perhaps the cameraman had gotten lost on the lot—couldn't find the right stage. The guard told him that he never had a pass for the cameraman so when he came he wasn't allowed on the property. They had to rush and call him at home. This time they made sure the pass was at the guard station. They finally did get that first show on film.

CHERYL: That's right. If you don't have a pass, you don't get on the lot. That's still true today.

JASON: Probably more now than ever.

SUSAN: It's like Fort Knox now. We went over to the studio where they filmed *Burns and Allen*. I don't remember what it's called today. They change the names every two years or so. Way back, when they were shooting it was called General Services. The stage they used has now been dedicated to George Burns.

JASON: It took a lot of chutzpa to put together the scripts that made the show off-the-wall perfect. They had a cast of writers backing them up including George and his brother Willie.

CHERYL: They had primarily the same writers for a number of years. A lot of them started with the radio show and knew exactly what type of material George and Gracie wanted. One of their writers was Paul Henning, who also wrote for *Petticoat Junction*. He had a long association with George, who was very loyal. Once they were in, they were in for a long, long time.

JASON: In some cases, after leaving, they were brought back at a later date. A couple of those early writers were Sid Dorfman and Harvey Helm.

CHERYL: Harvey passed away.

JASON: What about Norman Paul? Tell me about his rolling wastebasket.

SUSAN: Everybody we talked to had a Norman Paul story. He was one of those special, special writers. Some writers are good at jokes and one-liners. Others are good structurally. There was nothing Norman couldn't write and write brilliantly. Usually people that are creative tend to forget or ignore or are just totally unaware of mundane day-to-day things. One of the stories about Norm is this. He was always a chain smoker and he drove a convertible. Usually his car was full. Everything the man owned was tossed in the back seat of his car. There were old scripts. There was clothing. Whatever he had was thrown in the back seat. One day he was driving down the street and he flipped a cigarette out the window. Unfortunately, it flew into the back seat and landed on a pile of old newspapers. He was driving along, not paying much attention to anything except the road in front of him. Other cars were honking and waving so he waved back and smiled. He was totally unaware that the back seat was in flames. He finally glanced in the rear view mirror, saw the fire, but still oblivious to it he kept on driving. He saw a used car dealer, pulled in and traded cars. Then he threw what was left in the new back seat and drove to work. That was Norman Paul.

JASON: I have to wonder about the poor dealer left with a burning car.

SUSAN: I hope he put it out before it set the rest of his lot on fire.

JASON: It's a well-known fact that few worked harder than George and Gracie. Take me through what would have been a typical week for them.

SUSAN: They literally worked seven days a week. On Monday, George would come in around eight a.m. to work with his writers. Monday's job with the writers was mainly to get the story line down. They would work up just enough dialogue at that point to get the flow of information for the story. Gracie would be busy having wardrobe fittings. We estimated that she averaged three dresses for each show. She never wore the same dress twice. She was very tiny so it was impossible to buy her clothes off the rack. Everything had to be made to fit her so wardrobe fittings were a never-ending process for her. Between four and five, Gracie would be through with her fittings and George would be finished with the writers. He would be able to go home and relax a little. Gracie would be studying the dialogue for the show they would be filming on Wednesday, the show they were rehearsing. Tuesday would be another rehearsal day for the Wednesday show. This was the day when they would work with the cameras. The actors had already been spending a week on their dialogue. Every place an actor stood on the stage had to be exactly right or else the cameras wouldn't be able to pick them up. Wednesday would be filming day. It took about twelve hours from the beginning until the last shot was wrapped. We should mention at this point, we said earlier that they filmed with an audience. They discovered that because of the intricacies of Gracie's lines, it was very difficult to memorize that kind of material and shoot it complete with an audience. A couple of years into the shooting they stopped having an audience. They shot it the same way you would shoot a motion picture except they used three cameras to save time. Otherwise, it would take three or four days to make a thirty-minute show. By shooting it out of sequence, all of the things that took place in the living room set could be shot at one time. When those were finished they could move on to the kitchen, set up the lights and do those shots. When it was all assembled, they would run the finished show for a live audience to record their laughs and applause.

JASON: That presented the editors with another problem. They'd have to guess at how much time to leave for reactions. They were pretty much on target in almost every case.

CHERYL: George knew exactly how long a laugh was going to last. He had that magic of perfect timing. He'd know exactly how to deliver a line and exactly when to come back in.

SUSAN: He used his cigar for that too. He said in an article back in '57 that he relied a lot on his cigar to 'time' his jokes. It was a handy device. Here's how he put it.

****

If I get a laugh with a joke, I just look at it and twiddle it for a little while—while I'm waiting for the laugh to die down. If I don't get a laugh, it's something to hang on to. When a joke calls for a delayed laugh, I exhale my smoke slowly. If a laugh doesn't come at all, I swallow.

****

CHERYL: The worst part of it was the dialogue. With forty pages of script, thirty of them would be Gracie's.

SUSAN: After a twelve-hour workday on Wednesday the activity kept going. Thursday the writers would bring in pages from Monday's story meeting. They were always keeping one show ahead.

CHERYL: They had to because of Gracie's dialogue. There was no way they would risk having last minute changes for her to learn. The complete script had to be ready one week before each show.

SUSAN: George worked with the writers all day Thursday. They would take a lunch break where they figured was the worst place to go so they'd be back in thirty minutes. Then they worked on until four. Gracie actually had a day off. Thursday was her day off, but she didn't really have a day off because…

CHERYL: If she had an interview or anything, those people were waiting for her to be available. Thursday was the day they called her so she didn't often have a real day off.

SUSAN: Friday was a day to work some more with the writers and bring in the wardrobe people for final fittings.

CHERYL: Saturday was still a workday. On Saturday, George would take all the material the writers had been working on Monday thru Friday and bring it home. The scripts should have been about fifty pages long. The first draft could be anywhere from fifty-five to sixty pages. He would start working on the script, making cuts, getting it down to filming length. He would send it out with his secretary that night. A mimeograph copy would be brought back to the house. Sunday the secretary would be back along with the director to go over the script and make sure it was exactly the way they would shoot it. Once they locked down the script, no further changes would be made. By Sunday night, Gracie would be back studying lines for the rehearsal on Monday and it would start all over again. George was able to sit back and watch TV. He said it was his way to see what the competition was up to.

JASON: That's what he used to do on the television show, watch the competition as well as see what his own family was doing.

SUSAN: Right, his magic TV. That came along in the later years of the show. He had this wonderful TV set. It was almost like sci-fi fantasy. He could turn it on and, not only would Benny pop up from time to time but he could also keep an eye on Gracie. Then he'd plot his little schemes.

CHERYL: He could also keep track of Harry vonZell or his neighbors, Blanche and Harry Morton. Nobody other than Jack Benny knew about George's mysterious television set. George would be watching him and Jack would shout, "Now, cut that out!"

JASON: Jack was one of the few guests they had on the TV show.

SUSAN: The radio show was more conducive to having guests. The TV version was more of a family type sitcom and didn't call for guests, but because it was George and Gracie playing George and Gracie, they could get away with having their long time friend drop in now and then.

JASON: When Gracie retired after all those years of planned insanity, she was virtually worn out and had serious health problems.

SUSAN: She wanted to retire just about every year. Most people, when they get their contracts renewed by the networks, go out and celebrate, but for Gracie it caused anything but joy. George would come running home and say, "They picked us up!" She'd say, "Oh no, not again!" She had worked steadily from the time she was seventeen, not even seventeen. She never had a full week off until she was in her fifties. It was an exhausting schedule for her; also, most people don't know, she suffered violent migraines, but never said anything to anyone. You know, the show must go on no matter the pain. George was aware though. Each year he'd come to her and ask her if she really wanted to try it for another year. Until the last season, she always said yes, but finally she had to say no. He said okay, and that was it. He always respected her feelings. She also had a serious heart condition. She wasn't that old. She was just worn out. Her first reaction when she retired was that she wanted to sleep for six months. She also wanted to spend some time with her grandchildren and do some shopping.

JASON:　　The small things most of us take for granted were things she never had a chance to do. When she died, she was universally mourned. Even the *L.A. Times* ran a rare headline above their logo.

CHERYL:　　She was a person who didn't have an enemy in the world. It was really sad.

SUSAN:　　I don't think the world is aware of how much George loved Gracie. That was what made *The Burns and Allen Show* so special. The love they had for each other was so visible on the camera. He adored her on and off the camera. They just fit perfectly. You'd think, with so much closeness, they might have ended up in the divorce court. Just the opposite was the reality of it. After she died, George had a terrible time. He was so lost without her he couldn't get any sleep. They had twin beds at the end due to her health, and finally, almost out of desperation, he started sleeping in her bed. It worked. He's been sleeping soundly ever since. To this day, he goes every week to visit her in her crypt where he talks to her at length. He tells her everything that is going on in his life.

JASON:　　Here, in his own words, George describes how he felt about his years with Gracie.

****

Marriage was not our business. Our business was show business so our marriage was a byproduct of what we were doing on stage. The marriage worked perfectly. In those thirty-eight years we lived together, we ate together, we dressed together, and we worked together. We were not together thirty-eight years—we were together many times that. It was a wonderful time we had.

****

JASON: The house he lives in now is the same one they occupied for many years.

SUSAN: They never wanted more. They were not into material things. They were very generous with their donations to hospitals and such.

JASON: After he lost Gracie, George had some bad times professionally as well. He played Tahoe and Vegas a lot, but it just didn't seem to work for him as a single.

CHERYL: For a long time he was looking for a replacement for Gracie. He didn't quite trust himself to be out there on the stage alone. He paired with Connie Stevens, with Carol Channing and with Ann Margaret and anyone to play off him. Nobody could replace Gracie and gradually he realized that audiences were enjoying him. He didn't need that support system he was carrying around. So now, he performs by himself on center stage.

JASON: He got a big break when he got back into movies in 1975 in *The Sunshine Boys*, the story of two elderly vaudevillians trying to recreate their past glory. It earned him an Oscar.

CHERYL: It certainly did. A little later, he even played God.

JASON: And the devil.

CHERYL: And the devil!

SUSAN: I don't think you can pick up a magazine or watch TV without seeing him endorse a product.

CHERYL: The man has to be busy. He loves what he does. He says that anyone who is in a business he has to get away from for a few days is in the wrong business. He still works seven days a week and can't imagine any other way of life.

JASON: My favorite Burns quote is, "I can't die—I'm booked." In fact, he is booked at the London Palladium for his one hundredth-birthday celebration. I think he'll keep that date. He'll make it.

SUSAN: If anyone can, he will.

****

We know now that George Burns did make it to the century mark, but only by a few days. By then he said he wanted to die so he could rejoin Gracie. He did not keep his date at the Palladium. Both George and Gracie were taken from us by heart problems—but it was their hearts that kept them together so many years.

Just a note about *The Sunshine Boys*: before his death, Jack Benny had been pegged for the role George Burns eventually played. Their agent in common had much to do with the transition from Jack to George. That man was Irving Fein who did a fine job of looking after both men.

I would be remiss to leave the Burns' without mentioning at least two of the wonderful running gags on their shows.

In 1932, Gracie began a yearlong search for her missing brother, also named George. She showed up on nearly every other radio show and in many public places looking for him. The only person who found no humor in the routine was her real brother. He had to go into hiding for a time just to get away from it all.

Then in 1940, Gracie decided it was time for her to run for president. She conducted quite an active campaign including a whistle stop tour on which she made speeches from the rear platform of the Twentieth Century Limited. Of course, she did not win—but she did manage to garner 42,000 votes.

There is one other thing that should be clarified. When George would say to her at the end of each show, "Say goodnight, Gracie," she was often quoted as saying, "Goodnight Gracie." In point of truth, she never said that. She simply responded, "Goodnight."

For now, I would like to add my own closure. Goodnight George and Gracie. You have made our lives a happier place.

ACT II:
SCENE THREE
JACK AND GEORGE

As we know, Jack Benny and George Burns were the closest sort of friends for 55 years; so close that when George attempted to eulogize Jack at his funeral he only got a few words out before he had to retreat from the podium in tears leaving Bob Hope to take over for him. We also know that Jack was most vulnerable to anything he found even remotely humorous. Even though at times, no one else could understand what was funny. Of all the people who could tickle his funny bone, none was better at it than George.

In 1974, Irving Fein took over the same duties for George that he had been so successfully doing for Jack. Irving and George remained a team until George left us in 1996. Therefore, Irving is the best-equipped person to talk about the byplay between those two giants of comedy.

****

JASON: It's time to discuss some of the things that George did to break up Jack. There was one thing he did with regularity that most of us wouldn't find the least bit amusing, but it always worked on Jack. I think you know what I'm referring to.

IRVING: I do, I do. It was something that began in 1926, long before I knew either of them. It happened deep in the night after George and Gracie's wedding. Jack phoned their room.

****

JACK: George, this is Jack. I just called to
            congratulate—

GEORGE: We'll have breakfast at ten, in bed, scrambled eggs,
            bacon, toast and marmalade.

JACK: But… (*Line went dead*).

JACK: (*Calling back*) George, I wanted to …

GEORGE: And a big pot of coffee. (*Again he hung up*)

JACK: (*Third try*). George …

GEORGE: Don't forget the orange juice. (*Click*)

****

IRVING: Well, Jack didn't try again that night. While you
            and I wouldn't see anything witty about it, Jack
            was laughing hysterically. This sort of thing
            happened over and over again. In 1948, Jack was
            going to play the Palladium in London. As was his
            custom, Val Parnell, the Palladium's managing
            director, was hosting a party for him prior to
            opening night. During the party, he received a call
            from George, who was in Beverly Hills at their
            Hillcrest Country Club. George wished him good
            luck and hung up. That left Benny pounding
            the floor. I should mention he could never get
            even a chuckle out of George no matter how
            hard he tried. One year later, George and
            Gracie were about to open at the same venue.
            Jack thought he could get even, in spades.
            Unbeknownst to anyone, he went to London and
            secreted himself in the back room where Val

Parnell was throwing his traditional party. With
the aid of Jane Wyman, playing the part of a
transatlantic telephone operator, he rang George,
pretending to be in California. When George came
to the phone, Jack wished him good luck and
promptly hung up. Then he came into the party
room and stood there silent. He didn't get even a
snicker out of George, but he himself went out of
his mind with laughter.

JASON: I suppose every person has a different idea of what
makes for a joke.

IRVING: Here's a variation on the same theme. One time
Jack came home after three months on the road.
He spotted George parked across the street, honking
his horn. After defying traffic to get across to him,
when he got close, George rolled up his window
and drove away. It was something that happened
several times over the years, but Jack always bit on
it, leaving him in stitches.

JASON: Keep going. I know there's more.

IRVING: How about this one? Jack and George were having
dinner one night at Chasin's in Beverly Hills.
George said, "Listen Jack; let's play a joke on Dave
Chasin. When the check comes you say, 'If you let
George pay this, I'll never come in here again.'
Then I'll say, 'If you let Jack pay the tab, I won't
ever come in here again.' We'll see how he handles
that one.'" When the check came, Dave Chasin
came with it to ask if everything was satisfactory.
Jack said, "Listen Dave, if you let George pay, I
won't come back." George said nothing. Dave said,
"Okay Jack, if that's the way you want it," and
walked away. Another time they were sharing a
suite at the Plaza in New York. George woke up

Jack at four a.m. He shoved a deck of cards at him and said, "Pick a card." Groggy as he was, Jack did as he was told. With that, George picked up the rest of the cards, walked back to his room and went to sleep leaving Jack doubled over and wondering what just happened.

JASON: The amazing thing is that nothing you just told me would get a positive reaction from me. My reaction would likely be the exact opposite. There was some kind of weird chemistry between those two guys.

IRVING: It was a little strange, but it sure worked for them. I'm sure George wanted to give in at times, but he wouldn't do it. Later in Jack's life, he was once at his regular haunt, the Hillside Country Club. Someone asked him, "What was the best punch line you ever heard?" His answer stunned everyone at the table. He said it was something Larry Adler, the great harmonica player, said when they were on a USO tour during the war. They were staying in an old castle with a huge fence all around it with an iron gate. When they came in one night Larry said, "Don't forget to close the gate." For some unknown reason, that innocuous statement fractured Jack. I don't hear you laughing?

JASON: OK, so where's the joke?

IRVING: Right, only Jack could see it, but whenever he told the story, he was always overwhelmed. You have to understand, once he started laughing it was nearly impossible to get him to stop. There's so much more I could tell you. Suffice it to say, for fifty-five years, they were each other's best audience.

JASON: All I can say is, "to each his own." We don't have to understand it, but you must admit, they weren't your average every day guys.

****

ENCORE

I cannot resist adding one more bit that includes Jack, George and Gracie. This is about a long time sticking point between Jack and Gracie.

****

JACK: Gracie, for Heaven's sake, don't let out my secret. I don't want anyone to know I've been taking beauty treatments.

GRACIE: Don't worry Jack. They'll never suspect it.

JACK: Well anyway, don't you tell. If the newspapers get a hold of it, I'm cooked. You know how the gang would kid me on my program.

GRACIE: Oh yeah, your program. You don't want this to get in the papers, huh?

JACK: No. I'll do anything to keep it out... anything.

GRACIE: Good. Starting Sunday, George will sing on your program.

JACK: George? Sing? Gracie, I've heard prettier sounds come out of Carmen Lombardo.

GRACIE: Excuse me Jack. I'm going to telephone a little news item to the papers.

JACK: Wait a minute. You mean George Burns, your husband George? I don't suppose it would hurt to have George sing on my program.

GRACIE: I was thinking of having him sing every week.

JACK: Oh, no, no!

GRACIE: Ok, I'll call the papers.

JACK: Gracie, this is blackmail!

GRACIE: I know, cute of me, huh?

(*George enters the room*)

GEORGE: Well, well, Jack Benny.

JACK: Hello George, how's the juggling game?

GEORGE: I don't know how to juggle. Why doesn't everyone stop with that?

GRACIE: Oh George, don't get too excited. Jack has some wonderful news for you. Tell him Jack—well, Jack? I think I'll go call the papers.

JACK: All right, all right, I'll tell him.

GRACIE: Good. I'll go down and make some coffee.

GEORGE: Well Jack, what is it that you want to tell me?

JACK: Well, first I want to remind you that you're my dearest friend, George.

GEORGE: And you're my dearest friend, Jack.

JACK: I mean, you're more than a friend to me, George.

GEORGE: You're more than a friend to me, too, Jack.

JACK: I love you. I love you like a brother.

GEORGE: I love you like a brother, Jack.

JACK: I mean, I'd never do anything to hurt you George.

GEORGE: Thanks.

JACK: Wait a minute. I'll try that again.

****

I must add a sad note here. While this book was being prepared for publication, Irving Fein passed away at the ripe old age of 101 on August 10, 2012. He was a good man.

ACT III:
MUSIC–MUSIC–MUSIC

When delving into the performing arts it would be shameful to ignore the world of melody. Music and musicians present us with a wide range of possibilities to investigate. The diversity is infinite, from solo performers all the way to magnificent orchestral collaborations. While I have spoken directly and in some instances, indirectly with many devotees of musical endeavors, I have selected just four to feature here.

We will peek into the lives of one Big Band Leader, one master of the Motion Picture Score, one Latin singer and, last but not least, a noted composer, conductor and performer from the world of symphony and Broadway.

ACT III:
SCENE ONE
SWING IT!

The era of the Big Bands is now sadly, mostly history. It was a rough life for many of its protagonists, but also very rewarding for some of them. It was a life of continuous, tedious travel from one one-nighter to the next, in all kinds of weather—sometimes to remote locations all across our vast land and beyond. As the days and years passed by through the twenties, thirties and forties, the wheat rose above the chaff, due in large part to the exposure offered by the radio airwaves.

We all remember many of them. We recall the trumpets of Harry James and Louis Armstrong; the clarinets of Artie Shaw and Benny Goodman; the piano of Count Basie and many more examples.

One of them was a fine band with a fabulous singer, who eventually settled into a life of long engagements in a limited number of venues while their fame rose. I am referring to the Dick Jurgens Band and their unforgettable crooner Eddy Howard. From humble beginnings in Sacramento, California, Dick climbed to the top of the swing band ladder and stayed there for years until the general demise of his industry due to the ever-changing attitudes of the fickle public.

On February 10, 1987, I had a long discussion with Dick.

****

JASON: Let's start off way back in the twenties, Dick, when you were in an eight-piece high school dance band with your brother Will. From then until you showed up in the thirties at the Aragon Ballroom in Chicago, my information is a little sketchy. Fill me in if you will.

DICK: I started playing professionally around 1924 at the Tahoe resorts here in California. I played there for about eight years. In 1928, I got my first break, playing at the Center Hotel in Sacramento. Then in 1932, after I'd been playing Lake Tahoe for a couple more years, I got a chance to go to the St. Francis Hotel in San Francisco. That was really our first big job. From there I went to the Palomar in Los Angeles and in 1937, to the Drake Hotel in Chicago. We played a long engagement there, did very well. We were just sitting around at the Croydon Hotel in Chicago, waiting for a new break when the Aragon called me and told me that Freddie Martin was ill and they needed a substitute band for a few nights. We stayed seventeen weeks, believe it or not. That was one of our best jobs for years, the Aragon in Chicago.

JASON: It was a pretty steady booking for years. Let me go back to the St. Francis engagement. In 1934, you met someone who came to you to do some arrangements and stayed on for a long, long time—Lew Quadling.

DICK: Lew Quadling, yes. Lew was one of our arrangers. He was put in my band by fellows from MCA, (Music Corporation of America), to play piano and arrange. He was with me for many years. He and Carl Branch were my chief arrangers for many years.

JASON: Wasn't Lew with Kay Keyser when he came to you?

DICK: He was with Kay just before he came to me but he was with Johnny Hamp for a long time too. They were known as "Johnny Hamp and the Serenaders," a well-known band at the time.

JASON: When Lew joined you, it was supposed to be a temporary assignment but he stayed with you until 1943 when the war broke up the band.

DICK: Yes, he was with me until '43 when I went into the Marines. Most of the bands were separating then for similar reasons. When I came back in '46, he had his own band. I believe it was an all saxophone band. So I didn't try to get him back. I got some other guys to go with me and Lew continued to front his own group. I think he's still an arranger. I haven't seen him in three or four years. He's still in southern California.

JASON: He was a pretty busy arranger, doing two or three new arrangements every week.

DICK: He usually did two, Carl did two and I did one. That was five new arrangements every week just to keep up with the current songs. We had to do it in order to stay ahead of the crowd. The audience always wanted the new tunes they heard on the air.

JASON: Lew Quadling also wrote songs.

DICK: Quadling and I and also Eddy Howard wrote songs like "Careless," "A Million Dreams Ago" and "It's a Hundred to One I'm in Love." I wrote our theme song, "Daydreams" for a college exam in Sacramento. "Elmer's Tune" was written by Elmer Albrecht and myself. I kept pretty busy trying to write songs while we were at the Aragon.

JASON: "My Last Goodbye" was another one.

DICK: That was Eddy Howard's own song.

JASON: When Lew Quadling came on board, that gave you two piano players, Lew and Ronnie Kemper. That created a problem in some of the smaller towns.

DICK: How did you know that?

JASON: The story I heard had something to do with a washing machine.

DICK: A washing machine?

JASON: What I heard was that when you played Davenport, Iowa, Ronnie Kemper took ill, so one of the local people was brought in to play the ax rented from a music store in town. He looked at it and played a few notes. It didn't sound right to him and he said, "God, what a Maytag!" They became Maytags ever after.

DICK: I remember that story. I'd almost forgotten. Truth is we had those kinds of problems in a lot of small towns. Very seldom did they have two pianos. We were lucky if they had one. My brother Will, who was our manager, used to go ahead of us on the road and try to arrange to have two pianos and have them properly tuned so that when we got there we could just sit down and start playing. We also had a celesta that Quadling played, a little feature we always used.

JASON: There's a story told about the celesta too. If memory serves me, it happened at the St. Francis. Someone, who shall remain anonymous, did some switching around of the instruments and when they started playing it was a disaster.

DICK: I don't know where you're getting these stories, but, they're pretty good stories. I've heard that one too, but to be honest, I don't recall the incident. The celesta we had was much bigger than those little portable things. It was like a small piano. It was on rollers. We used to roll it up to the microphone then bring it back again.

JASON: By the late thirties, you were working a pretty regular schedule. The Aragon and ....

DICK: We started in late '36 at the Drake Hotel and, as I said, that led to our first Aragon booking. It was a regular booking every year until I went into the service in 1943. I came out in '46 and reorganized. We went back to the Aragon every year after that until 1955.

JASON: That was December through April most years, right?

DICK: Many acts played nine months there, Jason. We had long engagements. We were very fortunate. We often played the Aragon in winter then came out to California to play Catalina or the Claremont Hotel in Berkley. It was a good routine. We used to take two weeks a year vacation.

JASON: I remember the Aragon well with its old Spanish motif. When you were there with the lights set right, it was like being outside under a starry sky. In recent years, it has been used for everything from a roller rink to a boxing arena.

DICK: I'd hate to see it now because that was a beautiful floor. Every one of the boards in that floor was curved. It was an ideal place to dance. It was on springs, beautiful, beautiful ballroom. One of the cleanest I've ever been in. I think the Aragon was the greatest of all the ballrooms I ever played.

JASON: I remember it well. I also remember the Trianon.

DICK: That was on Cottage Grove. That was the sister ballroom. In fact, it was the first of the two. They built the Trianon and then saw a need for a ballroom on the north side of Chicago so they built the Aragon. Wayne King opened the Trianon and had people there with him like Rudolph Valentino. The story goes that women came to see Valentino and threw their wedding rings at him. It was a beautiful place but I always liked the Aragon better. Lawrence Welk played the Trianon a lot when I played the Aragon.

JASON: Another of your familiar haunts was the Elitch Gardens in Denver, also the Baker Hotel in Denver.

DICK: Elitch Gardens was a big amusement park, much better than most amusement parks, Jason. It was a fresh, clean beautiful place where families could go and spend the day, then dance at night at their outdoor pavilion. I played seventeen consecutive summers at Elitch Gardens. They've now taken away the area where the dancing used to occur. They put more rides in. It used to be a beautiful place for the whole family.

JASON: Most amusement parks were quite different then than they are now. Riverview Park in Chicago, which is no longer in existence, used to have a dance pavilion as well.

DICK: In Denver the slogan was, "Not to See Elitch is Not to See Denver." That was so true. They used to have a big garden and their flowers were sold commercially, orchids and stuff like that.

JASON: In the early forties, throughout the Midwest, you were out-drawing all of the other bands including Glenn Miller, Tommy & Jimmy Dorsey, Harry James and Benny Goodman.

DICK: It started in about '38. We started to write songs, started to get big crowds at the Aragon. If you could go to the Aragon and stay there for any length of time and be on WGN every night as we were, you couldn't miss. We used to play there for weeks on end and then go out and tour Illinois, Iowa and Wisconsin. We did well on those one-night stand things.

JASON: Including the Orpheum here in Madison.

DICK: Yes, we used to play theatre dates in Madison. We'd play "It's Dark on Observatory Hill." I believe that's the name of the hill at the university.

JASON: You also played some dates at the University of Wisconsin.

DICK: Many dates.

JASON: One in particular was pretty sensational. You were booked with Glenn Miller, Harry James and Benny Goodman, all on the same bill. Lew Quadling said it was the best date your band ever played while he was with it.

DICK: I guess that's right. We were all there that night.

JASON: The total fee for all four bands that night was $15,000, which was a sizable sum in those days.

DICK: That was a lot of money in those days. We saved a lot of money too.

JASON: You never had much time to spend it. You were so often on the road.

DICK: Well, yeah, we were working hard, but that's what the guys wanted and that's what I wanted. My brother was always ahead of us booking. He knew every booker in the business. Will was a great manager. He passed away about three months ago.

JASON: I'm sorry to hear that. In 1942, there was an occasion when you were rushed to Frank Daley's Meadowbrook in New Jersey. You replaced a band that was bombing, but in all fairness, they were a band that was just getting started in the business. Do you remember who that was?

DICK: Remind me.

JASON: Stan Kenton, but I repeat they were just beginning what turned out to be a very successful career.

DICK: I remember now. That was our first appearance in the East. I expected to see a great big place with springs and waterfalls. It wasn't like that. It was a sort of roadhouse. It was a nice place to dance, but it was nothing like what we had in Chicago or California. We did good business there for Mr. Daley.

JASON: And yet, it was one of the better-known band venues in the country.

DICK: That's because they had a fine wire out of there to broadcast. That meant an awful lot to bands in those days.

JASON: That brings up another question since you mentioned radio. All of the bands were doing as many remote broadcasts as they could get. You had a theory about recording arrangements that were the same as what could be heard on the air. It was a good plan.

DICK: In some cases we didn't. We tried out the tunes before we recorded them. If we didn't like the arrangement, we'd change it before we recorded it. The version on the record is the one that made the money.

JASON: In other words, live performances were a sort of test lab.

DICK: Testing lab is right. Sometimes we just arranged one chorus to see how the people liked it. If they liked it, we'd do a full arrangement. We used to call that a scratch arrangement, one chorus. Quadling would make it so we could play it and then improvise the rest. Eddy Howard might have wanted a different key or something so we'd change it. We had a lot of things going. We tried everything.

JASON: You ran a contest one time when you were playing Catalina. You were getting the autographs of fans. Along with their signatures, they had to add, "I like Dick Jurgens because …" I understand the post office was flooded.

DICK: I don't know where you get your information, but it's pretty reliable. That was also one of the finest places we played, Catalina. It was a beautiful place. I don't know if you've ever been out there, but, it's twenty-two miles out in the blue Pacific, away from everything as they say. It really was. It was on the island of Catalina and it was called Avalon. It's a huge casino-ballroom. The ballroom was right out over the water. It was round and cost about four million dollars to build. That's a lot of money even now, but it was a whole lot more back then. Mr. Wrigley built it. Before we'd start work each night, we'd go up to the third floor where the dance area was. We'd go out on the huge balcony right over the water. We'd take out our horns and play our theme song and we'd play "In a Little Spanish Town," "Avalon" and "Harbor Lights." We could watch the people coming up the path. No cars were allowed on the island. They'd have to walk. The boats in the water would blink their lights. It was a highly romantic setting.

JASON: And at that time, you could probably see the mainland from there. We lived in the Corona Del Mar area for almost five years in the sixties and in all that time we actually saw Catalina Island a total of two times, too much fog and smog. There was another facet of the band business that you were all involved in from time to time and it had to be one of the hardest grinds you had to endure. I'm talking about movie theatre bookings. The Chicago and Oriental Theatres did them all the time as well as the Strand in New York and many more around the country.

DICK: The Paramount and the Capitol.

JASON: The thing is you'd have to play as many as eight shows a day, starting early in the morning and not finishing up until around midnight.

DICK: We started at eight-thirty in the morning when everybody in the place was asleep. The drunks off the street would come in while we were playing.

We'd finish around eleven thirty each night. It depended on how well we were doing. If we were drawing well, we'd do more shows. If you had some nice acts to go with the band, that helped. I went in once with Dick Powell. It was a great show. Everyone seemed to like it so we did nine shows a day.

JASON: You were doing nine at the Strand, at least on weekends.

DICK: I can believe it. That was quite a show place for the bands.

JASON: You had about an hour and ten-minute break while the movie was on.

DICK: You couldn't go anyplace. You'd just sit in your dressing room and relax for a few minutes. Then you'd be on again.

JASON: And it was seven days a week.

DICK: Those dates would last about two or three weeks. By the time they were over, we were exhausted.

JASON: Let's talk about some of the others in your band from your hometown area around Sacramento. Eddy Howard was from there, as were Ronnie Kemper and Carl Branch, who did arrangements and also played violin and sax.

DICK: Eddy Howard was from a little town called London, right near Sacramento. He came to town with a band from San Jose, which is also nearby. I picked him up at the Sacramento Hotel at Tenth and K. He liked my band and I liked the way he sang. We got together and we stayed together for about fourteen years, from 1927 until 1941. Ronnie Kemper went to school with me in high school and junior college. He played piano and I liked his work. He started singing when he first did "Cecilia." Carl Branch was another local boy, very talented in many ways. We had about eight guys from Sacramento. We were all together from 1928 until 1940. Then we changed some personnel.

JASON: Is there any truth to the story that when Ronnie Kemper first did his C-C-Cecilia thing, he had new caps that made him so sibilant?

DICK: The lisping, you mean? I don't think so.

JASON: Another story that's just a story.

DICK: I think he was trying to imitate another guy called Little Jack Little. He was an admirer of that gentleman. He started singing it that way. I said, "Keep it in. We'll record it that way." We did and it was an instant hit.

JASON: A lot of other people recorded that song as well, which was the case with most band music then.

DICK: Right. One time Glenn Miller called me. He said, "Dick, you're playing a song down there at the Aragon. I'd like to make a record of it. It's called 'Elmer's Tune'." He added, "You have to have a lyric for it?" I told him it never had a lyric. It was just an instrumental. He said to get one. I got on the phone. I called a songwriter I knew and asked him to come to the Aragon. I told him why. He said, "I can't write a lyric for a song with a title like 'Elmer's Tune'." I said, "Try it." He got on the elevated and came out there. I gave him a copy of the song. He called me about twenty minutes later when he was back in the loop. He said, "Here's your lyric." He sang it. We never changed one word of it. That's the story of "Elmer's Tune." It was on the Hit Parade for seventeen weeks.

JASON: When Eddy Howard joined you, he was a guitarist, just a fair guitarist, but when he came to you, didn't he break in with a different instrument because you didn't need another guitar?

DICK: It was trombone.

JASON: And of course, he couldn't read music.

DICK: He couldn't read, but he sure had a tremendous ear. You just had to do anything once for him and he had it. In the professional band business, where you have at least five new arrangements to deal with each week, you had to be able to do more than just think. He did most of the singing, as you know. We wrote him some parts and then he memorized them with the help of some of the other guys in the band. We let him play a few solos on trombone. He was quite a guy, one of the best band singers I ever heard. He never had to warm up. He'd just get up from the pit and start singing.

JASON: Carl Branch said that Eddy Howard would just open his mouth and a beautiful tenor would come out.

DICK: He used to thrill the women, I'll tell you that.

JASON: He was my favorite too. I heard him at the Aragon on several occasions.

DICK: Everybody thought his wife died when he wrote "My Last Goodbye." It sure sold the song, but it wasn't true. He and his wife were very happy and lived many years together after that.

JASON: Over thirty-seven years you had some sizable changes of personnel. Some that left were Dan Newman, Al Iavoli, Al Grimes and Art Modell. You also dropped the third violin somewhere along the way.

DICK: Those were all Sacramento guys who went home. I replaced them with different guys, mostly from around Chicago. Eddie Kaylor came from Denver. He was one of the best first trumpets I ever had.

JASON: Another trumpet was Joe Conterci.

DICK: Joe was our hot trumpet, he was second trumpet.

JASON: The new drummer was Frank Sayer.

DICK: Frank was a great drummer too.

JASON: Sweet Lund on bass and Charlie Hands on tenor.

DICK: Hey, you've got them all, haven't you? We had some great guys. When Ronnie Kemper and Eddy Howard left, I got Buddy Moreno and Harry Cool. Harry Cool came out of St. Louis. He was on staff at KMOX in St. Louis. I asked Perry Como, who was with Ted Weems at the time, if he knew of any good vocalists, like himself. He told me about Harry Cool. So I had him come in for an audition one afternoon. I'll never forget it. We had him sing a couple of songs and then I said, "I understand you play baseball." He said, "Yeah...why, what's that got to do with it?" I said, "What position?" He said, "Pitch." I said, "You're in, Harry, you're our new vocalist." We needed a pitcher for our ball team.

JASON: You just unwrapped a whole new ball of wax. There was a more or less regular league of band baseball teams.

DICK: A lot of bands had teams we used to play.

JASON: I remember seeing a box score from when Harry James was still with Goodman. He hit two doubles, a triple and a home run all in that one game.

DICK: He was a good ball player. He was crazy about baseball.

JASON: The Lionel Hampton band was their victim that day. Getting back to your band, Harry Cool had an entirely different voice than that of Eddy Howard. It was a bit stronger.

DICK: He was a much different singer, but what could we do? When Eddy left, I didn't know what to do so I finally decided to take the opposite angle and hire a girl vocalist, which I did, a girl named Gloria Gilbert. She had a very nice voice, did a good job. I bought her a lot of clothes and she sang with us for four or five weeks, but people didn't want a girl in my band so she was the last, the first and the last. That's when I got Harry Cool.

JASON: Coming up to the present, the obvious thing, at least around here, is that your band or at least its backbone is still very active. Don Ring, a local man, is fronting today's version of the Dick Jurgens band. He's working with your whole book of arrangements.

DICK: Yes, I started playing Don's bar when he first had it around 1970. It was one of my later bands. He admired the group. He always wanted to sing with us. I let him because he was a nice guy and he had a nice voice. He told me that if I ever left the band business he'd like to buy my library. That's how it ended up. About a year and a half ago, I sold it to him and he's done very well with it. He's got some good men. I told him that if he treated that library well, he'd do as well with it as I ever did. I understand he's doing fine at his Ponderosa Ballroom in McFarland, near Madison. I wish him luck.

JASON: They just got back from a tour here in the Midwest. He told me it went quite well. Next month they're booked for a Caribbean cruise on The Song of Norway, a well-known cruise ship.

****

After Dick Jurgens broke up his band in 1956, having seen the writing on the wall, he remained on the fringes for the rest of his life. In the late sixties, he assembled a new band, with which he recorded and played sporadic engagements.

We lost him in 1995, but his library of arrangements and original songs lives on.

ACT III:
SCENE TWO
THE MUSIC MAN

We sometimes take for granted the fine melodies that bind together the scenes of most any motion picture; yet, without those often-mysterious airs, continuity would be lost. It takes a very special talent to tie together and create the all-important harmony that helps to make the story line flow.

I present, for your enjoyment, a man who admirably accomplished that task and who, during the course of his long career, was rewarded with five Oscar nominations for his work. His abilities ran the gamut of musical possibilities as well as many appearances in acting roles.

He did pop arrangements for the likes of Nat King Cole, Ella Fitzgerald, Tony Bennett, Dinah Shore and lots of others. His original songs, his arrangements and his incidental music for films remain in the minds of many who, while they may not connect his name with his work, wish they could do just that.

His name was Frank DeVol. We spoke on July 29, 1987.

****

JASON: Today we're talking with a universally known musician, universally that is, among his peers. Frank DeVol has just about done it all in radio, television and motion pictures. He is also the president of a very interesting group in California called Pacific Pioneer Broadcasters. That seems like a good place to start.

FRANK: It doesn't go back to the early days of radio, but its members have to have been in radio for at least twenty years or television for twenty years. It doesn't accept motion pictures in the same vein. It's an organization that was formed around 1973 by people from the days of radio, *Ma Perkins, Meet Corliss Archer*, all of those people you can think of from those wonderful soap operas and dramas and comedy shows. Also, people from the early days of television before TV went network. It's a cross section of people who were actors, engineers, advertisers and studio heads. When you go to their luncheons, which generally include about seven hundred and fifty members, you see people you have worked with, from every category. It's a marvelous group to be with.

JASON: I believe it was founded by Edgar Bergen.

FRANK: Yes it was. He was a charter member and one of the founders. You'd also be interested to know that Jim Jordan (*Fibber McGee*), who is ninety, usually sits on the dais with other people who are there to honor our guests

JASON: The most recent newsletter I have from PPB, which is kind of old now, lists Jim as Chairman of the Board.

FRANK: He took over for Edgar Bergen when Edgar passed away. We were going to elect Charlie McCarthy, but it didn't seem right.

JASON: Charlie is sitting in the Smithsonian these days along with Effie Klinker and Mortimer Snerd. They're also on display at the Museum of Broadcast Communications in Chicago.

FRANK: I didn't realize that. They keep going, I guess. By the way, I think they're made out of redwood. That's the reason for their longevity.

JASON: If you say so, but just off-the-cuff, weren't they actually carved from beech?

FRANK: I thought that was supposed to be a secret, but now that you've let it out of the bag, it will be in *The Enquirer* next week.

JASON: Let's talk about Frank DeVol. People remember you, not only for your music, but also for the fact that you were the perfect foil for a lot of comedians on a lot of different shows and the brunt of a lot of jokes.

FRANK: Correct. You see, in the early days of radio, usually the orchestra leader was the butt of many jokes. That was because they didn't have to pay him any more to speak than they did for arranging and conducting. So it was a combination of things, mostly monetary. If he could play music and his voice was distinctive, they would use him. I was happy to do it because acting was always an avocation for me. I wanted to be two things when I was a kid. I wanted to be an orchestra leader like my father and a burlesque comedian.

JASON: You played a few regular roles on some shows. I know you were a panelist on *Pantomime Quiz*, but that was not what I had in mind.

FRANK: That was started in 1949, before network television and it was something else. Television was just a toy, just as radio was suspected of being when it started. We never got paid on those shows. We were given—I think for the first six months—a box of Ronson Lighters, beautifully displayed. A lot of people had to take up smoking around Christmas because they received lighters that I had been paid with. Often times we were sponsored by Gold Medal flour. I went home with bags filled with cake mixes and noodles and flour, that sort of thing. It was a joyous occasion, unrehearsed.

JASON: In the early days of radio, people were also sometimes paid in product rather than cash.

FRANK: That's true. On radio shows or TV shows like *Truth or Consequences*, you were either paid scale or there were gifts you could choose. In other words, if you wanted a refrigerator, washer or range, you got them without having to pay anything because the sponsor paid the tax. There was also a long time when the writers were encouraged to mention the name of a product in a script. Some of those writers ended up with garages full of soft drinks or whatever they thought they needed and put it in the script.

JASON: I remember one prime example of that and it wasn't even written in the script. It was strictly ad-lib. One time during his radio show, Jack Benny called his home and told Rochester to plug in his General Electric blanket so his bed would be nice and warm when he got there. Rochester said, "But boss, we don't have a General Electric blanket." Benny replied, "We do now!" A short time later, every member of the cast had one—gratis.

FRANK: They just slipped it in. Nobody ever thought about it because it was just every day speech. You talk about all the product names at home. It took a long time before they clamped down and said no products could be mentioned on the air, except the sponsor of course.

JASON: Let's talk about your music. It's the biggest part of your resume. You began as a sax man and arranger for Horace Heidt, if I'm not mistaken.

FRANK: That was my first big band, but it was not my first band. I was with little bands before the big bands came into being due to their access to radio airtime. They were called road bands. They were small bands that traveled from city to city. Many were the same ones that later became big bands. They were groups of eleven or twelve or maybe thirteen men. They had names that people just don't remember anymore. I do because I used to see their cards in various store windows, grocery stores and so on. People like Whitey Coughlin and Tommy Christian who I'm sure you never heard of. Then when radio started, I went from Canton, Ohio, which was home, to Cleveland and joined Emerson Gill and his Orchestra in 1931. I was with them for three years. About 1935, I joined George Olson and his big band. He was a man who had several musicals on Broadway. Then I went with Horace Heidt. I studied arranging, just by myself. I copied records and joined the Musicians Union when I was fourteen. I was with Horace, off and on for about five years. Then I moved on to Alvino Rey and his orchestra with the King Sisters. I met those ladies in 1936 and am still very friendly with them. Some of them live close by and the others are not that far away.

JASON: Alvino was also from the Horace Heidt organization.

FRANK: Yes he was. Alvino was born in Cleveland and his name was Alvin McBurney, but because he played the steel guitar, he thought it might be better if he had a Hawaiian name. He took Rey, which means king, and became Alvino Rey. He combed his hair straight back. He had long shiny black hair. He was the inventor of the electric guitar or at least the developer of it, a very nice man. He married one of the king sisters, Louise.

JASON: There were others who came out of the Horace Heidt Band. I'm not sure how the timing fits your stay there. One of them was Ernie Passoja on trombone.

FRANK: We were both there at the same time. He was from Chicago.

JASON: Then there was Fred Lowry, the famous whistler, and Frankie Carle, Bobby Hackett and Bill Finnegan, doing some arranging.

FRANK: Hackett and Finnegan came after me. In our band, we had Larry Cotton who had a few hit records. We had Art Carney. Art joined us at seventeen. He was an impersonator. He was marvelous at the time. He's done a great job with his career. I'm sure you've seen him in pictures since he got older. If you ever noticed, he limps. The limp is from a wound he got in World War II. When I was in New York, I went to see him. He told me about when his leg was wounded. He was in a cast up to his hips. He was in a ward with people with similar injuries. He said it used to itch so far down their legs that they would tape tongue depressors together and then push them down into their casts to scratch their itch.

JASON: When you got to radio, you worked on a kind of strange show, *Tommy & Betty Lou.*

FRANK: You mean *The Ginny Simms Show.* That was the show they were on—a ventriloquist and Betty Lou, his dummy. I did another year with Ginny and Donald O'Conner. I was doing comedy at the time and so was he. He was the star, but I was always included. When I became an orchestra leader back in 1945, I was on KHS in Los Angeles. In '45, I had a call from Rudy Vallee who had heard the program while he was in the Coast Guard. He was going to go back on radio so he asked me to do the music for his show. I did that show for a year. Then I went with Ginny Simms for two years, '46 and '47. After that, Dave Bullock and I went with Jack Carson and Eve Arden. That's how I got on *Pantomime Quiz.* I did that show with a group from Jack Carson. They used a different group each week for their charade thing. I was with Jack for two years. The last year overlapped with Jack Smith and Dinah Shore on *The Oxydol Show* and I had that for five years. Then came television with Rosemary Clooney, *The Colgate Hour* with Martin and Lewis, *The George Goble Show* and finally, *The Danny Thomas Show.* I also did a special called *The Wonderful World of Burlesque.* Then I started into motion pictures. I got mostly into background music, but I did some acting too. I've done over fifty TV shows and four or five movies. They were all bit parts, but enough to get me pensions from AFTRA and SAG. (American Federation of Television and Radio Artists and Screen Actors Guild).

JASON: One of the characters you played was Mr. Bannister on *I'm Dickens, He's Fenster.* Another was Doc on *Camp Runamuck.*

FRANK: How did you know that? That was just the pilot. I was only in the pilot. I must tell you something funny. The man who wrote and directed *Camp Runamuck* was David Swift, who also created

Mr. Peepers. I just recently had lunch with David Swift, Livingston and Evans. Those last two wrote *Mona Lisa* and *Silver Bells* and many more. We were talking about *Camp Runamuck.* After the pilot we got the go ahead and were supposed to start production the following Monday. The Saturday before that, I had a heart attack. I was in the hospital, so they had to hurry around and find someone else to play the role of "Doc," so I was never really on that show. When I saw the series and saw the things they put the doctor through, who at that time was Leonard Stone, WOW! They had him flown on wires across water and they were constantly running him up and down all kinds of places. If I hadn't had the heart attack, I would have been dead. I would have had a full motion picture of it, but that wouldn't have done me much good, would it?

JASON: Not at that point. I only vaguely remember that show but I do know that it was pretty active.

FRANK: I enjoyed playing Mr. Bannister on *I'm Dickens, He's Fenster.* I met a lot of nice people on that show. You know, I always played myself. I always did deadpan humor. I studied acting at three times in my life, in 1939 and 1948 and then again in 1972. I found that I was not an actor, *per se.* I could not portray anyone, but myself. I am an after dinner speaker now for conventions and such. I talk about Hollywood, the Old Hollywood, the New Hollywood and the music business and I do it in a humorous fashion.

JASON: Speaking of film scores, we could assemble quite a long list of your credits. Many are well remembered. There were some excellent pictures like *Guess Who's Coming to Dinner* and another one I cannot personally forget for reasons close to my heart, *The Flight of the Phoenix*. At one time in my life, when I was a professional pilot, I worked closely with Paul Mantz, who was killed doing a scene near the end of *Phoenix*.

FRANK: Yes he was. A lot of people remember that movie out of the many that Robert Aldrich did, but he did many others. He made *The Dirty Dozen, What Ever Happened to Baby Jane?* and *Hush, Hush Sweet Charlotte*—just to name a few. I did the song for *Charlotte* along with Mack David. I also did the score. We were both nominated for Oscars. We didn't win, but when you consider that you were one of over two hundred and fifty people who wrote scores and backgrounds in any given year, you can feel rather proud. Although I don't have any of the hardware that goes with any of my five nominations, I still feel good about being considered.

JASON: That's an interesting point. Just to be on the short list is an honor.

FRANK: Correct. You are nominated by your own branch of the industry. That's one thing most people don't know about. Composers nominate composers. Actors nominate actors. Cinematographers, costume designers, you can just go right down the line. They are each nominated by their own branch. Then the entire membership votes on everything. Well, each member is not familiar with what other branches do. I myself have to vote on color photography, set design, etc, many crafts for which I can only say, "Oh yeah, that looked nice." So if you're nominated by your own cohorts you know you must have done something right.

JASON: Heavy acceptance by a jury of your peers.

FRANK: Yes, we're all fans of each other. In the music business, nobody is jealous of another person. I think the reason for that is that we each have an agent who has all of the scripts sent to him for all of the pending motion pictures and television shows. The agent then calls the producer and says, "Seems to be a comedy picture. I have so and so or so and so." The producer asks what they have done. In the end, you're put in according to what your specialty is because you do get type cast. It's trimmed down that way. Sometimes you don't even know you're up for a picture, so you're never jealous of anybody and you have a real good time. I'll tell you, the wrong impression of Hollywood is gotten in many instances. I myself have never been to any party where there was any dope or any drugs of any kind. I never worked with a band that had any alcoholics or drug users. I think you tend to gravitate to people with like tastes when you're out here. Some people want to live in Beverly Hills. They love the high life, love to go to all the five hundred dollar a couple parties that are held often every year. I probably get six invitations a month for parties, which range from two hundred to two-fifty a person. It's ridiculous. As a rule, I just tell them that I give to my own charities. I'm not going to support any boiler room group begging for help. Most times the money doesn't go where they say it will. Some of the most talented people, especially actors, act like they think stars should act. They get carried away with their own image. I would say that forty to fifty per cent of their gross is paid out just to make that image. They must live like they make one or two or three million a year. They live like that for the general public, not particularly for themselves. They're living on a lot less than you might think. It's still a lot of money but not the amount we read about in the papers.

JASON: Another big misconception people have about Hollywood is that marriages don't ever last there. The last six people to whom I've spoken out there have all been married no less than forty years.

FRANK: I've been married for fifty-two years.

JASON: There it is. You just added credence to my point. Just last week I had a conversation with André Baruch. He and his wife, Bea Wain, just celebrated fifty years together.

FRANK: We had a fiftieth anniversary dinner with all their children and grandchildren. There were Bea and Major André Baruch, Norman Cousins and his wife and my wife and I. The three couples at the table boasted over one hundred and fifty-five years of married life.

JASON: It's more the rule than the exception, but it's the exception that we hear about in the news.

FRANK: If people lived up to everything you read in the paper, they wouldn't have time to eat, sleep or do any of the things they have to do. Jack Carson used to read the columns in *Variety* and *The Hollywood Reporter.* He used different language, but he said, "It's funny, you read this and you know that ninety-five percent of the stuff is pure—." He added that if you don't read it, you might miss the five percent that's true.

JASON: So you learn what you've been doing that you didn't know you were doing.

FRANK: I had a press agent who also handled six or seven actors and actresses. I was always in the papers, at least once a week in Hedda Hopper or one of the other writers of the time. I would be with one of the agents other people, maybe an actress. We were going to produce a picture. She was going to sing in it and I was going to write the score. There would be all these things and there would be a funny line for me at the end, what Frank DeVol said. I read *The National Enquirer* while I'm waiting for the checker to do her thing. I read all about things supposedly said by Pia Zadora or whoever. If they don't read it, they won't know what they said.

JASON: There's a certain element among us who have to have that sort of information. I never quite understood it. They have to know that most of it is pure fantasy. They live for sensationalism.

FRANK: I remember when I was a kid, the guys I hung around with always had older sisters who used to read *True Confessions* and eat chocolates. That kind of went together. They became rather heavy-set, fleshy as they say.

JASON: With a movie magazine in the other hand.

FRANK: Without a doubt. Everything is at such a high pitch now. It's changed the music business. I think synthesizers are taking over, unfortunately. They're still in their infancy as far as technique is concerned. It's a marvelous thing, but also unfortunate. It's like the industrial revolution for music.

JASON: It's taking a lot of jobs from musicians.

FRANK: I think a lot of side men had to sell their airplanes. They were used to great salaries. So many of them thought it would never end. When it ends, it's very difficult if you're leveraged, meaning small down payments with big payments after that. They'd get pretty deep in debt. I was brought up in Ohio. We didn't think that way.

****

Frank DeVol was a master at his craft and a man with a great sense of humor, something that may not show up well in print.

As he stated, he never played any major acting roles, but he used to pop-up all over the place in bit parts and small continuing character roles. You might have noticed him with Don Adams on *Get Smart*, with the Cartwright's on *Bonanza*, or on *Fernwood Tonight* as the bandleader. You could have caught him with Barbara Eden on *I Dream of Jeannie* or on the big screen with John Wayne in *McLintock*.

You would have heard his musical scores behind films and TV shows as diverse as *Krakatoa, East of Java, The Love Boat, McCloud* and another movie, *The Frisco Kid* with Gene Wilder.

He earned five Oscar nominations in all, quite an achievement: In 1959 for the score behind *Pillow Talk* with Doris Day and Rock Hudson, and in 1964, a double for his work on *Hush, Hush Sweet Charlotte*, one for the song and the other for the score. In 1965, he was again honored for *Cat Ballou* with Jane Fonda and Lee Marvin, and the final one, *Guess Who's Coming to Dinner* in 1967.

In 1995, Frank died of congestive heart failure. Only time can write his true epitaph.

ACT III:
SCENE THREE
LIVELY LADY

There are not many people who simply exude zest and happiness from their first hello until a reluctant goodbye. One of those was a lady, who oozed joy from every pore. She was a member of an exclusive group of entertainers. That group was the girl singers who worked with the many pop and swing bands from another era. In those days, we could have heard Margaret Whiting, Helen O'Connell, Kay Star, Martha Tilton and so many others. They were all stars, each in their own unique style.

For me one stands out because she was so different from the rest. She had a relatively short career on the bandstand due only to her own wishes. She was always bouncy and vivacious when performing, whether she was singing or just watching between songs. She was still like that when we spoke for hours on August 1, 1986. I was thoroughly entertained the whole time we talked. I did not want it to end.

The lady in question could be called "Latin Dynamite." She was Lina Romay, who did most of her band singing with Xavier Cugat—but that was not the end of her story.

****

JASON: Lina, I understand your career started with a surprise.

LINA: What happened was–my father was with the Mexican government–sort of a consul. At the time, we were living in Detroit and I was finishing school. I remember that Xavier Cugat was appearing at the Statler Hotel. I thought he was one of the most wonderful musicians. At that time, he was getting very popular. It was a great era for the rhythms of the Rumba and the Conga. My father was at the consulate in Detroit at the time. I remember we had to appear at one of those Pan-American receptions and my father was the major speaker. Whatever happened, someone asked me to get up and sing a couple of little Mexican folk songs, which I had grown up with. I sang and there was a news reporter, Hershell Hart, from *The Detroit Free Press*. He liked what he heard, so much so that he said to my father, "I think we ought to take her to the local radio station. I really think they should hear her. That music is big now with Cugat at the Statler." To make a long story short, my father said, "She's still in school and I was planning to go back East." Mr. Hart said, "I'd like to take her up there and just introduce her to those people at the station." When I heard that, I got so excited that there would be a chance for me to talk to anybody who had anything to do with singing and music. So I did go and they liked me so much they gave me a little program, part of a homemakers program, on which I sang Mexican, and Spanish and American songs, a combination of all three. They had this orchestra, the Don Del Rio Orchestra and I sang with them. Mr. Cugat was still at the Statler and was listening to his radio while getting ready for his evening show. He heard me and got all excited because here was a brand new voice. He called the station and they told him I was the daughter of the Consul from Mexico. Then he called my father at the Consulate and made a date with him to bring me to dinner at the hotel on the next Friday, which was guest night. It was the most exciting night for me. I can't ever duplicate that particular night. It was so much fun for me. I got up and sang the same little songs that I did at the Pan-American dinner. Mr. Cugat was impressed and the audience reception was wonderful. Hank Greenberg was in the audience, handsome baseball player, hands like you wouldn't believe. He praised me too. So that was really, truly how I got into the business. That was my first big chance. I didn't go with Cugat at that time. He wanted me to but he wanted me to share the spotlight with his niece. I immediately balked. I said no. I have to sing by myself. I can't sing with anybody else. Time went on. We were sent back to the New York office. My father was back as Consul in New York. I went back with him planning to go to school again, to college. Two weeks after we moved, Mr. Cugat got in touch with us again. Somehow, he got our home phone number from the Consulate. He called me at home and asked me to meet him for dinner at the Waldorf Astoria, where he was playing then. He wanted to discuss the possibility of my joining the band. That's how it happened. That's how I became Xavier Cugat's vocalist.

JASON: You had to be a good singer to get so much attention from him.

LINA: I don't know about good. I'm not a coloratura or anything like that, but I had a lot of verve.

JASON: Did you ever have any formal voice training?

LINA: No, I never studied anything, anything at all. There are a lot of people in our business like that–Crosby was one, just a natural talent. We were able to get up and interpret the lyrics and have people respond to the feelings.

JASON: You did work with Crosby on his show. We'll get to that later, but for now, I want to go back to Cugat.

LINA: Well, of course. You have to go back to Cugie at the Waldorf.

JASON: And even before that. He was initially brought to this country by Enrico Caruso.

LINA: Oh, yes? I don't know very much about his background. I do know he was born in Cuba of Spanish parents.

JASON: And he was a Chihuahua breeder?

LINA: That was a long time later. That was when he became popular on the screen at M-G-M. He never had a Chihuahua at the Waldorf. He had a great big Norwegian Elk Hound—Simba. That was his name. I'll never forget that.

JASON: One thing he did do was draw cartoons and characterizations. In fact, his work was syndicated by King Features.

LINA: He was wonderful at that. I loved Cugie. He was a grand character. He's eighty, something now. He's in Spain thinking about starting the band again.

JASON: When you were with him, didn't you work with Miguelito Valdés?

LINA: I did. He was a singer and a Boccoterro. A Boccoterro is someone who plays the Conga drum. He was wonderful. He sang "Ba-ba-loo" and all those great Cuban rhythms. It was a tremendous band in those days.

JASON: Miguelito was the one who actually introduced the Cuban beat here.

LINA: That was while I was still in Detroit with my father and mother. I was on WWJ, an NBC subsidary in Detroit, doing my Latin songs. During that time, we did some experimental television for Philco. I found that to be very exciting because television was just beginning. TV didn't really take hold until the late forties. I'll never forget the first time I saw myself on the monitor. Everything was brown and beige. It didn't matter what I had on. It was brown and beige. It was really funny. Then, as you know, I went back to New York and was on with Cugie. We did a lot of theatres around the country and we recorded for Columbia.

JASON: You worked quite a bit on *Spotlight Bands* on radio. Then you were with Dick Haymes on his show. Along with singing, you did a number of character voices.

LINA: I did a lot of character voices and I did a lot of dialects. That was *The Autolite Show* with Dick Haymes. I did four or five with Ozzie and Harriet and then with Red Skelton. He was such fun. I did quite a few with him. I did a couple with Frank Sinatra when he had his short-lived show. I also worked with Meredith Willson. He was a great musician.

JASON: And Paul Whiteman.

LINA: Oh, Paul, the 59th Street Theatre. I could never forget. It was tremendous. It was the first time I had so many musicians backing me up. I stood on a high platform and sang a couple of Latin songs. Then I also did "Come Rain or Come Shine" from *Porgy and Bess*.

JASON: A nice thing about Whiteman was that he always gave his guests time. He never cut them off. He gave them the extra time he would have used himself.

LINA: He was a charming guy. Another person I loved very much was Guy Lombardo. I recorded four sides with Guy. He loved Latin music. He was someone who became very personal. Anyone he liked, he'd invite to his home on the Island. He had a big boat. He and his wife were wonderful. I was young. I wasn't attached to anyone at the time. I used to date one of his brothers. It was a long time ago. I can't remember which one. It was a wonderful career while it was active. I made quite a few nice movies. They were good ones, not just scraps.

JASON: One of them was with Ginger Rogers and Lana Turner, *Weekend at the Waldorf.*

LINA: That was the second movie I did at Columbia. Then I was in *The Heat Is On* with Mae West. Mae West was absolutely the funniest lady. She could do anything with lines.

JASON: Did she have a problem with her glasses?

LINA: I don't remember that. I don't remember her having glasses.

JASON: This comes from a conversation I had with Arch Oboler who brought up the subject. She did a skit on the Bergen and McCarthy show, the now infamous "Adam and Eve" skit, after which she was banned from the media. The reason behind the problem, as Arch explained it, was that she would never wear her glasses in front of an audience.

Soooo–things didn't come out quite the way they were written. Her double entendre was classic Mae West.

LINA: That's funny. Things are so different today. I started wearing glasses about four years ago and I really love them. My fans don't mind them either. Anyway, to get back to Columbia, after *The Heat Is On*, which was quite an experience, I did *You Were Never Lovelier* with Cugie. That was followed by a seven-year contract with M-G-M. They came to the Waldorf and asked me to dance. Then they asked me if I'd like to join MGM and become a star. I said I'd like to try. So I signed with them.

JASON: Tell me about *Stage Door Canteen*.

LINA: That was during the war; consequently, all of the Hollywood people were involved in it.

JASON: I'm sure you must have worked in the canteen as well as being in the movie.

LINA: Quite a lot. We all took part, all the singers—all the bandleaders—all the actors, producers and directors. I was there when Bette Davis took a pie in her face. The guys loved it. They screamed at a big actress taking a pie, a custard pie. I'll never forget it. At any rate, I got to go to MGM. We did *Two Sailors and a Girl* and *Neptune's Daughter*. I did *Love Comes to Andy Hardy* with Mickey Rooney. What a talent. That was my favorite. Then I did a dramatic film with Clark Gable when he came back from the service. It was his first film after the war. It was called *Adventure*. "Gable's Back and Garson's got him." ... Greer Garson. That was the tagline. It was an exciting movie. It got a lot of nice revues. Then there was *Man*

Behind the Gun for Warner's with Randolph Scott. In the interim, I had done *Honeymoon* at RKO with Shirley Temple and Franchot Tone. We still see reruns of many of them on late night TV so that's kind of fun for me. After MGM, I was presented with a lot of good comedy shows on radio. I was on a show with Ed Gardner, *Duffy's Tavern*, and as I said earlier, *Kraft Music Hall*. I was on there for twenty-six weeks with Bing. He chose me from all the vocalists. He wanted someone exciting and he picked me. I did *Bob Hope's Comedy Hour*, in fact that was the last show I did. I told Mr. Hope that I couldn't go back East to do the extra shows I was signed for. I wanted to stay home. I was getting married.

JASON: You are one of the few people who did that and stuck to it.

LINA: That was 1953. I'm still with the same man.

JASON: I meant about canceling your public career.

LINA: I really did it. I went from one life to another. I guess, in the final analysis, it was because I never had to work too hard to get what I wanted. It all just came easy. I never spent any money on my career at all except for a few arrangements.

JASON: You are a very exceptional case. So many people bang their heads against the wall for years and never get anywhere.

LINA: I think there must be some other people around like me. I can't be an original.

JASON: In my book, you are an original Lina, but you're right about there being others who found it easy.

Ozzie Nelson was one. He went right out of law school into the big time. He had a law degree but he never used it.

LINA: You know another funny thing? Everybody thinks I was married to Cugat. A lot of people think so, but I was not. When I joined the band, he was still married to Carmen Castillo, a beautiful lady. When I came on the scene, they'd been married for at least seventeen years. I guess they were having some troubles. They were divorced a little later. I think he always liked me very much, but I was very young and just not interested. To me he was an old man. Let me tell you something that happened recently. I joined Pacific Pioneer Broadcasters back in 1974. They were having luncheons every couple of months. I decided I wanted to do something with all the girl singers who had been popular during the thirties, forties and fifties. I presented the idea to the president reminding him how good they all were. People like Margaret Whiting and June Christie and Peggy Lee and all the rest. He said if I would put it together, he would be glad to do it. So I worked for three months. I got all the girls on the phone and signed them up. I had about eighteen of the most marvelous girl singers on the dais. It was a big success. A lot of them got their old bandleaders to come and see them. I called Las Vegas to talk to Cugie who was appearing there with Charo. I said, "I want you to be here to represent me, but **don't bring Charo!**" He did come. He really did.

JASON: There's something else I know you really like to talk about. That's about what you're doing now and have been doing for the last six or seven years.

LINA: My current effort? I can't believe I'm still doing it. I was hired in March of 1980. Someone found out that I speak perfect Spanish and perfect English. They were looking for someone to go on the radio and give the results of the horse races—thoroughbred races at Hollywood Park, and they weren't able to find anyone. I don't know why. There should have been someone besides myself. At any rate, I was very negative. I had no concept of thoroughbred racing. I didn't know anything about it except to go to the Turf Club once in a while. They kept after me until I finally said it looked like a real challenge. I was tempted to try it. It could be fun. I love radio and I knew I could do that part of it, but I didn't know anything about horses and you just don't have time to study. The race is run and you just have to do it. They said, "Do it–we want you to try." They hired me to do it in Spanish at first. That's what I did. I'd never done anything like that in my life. I don't know who was standing over me to tell me what to do–obviously someone was. It was a whole new ball game to me. I just watched every race and followed it with the winner, the time and whether it was a gelding or a little two-year-old filly, who the jockey was and if anything spectacular had happened. Then I'd give the prices, you know, the winner, the placer and the shower, along with any other bit of news that I could give in the time I had on the radio. Now I've got ten or twelve stations I report to. It's really fun. I love it. All of the sudden I realized that I'm a senior citizen. My picture was in the *AARP Magazine* with an article titled "She's a winner."

JASON: Overall, your career in show business was only ten or twelve years before you walked away from it.

LINA:	That's just about it. I signed with MGM in 1944 and I was with Cugat for two years before that. That's all the time I was with him, but I'll tell you, Jason, with Cugat it was like putting a glove on your hand. We suited each other perfectly. It was wonderful. I could feel the music and knew what he wanted. I could project those feelings in the lyrics. He didn't like it when I left. We had something good. Naturally, he wanted to continue with it, but I had to have my life go on. I had to go ahead and do what I had to do for me.
JASON:	Was Miguelito Valdés still with the band when you left?
LINA:	A little longer than me. I can't say how long… maybe another two or three years. All of the boys are gone now. It's terrible to have to say that. All I have is pictures. Capalino, who longed to play the maracas and Pregnico, the other Boccoterro, are gone. Of course, for me it was the clave. I loved the rhythm of the clave. The boys let me play it. I never sat down. I had a chair, but I never used it. I was always bouncing around on the bandstand. Poor Cugie!
JASON:	Talk about someone who is young at heart. Don Ring told me that the main thing he remembers about you is that you are dynamic.
LINA:	Bing Crosby used to ask my mom, "Where does she get the energy?"
JASON:	You haven't lost any of that energy, Lina. I can feel it from two thousand miles away. Don't ever change.

****

It was a short, but very intense ten or twelve years that Lina Romay invested in her career. It would be hard to imagine that she could ever have done anything at less than mach speed. To the best of my knowledge, she never ever slowed down even after she left show business.

Sad to report, Lina passed away one week before Christmas in 2010. She was ninety-one. I am quite sure she is back on the bandstand somewhere with Cugat, still jumping around while she plays her clave with gusto.

ACT III:
SCENE FOUR
THE MAESTRO

He lived his life to the fullest measure, from the first downbeat to the final coda. He always wanted more and, for the most part, through his own tenacity and some might say, arrogance, he reached his goals. No matter what one might think of him on a personal level, it would be criminal to deny his unquestioned genius in his chosen field of endeavor. He was one of, if not the best of American composers and conductors as well as a virtuoso on piano. His work can never be set aside for any competitor.

I could only be talking about one monumental talent. His name was Leonard Bernstein.

As busy as his life always was, it proved to be virtually impossible to catch up with him for even the briefest of chats. Not to be denied, I called on Joan Peyser, who had recently released the most honest and definitive Bernstein biography of the many available. She was well informed and very helpful. The date was April 23, 1987.

****

JASON: He's been called many things by many people, but perhaps his own mother described him best when she said, "Scratch any part of him and he oozes talent." He is the subject of this discussion along with a very recent, very readable, and I must add, very successful book, *Bernstein: A Biography*. Please meet the author of that book, Joan Peyser.

JOAN: There have been many written, many biographies before mine, but they are mostly the sort of book that has always been written where music is concerned, very appreciative, very admiring, but not capturing the true essence of the man, which this book does.

JASON: Your book definitely does capture the man himself as well as his contributions to music. Let me ask you a bit about your own background. I know that this is not your first book and also that you are very capable of handling material in the field of music.

JOAN: I've been in music all my life. I started to play piano when I was five. I played in Town Hall, which was a major house in New York at the time. It's still in existence, but does not have the prestige that it did then. I was thirteen then. I majored in music at Smith and Barnard Colleges and then got my Masters in Musicology at Columbia University. When I emerged from that, I began writing about music and found that I liked writing better than I liked playing. I've been writing about it for many, many years. In general, I try to illuminate a time and place, the music of a time and place, through the person. I've done that in each of my books. The purpose of this book was to try to reveal as much as I possibly could from the thirties to the present day through this sweet, likable man, who seems to have found the Fountain of Youth and Dante's *Inferno* as well, a man of force, talent and achievement, devil and angel. He certainly crowded more experience into his life with incredible intensity than any other man I know of. Bernstein regularly stays up until six a.m. The people who are close to him say that what he calls insomnia is his inability of bearing the idea of losing a minute

of time. He thinks if he goes to sleep, he'll miss
something.

JASON: His life has been crammed with activity right from
the very beginning. He was a pianist long before he
was a conductor or composer, a very fine pianist.

JOAN: Most professional musicians start when they are
four, five or six years old. Leonard Bernstein didn't
get near a piano until he was ten, when his aunt, in
the process of getting a divorce, simply had the
movers leave an upright piano in his parent's house.
As soon as he hit those keys, he knew he was
destined for a life in music. He felt that it was
then that he began to grow strong and big. He
claims he had been frail and sickly before that.
He immediately showed a tremendous affinity for
the piano, studying, as was usually the case, with
some neighborhood women. Then he moved on
to a woman who still serves him as his private
secretary, a woman in her late eighties today,
Helen Coates, who was assistant to Boston's finest
piano teacher, Heinrich Gebhard. Then he studied
with Gebhard and continued with his piano when
he went to Harvard. He was really bound to have
a career in those early days as a concert pianist. I
have a little incident in the book in which he wrote
to a friend–he called her Myra Hess and signed it,
Josef Hofmann. That was his fantasy when he
was fifteen. It wasn't until he entered Harvard that
he discovered the other world of conducting and
composition.

JASON: You're talking about two of the premiere musicians
of the time, Dame Myra Hess and Josef Hofmann.

JOAN: Not just of that time, but of any time. It was a fantasy
no less than awesome. It's just that his feelings

changed. At the time, in his mid-teens, his dream was of being a renowned concert pianist. That all changed during the time he was at Harvard.

JASON: Two of his talents are things that cannot be taught. I'm talking about his ability to sight-read music and also his ability as a mental arranger.

JOAN: He certainly was a phenomenal sight reader. I can tell you a story about that. He was applying to the Curtis Institute and Fritz Reiner, a fearsome man, so austere and rigid. Reiner put Brahms' *Academic Festival Overture* on the piano for Leonard to read and he just went right through it. In fact, when Reiner asked him to identify it, he did so with a sort of a poem. He had learned that piece while in grammar school. The poem was something to do with Santa Claus and hooves. The kind of thing we all had in music appreciation. You could put a stack of pop music of the day on his piano. Bernstein would go through it, eating it up and loving it all. He didn't make a distinction at the time, you know, Brahms is good and the other bad. He just devoured all kinds of music. There was a man, who when Bernstein was fourteen, put a copy of Stravinsky's *Petrushka* in front of him. Bernstein had not heard the work before, but he played through the piano version without missing a beat. He had incredible gifts from the start. The gift of enormous musicianship, innate musicianship with which he was born, combined with remarkable aggression that I attribute to the struggle he was continuously engaged in with his father in addition to a sort of powerful sexuality. This all combined to make Bernstein the figure he is, certainly the most important musician in the United States, probably in the world today. I would go that far.

JASON: You made an interesting point when you mentioned pop music. He also had a love for jazz.

JOAN: Yes, he did quite a lot of that. At his *Young People's Concerts*, he devoted several to the exploration of jazz. I traced in detail what kind of pleasure he found in jazz when he was a young man living in New York before his career took off. In the early forties, he would go to some of the clubs with his friend Marc Blitzstein. If you speak to people about that kind of jazz, several would hedge a bit. He himself is not the perfect jazz performer because he is not an ensemble person. He doesn't know how to do anything without taking it over. One thing about jazz is that everyone has to blend in. When Bernstein is in the room nobody else can breathe. He just takes over. He has that kind of heat and energy that radiates from him when he enters a room. His sister has said that when comes in the room, the temperature rises several degrees.

JASON: He did considerable work for the Broadway stage. I'm referring to *On the Town*, *Wonderful Town*, and of course, *West Side Story*.

JOAN: I feel that his most productive years were those when he was involved in Broadway. He began in 1943 with *On the Town*, then *Wonderful Town* in '53, *Candide* in '56 and *West Side Story* in '57. The reason for the hiatus between *On the Town* and *Wonderful Town*, I explain in my book. In 1943, Koussevitzky had grown to really love him and hold his musicianship in the most enormous esteem. He was trying very hard to help him with his career as a conductor. In '43, Bernstein got the post of Assistant Conductor with the New York Philharmonic, which was an incredible achievement, something Koussevitzky had a big role in. As it happened, Bernstein had written *On the Town* for Broadway and when it opened in Boston, for it's out of town trial before the official opening on Broadway, Koussevitzky came back stage and spent three hours railing at him for wasting his time on what he called jazz. Bernstein pronounced it 'jezz' because that was the way Koussevitzky said it. He made it clear that if Bernstein wanted to continue to have his support as a conductor of European music, he had to stop this other arena, which he considered the "Rot of Broadway." So Bernstein did not write again for the stage until Koussevitzky's death in 1951. I feel it was a great loss for all of us because the collaborators for *On the Town* went on to write any number of shows using other composers like Julius Stein and Morton Gould. One can only speculate as to what those shows might have been transformed into if Bernstein had been the composer.

JASON: You mentioned a couple of people who had a big influence on Bernstein's life. The most obvious one was Serge Koussevitzky.

JOAN: I think Koussevitzky was a tremendous influence. He gave him the kind of warmth and support for a career in music at a time when he certainly had not received it from his father, who was very upset when he discovered his son was really serious about the field. He predicted he would end up playing the piano under a palm tree in a cocktail lounge. Before meeting Koussevitzky, Bernstein, as a sophomore at Harvard, met Dimitri Mitropoulos. He was a tremendous influence as well. I would say Mitropoulos was second only to his father in the effect he had on Bernstein's life. The relationship had some very dark disappointments. At the

moment when he expected Mitropoulos to come
through with a job in Minneapolis, he did not.
That was a dark moment. He went to interview
with Koussevitzky to see if he could get into the
Tanglewood-Berkshire program. Koussevitzky
simply embraced him and understood immediately
that this was no run-of-the-mill student. He was
someone very special. He supported him enormously
in an effort to develop a career as a conductor.
In fact, he was trying his best to maneuver the
situation to get him his post at the Boston Symphony
when he left, but the BSO didn't want Bernstein.
There were a million reasons they didn't want him,
but certainly the most obvious was that he was
much too young to be considered by any orchestra
as music director. He didn't get the Boston job.
It went to Charles Munch in 1947. One of the
things most people don't have a clue about is the
enormous amount of time between his eruption
onto the music scene, filling in for Bruno Walter
when Bernstein was his assistant in New York, and
his later success. Walter was a guest conductor in
1943. He took sick and Leonard had to take his
place. It was a concert that was broadcast on CBS
on a Sunday afternoon. He did not get a regular
conducting job until 1958. People somehow
picture that Bernstein just bounced into the
conductor's world and had it 'made' from the start.
He didn't at all. He spent those fifteen years as a
guest conductor. He certainly ran around and even
went to Europe, but, in a sense, nobody wanted
to live with him. He was very good as a fill in
conductor, but not permanently. He was very
insecure financially and emotionally. It wasn't until
1958, when he got his tenure that he knew he had
a big steady income and that it would be smooth
sailing. At least that was what he had every reason
to believe.

JASON: That's a field where there isn't too much money unless you reach the top, music in general, for that matter.

JOAN: Music is very, very hard, very hard to make a living. As a composer, it's incredibly difficult. I don't think most of your listeners have any sense of what it costs a composer just to be a composer. He might get a commission to write a piece and then he has to have all the parts copied for a large orchestra. You cannot be in the music business unless you have no choice. That it gives you oxygen. That you can't do anything else because something inside forbids it.

JASON: Unless you're prepared to starve for a long time, maybe forever.

JOAN: Right, maybe forever. Unless you're like Charles Ives, who had his insurance company and did composition once in a while. That's an odd situation.

JASON: By mentioning Ives, you bring up another subject. Leonard Bernstein has a great penchant for American composers, but the music of one he refused to play, a guy who won a couple of Pulitzers, Samuel Barber.

JOAN: Yes, well, Bernstein is very competitive in spirit. I don't think anyone could get where he is without being competitive. It means, when he sees a man like Barber, who's music was performed by Toscanini and Horowitz and Steber, the great artists of the day, whereas, whatever he wrote for the classical world, nobody would play. Not even his mentor, Mitropoulos, would ever conduct anything by Bernstein. The great conductors tended to look askance at Bernstein's art music, something I think he has suffered from tremendously. Then he would look at Samuel Barber, who had the advantage of being elegantly raised, the best education, seeming to have been born with a silver spoon. He went to Curtis some years before Bernstein. As soon as he began to write, everybody performed his work, so it's certainly understandable that Bernstein felt very tense about that and he didn't go out of his way to increase Barber's performances.

JASON: I want to go back to Marc Blitzstein. His is a name that that has come up in several other interviews, particularly one with John Houseman. I'm quite sure you know the reason there. Leonard Bernstein did his own version of *The Cradle Will Rock* not long after the original, that looked for a while like it was going to be a disaster, but turned out to be a bit of theatrical history. I understand that the second version, the Bernstein version, was done in a similar fashion.

JOAN: Yes, Bernstein assumed the role of Blitzstein, sitting at the piano. Not the way it was originally staged, but just the way it actually turned out, which was him sitting on the stage with his sleeves rolled up and having the various actors stand up in the audience to do their parts. Blitzstein heard about it and went to see the second performance. He was absolutely thunder struck by what this undergraduate had done to bring his beast back to life. It began a friendship that was very intense and lasted until the bitter end, until Blitzstein's tragic death in Martinique about twenty years ago. He was murdered. It was a terrible death.

JASON: You said that Dimitri Mitropoulos disappointed him on one occasion, but in reality, he let him down many times. I don't think he ever came through for Leonard.

JOAN: No, he didn't. But you know that's what usually results when the younger man adores an older remote figure. It doesn't result in the younger man turning his back on the older one. It just means that the younger one, in many ways, is seeking approval. He didn't get it. What finally happened was that Bernstein's aggression came to force. I don't think it was a complete accident that when Mitropoulos was pushed out of the New York Philharmonic, it was Bernstein who took over.

JASON: It was a bit of a turnaround for Koussevitzky as well. The admired became the admirer. I can think of a statement that Bernstein made when he was attending an earlier concert conducted by Koussevitzky. He sat there in tears. He didn't like it.

JOAN: He didn't applaud enthusiastically so his companion asked him why? He didn't say he didn't like it. He said he was just so jealous. He was young and talented. He just wanted to 'be' those men. He wanted those men to help him become what they were. It was one of those complicated interactions between a very young gifted person and a figure who had already achieved world renown. I think Mitropoulos was very put off in many ways by Bernstein's abrasiveness. In the beginning, he was awed by his gifts, his charm and his good looks, all of the things that rolled up into a pretty impressive package. Bernstein, in the thirties and forties, was something that must have been quite unbelievable for anyone who was in his presence. If you get close to him in any kind of relationship, you find that there is a price to pay because he can be pretty rough.

JASON: One thing that most people don't realize is that

symphonic conducting is a very physical job. You must be in good shape to do that kind of work.

JOAN: When he finishes a concert, people say how terrible he looks, he must be sick. No, no, no! Look at what he does. Active conductors live a very long life and there's no reason to believe that Bernstein won't. He doesn't look like he'll ever get into physical trouble to me, but after a performance, he looks like he may die in twenty minutes. He's so spent. He's lost so much water. His sweat has been overwhelming. One time he told me he loses ten to seventeen pounds during a performance. That wouldn't surprise me. He sits in his chair. He doesn't make an effort to stand and receive people in his dressing room. He literally looks weak. After a few minutes, he comes to life. Twenty minutes later, he bounces into a reception. He looks perfect.

JASON: Similar to an athlete after a big game. No question that conducting is an athletic endeavor.

JOAN: No, there is no question at all.

JASON: The first piece of music he conducted when he filled in for Bruno Walter on that early Sunday afternoon concert was a bear. He had to start the beat on syncopation in the middle of a bar. After his correct downbeat, the rest was easy.

JOAN: He said that that was what he worried about. If they hadn't come in exactly on his cue, he didn't know what would have happened, but he said they came in like angels. From that point on, he knew all would be good. As a matter of fact, he says he does not remember the process itself. He remembers the beginning and he remembers the end with everybody on their feet screaming. I certainly don't mean to suggest in any way that any of my experiences as a performer can compare to his, but I felt that same way in that first performance of mine as an adolescent. I remember going on stage. I remember the importance of it. I must have gotten through it okay because there was applause, but I don't remember the actual playing. Something happens to you. The music takes over in some ways it's rather mysterious. You're not aware of the physicality of playing or conducting. That was how he described that incredible debut that launched him on his career that certainly can be said is the most successful career in the history of music. In fact, William Schuman, the composer who had been the head of the Lincoln Center for a number of years, has defined Bernstein's career in exactly those words.

JASON: He is a man who has done everything in the field of music.

JOAN: He's done everything where everything is concerned. That's what is so remarkable about him. He's on every side of every issue. He has to experience everything. It all matters to him when it comes to composition, be it chamber music, a symphony, music that sells, *On the Waterfront*, conducting, being a pianist or being an educator. There's nothing he won't try. He's a tremendous risk taker and generally, he succeeds. The only area that he would probably say he felt disappointed in, in terms of his achievement, is the area we spoke of earlier when we talked about Sam Barber. That would be the area of classical composition. My own feeling is that he is unnecessarily hard on himself because the way I see it, is that art music is slowly grinding to a halt. The kind of music we have associated with concert halls for hundreds of years is winding down. I do not mean that we won't always be in concert halls listening to Schubert and Mozart. I'm just saying that contemporary composers are not making the kind of music that is as enhancing of life as was the Mozart and the Schubert. I would say that Mr. Bernstein's Broadway works have a greater chance of survival than the art music of a figure like Elliott Carter.

JASON: The main point that I have to make here is that there is no way in the world that we can cover, a subject as complicated as Leonard Bernstein, or even "scratch his surface and watch the talent ooze," as his mother once said, in the time we have.

JOAN: The man is many things and he's not just all music. He creates out of what he is and what I've tried to do is show "what" he is in all of his complexities, in all of his manifestations and then describe how "what" he is, has affected what he does during his lifetime.

****

Sometimes the best approach to a subject takes an indirect path. I believe Joan Peyser was the best person to aid my humble effort to quantify and qualify the life of a very complicated and often obtuse man. As Joan said, "He was into everything and anything that caught his interest and just about all of it did just that." A short five days, after he retired from public life pneumonia took him from us, but not even death can take away the massive body of work he left behind.

I must confess that when it comes to music, my tastes are extremely eclectic, but rising to the top of the pile has always been the world of classical music. The amazing continuity of so many master technicians working in perfect unison under the direction of one man or one woman is truly something to behold.

As I write this, I am listening to the incredible recording of Beethoven's *Symphony Number Nine* with a multinational orchestra and chorus. The performance was at the celebration of the fall of the Berlin Wall on Christmas day in 1989. In the final movement, Bernstein took a small liberty with the "Master's" work. The *Ode to Joy* became the *Ode to Freedom*, to commemorate a joyous event after so many years of strangling control.

Act IV:
Toons

There is a large group of performers who entertain us—but we never see them. It is a society of mystery voices who have worked together and separately for years. You may not recognize names like Daws Butler or Don Messick or George O'Hanlon, but if I were to say Spencer Cogswell or Astro or George Jetson you would probably know them. What I am referring to is *The Jetsons*, a show that has enjoyed a long, long run in spite of some early roadblocks.

The history of animated programming dates way back to some early Disney productions. Many of the voices you hear in cartoons and animated feature films are part and parcel of that close-knit group of folks who portray a variety of strange characters. In this act, we will hear from just two of those special people. Each has many radio, television and movie credits beyond their animated work.

ACT IV:
SCENE ONE
MORE THAN JUDY

When considering impersonators of multiple personalities from the genre of animation, many names come to mind. Being able to do two or more characters in the same production is a definite plus for anyone involved in the industry. One of those people is a charming lady who rates at or near the top of the list. Interestingly enough, she also played many roles during the Golden Age of radio, which is similar in one important way. We could not see the person who was speaking those many voices.

I am not ignoring her vast radio experience, but for now, we will consider only her other vocal personas.

It is time to meet Judy Jetson, better known as Janet Waldo. Our first, but by no means the last, discussion took place on May 18, 1987.

****

JASON: Janet, I get the feeling that you've adopted Judy Jetson.

JANET: She's the easiest character I do because she's pretty much me. Maybe a little more animated and a little more excited. After all, she lives in outer space.

JASON: You've been doing *The Jetsons* since 1962. Then last year you did a whole bunch more with the same cast. I hear there's also a new special on the horizon called *The Jetsons Meet the Flintstones.* That's mixing the future with pre-history.

JANET: That's right. It's a wonderful two-hour special. There's that one and we also did another special called *Judy Jetson and the Rockers*. It's about Judy becoming sort of a rock star. It's just an adorable script. In *Jetsons Meet Flintstones*, they change places. Something gets mixed up. The Jetsons go back to the Stone Age and the Flintstones move into outer space.

JASON: That's really life in the past lane for the Jetsons.

JANET: Not so easy for the Flintstones either. Do you realize that some of the things we talked about on *The Jetsons* twenty years ago have now come true? Now we have to think up a whole bunch of new things so we can predict that will happen in the future. We talked about laptop computers. Now my husband has one. I'm waiting for the seeing-eye vacuum cleaner that just runs around and cleans. You just had to set it and it took care of everything by itself. Moving sidewalks weren't even around when we did the first *Jetsons*, but now they're everywhere. It's wonderful to predict the future. And, as you said, we did recently make many new *Jetsons* with the same cast.

JASON: That would be George O'Hanlon, Penny Singleton, Daws Butler, Don Messick and of course, Janet Waldo.

JANET: Don Messick plays Astro, the dog. They invented a new character for the new ones called Orbitty. Frank Welker plays Orbitty.

JASON: Until we spoke briefly the other night, I wasn't sure how the old shows would still be used with so many new ones.

JANET:	They are interspersed. We made forty new ones last year and then we just did ten more when we did the specials. They didn't put Orbitty in the new ones, but he was in the other forty. They keep inventing new characters. There's a wonderful new character called Di-Di. She's Judy's diary. Judy confesses all her problems and all her romances and all her other secrets to Di-Di. Brenda Vaccaro plays Di-Di. She's wonderful. She's got that very throaty low voice, a sort of blasé voice.
JASON:	What I'm looking forward to is a work schedule like George had. Anything over four hours was overtime. All he ever did was push buttons. All anyone did was push buttons, and complain about it.
JANET:	Jane was always complaining that her index finger was fatigued because she was tired of pushing buttons. She wanted to get out and live a little.
JASON:	As Judy, you had your own share of problems. On one of the shows when George and Jane left for a vacation in Las Venus, you had to run the house. Pushing buttons was just too taxing to get anything done.
JANET:	Absolutely exhausting. You see, they were a little spoiled in outer space, but they have a lot of other things going on so they don't have time to do the things we do today.
JASON:	Let's go back to the beginning of *The Jetsons*. You seemed to think that it wasn't going to go anywhere.
JANET:	Joe Barbera and Bill Hanna had such a success with *The Flintstones* about the Stone Age that they

decided, being thoughtful gentlemen, to try the opposite. Their shows are often about families. Joe feels that is why they're usually successful. So they decided to do a family in outer space. They were all excited and they had wonderful scripts. They opted to make some episodes and call it *The Jetsons.* It was going to be a prime time show to be on at eight in the evening. They were thrilled with what they had made so they put them on the air, but at the same time, another network ran *The Wonderful World of Disney.* They clobbered us in the ratings, so we switched to Saturday mornings. They only made twenty-four to begin with.

JASON: That was twenty-five years ago. They're still running.

JANET: They never stopped running. It's the most amazing thing. That show has never been off the air. It became quite a cult, so they were rather forced to make more episodes. I don't think many people realized that there were only twenty-four.

JASON: It got to be like watching Bob Newhart reruns. They had them memorized, but they remained fresh.

JANET: They are still fun for me to watch too. If I haven't seen them for a while, I love to have a sort of refresher course. My favorite was the one about Jet Screamer. That was the very first one they ever showed. They still play it a lot. It's become a classic.

JASON: That was when Jet didn't have time for Judy when they went on their date.

JANET: And George follows her because he feels that something is going to go awry. He doesn't like his little girl going out with this rather worldly Jet

Screamer, who is a matinee idol, a rock star. He follows her and then he plays drums in the rock group. Have you seen it?

JASON: I have. He was a pretty good drummer, in fact, Jet wanted to take him on full time.

JANET: And he got totally hooked by the whole thing. Some of the new ones are just as charming. In *Judy Jetson and the Rockers*, she gets a crush on a guy named Sky Rocker. It's sort of an imitation, Jet Screamer revived. She writes a song again as she did in the original one and wins the contest. She becomes quite famous as a writer of rock music. It has some wonderful music in it.

JASON: Cartoons are similar in some ways to what radio was in its heyday. You're doing a voice, but you can't be seen. We're able to use our imagination like we did with radio.

JANET: That's why I love it. I love the use of imagination. You can play anything you can sound like. Very often, they show you a storyboard or a drawing of the character you are supposed to portray. You take a look at the character and put your imagination to work to create a voice to go with the drawing. Another reason it's like radio is that you don't have to memorize a script. You just read it as we did on radio. The main difference is that it's more of a caricature than radio. The characters are broader. Radio was so real. On radio, we always prided ourselves on being real and talking like real people, but in cartoons, it's just accelerated a little more. It's a little more oomph in order to print, what they call print. They have to have something fairly big in order to register.

JASON: Isn't it true that the final characters are sometimes drawn after the voice track is laid down? Mel Blanc told me that many of his characters were designed according to the way he sounded.

JANET: I know, in my experience, especially in the early *Jetsons*, the animators would come down to the studio and watch us perform. They would give the characters some of our mannerisms so that the movement would go with the animation and the voices. Generally, before we play a role, they give us an idea what the character is like. Joe Barbera used to show us the storyboard, what the characters were doing at the time and how they looked. They changed them as we progressed. Mel probably did give them a lot of inspiration. As you know, he did some pretty wild voices.

JASON: I think we may be saying the same thing in different ways. Incidentally, we both forgot to mention Mel when we talked about *The Jetsons* cast. He was George's boss, Cosmo Spacely. His catch line was, **"Jetson, you're fired!"**

JANET: He's definitely still on the show and as wonderful as always. Daws Butler does doubles. He does Henry, the Handyman and he does Mr. Cogswell. Don Messick does a lot of doubles and I do a lot of doubles. I do robots and I do Mr. Spacely's secretary. I do whatever voices I can get.

JASON: It works out well. Some of the old radio shows had only one or two people doing the whole thing. Mel did many cartoons by himself, all the voices.

JANET: Yes, he did, however the industry is so crowded now that I don't know if that will ever be possible again, in spite of his tremendous talent. People are panting to do these voices. The competition is so great that I have a feeling that for one person to do a one person show with all the characters would be a very exceptional thing. He was so unique when he started in the animation business. Now there are so many people who can imitate what Mel does. Naturally, it isn't as good, but they try.

JASON: I can tell you from first-hand knowledge that he's not too happy about it.

JANET: I used to do *The Addams Family*. I did all the female characters on it. I still do a series where I do all the female and some of the little boy voices, *The Little Prince*. They have a sort of stock company. They hire me to do all of the female voices and a couple of men to do the male voices, three of us in all. It's wonderful when it works that way. That's fun for the actors, but there aren't too many shows that do that now. Mostly, they have a cast of thousands, even *The Jetsons*. On the last few recordings we made, there were twelve to fifteen people in the small recording room.

JASON: You do several voices on *The Smurfs* including a ravishing little witch.

JANET: Actually, Hogatha is not so terribly ravishing. She's pretty repulsive looking. She sort of snorts and has a horrendous laugh, sort of a wicked witch. I also do a little thing, which I enjoy doing, called Labeth, sort of a mite on the show. She hasn't been on as much as Hogatha. When I was doing *The Jetsons*, I had never done any other voices. In working with all the people, Daws and Don and Mel, and seeing them all doing all those voices, I thought maybe I could do another voice or two. So I asked Joe Barbera if I could and he asked me to make a tape. I did and he started giving me other voices. Some of them were close to what I myself sound like, but one of the first voices he gave me was a big stretch for me. It was Fred Flintstone's mother-in-law. "You know Wilma, that Fred Flintstone can never keep a decent cave over your head." I was thrilled to do something that far-out. Another character he had me do was Penelope Pitstop. She'd say, "Help! Help! Won't somebody please help me?" That was one of my favorite things to do.

JASON: You worked with Paul Lynde and Paul Winchell on that show.

JANET: They were both wonderful. That was one of my favorite shows. In fact, I think Penelope Pitstop is very close to *The Jetsons* in popularity. So many people remember *The Perils of Penelope Pitstop*.

JASON: How about *Josie and the Pussycats?* I understand that was also one of your favorites.

JANET: I love *Josie and the Pussycats*. That played forever. We did a great many of those. I did one called *Jennie Jet* and *Granny Sweet*. Granny was an old lady on a motorbike she was goin' on about eighty years old. She'd ride around with her marvelous doggie. He was called Precious Pup, who was played by Don Messick.

JASON: You worked with a lot of animals. You did *The Grape Ape Show* and *Jabberjaw* and *Scooby-Doo*. Then you did *Dino Mutts*. There were many others, *Roman Holiday* and as you said, *The Addams Family, Inch High Private Eye*, which was a great title, and *Help! Help! It's the Care Bear Bunch*. There was another one you brought up the other night that I'm not at all familiar with. That was *Miss Switch to the Rescue.*

JANET: That was made in the early eighties. I think it was in 1982. I loved doing Miss Switch. She was really sort of a witch who was a schoolteacher and could do all kinds of witchcraft. It was a two-hour special. I wish they'd make a series of that. I keep hoping they will.

JASON: When we discuss *The Addams Family*, I think we should clarify that it was the animated version.

JANET: I played Morticia. You know, "Gomez, darling, please get me some bat wings." She was a fun character to do. I also did Grandmama and any other incidental voices I could manage.

JASON: If I'm not mistaken, some of the people from the real life version were also on the animated one. I'm thinking of Ted Cassidy and Jackie Coogan.

JANET: Yes, Ted was Lurch and Jackie was Uncle Fester. Do you know who played the little boy? It was Jodie Foster. Are you ready for that?

JASON: I didn't know that, but I do know that she was on another show called *Amazing Chan and the Chan Clan* with Keye Luke and a few others. It can be intriguing to go through the credits for many of the animated shows. You're bound to find some names you don't expect. Bob Hastings was one. You worked with him on *Crime Club.*

JANET: Just about everyone gets into animation sooner or later. Just the other day I worked with Kathleen Freeman. I worked with June Lockhart and a lot with her daughter Ann Lockhart. I did a special for

Jack Grey Productions. There I worked with Jonathan Winters, who also plays Grandpa on *The Smurfs*. I played with him in *Alice, Through the Looking Glass*, along with Phyllis Diller. I played the Red Queen, but I also played Alice. We just did a couple of pick-ups the other day. A new scene they wrote for it.

JASON: I want to see *The Canterville Ghost*. I particularly like Dick Orkin's voice. I know he was involved in that one.

JANET: That's the one Kathleen Freeman was in. It was a Christmas special. Dick played the ghost and I played the mother, for which they wanted a sort of Billie Burke sound. I love doing Billie Burke any chance I get.

JASON: Back in 1966 and 1967, you did *Shazzan* and *Space Kidettes*.

JANET: *Space Kidettes* is the one Jennie Jet was in. Jennie was a little girl. I remember that one well because I played one of the lead roles. Then in *Shazzan*, I played the part of Nancy. Their leads were …

JASON: Barney Phillips and Jerry Dexter.

JANET: And also Marvin Miller.

JASON: Marvin was in everything until he died, I think.

JANET: It's interesting the way things happen. Marvin was originally cast as *Shazzan*, the big voice. Somebody at the network didn't like him. They were crazy. Hello network! Anyway, they recast him and Barney Phillips played his part.

JASON: It's interesting, when you mention Marvin Miller. People usually think of *The Millionaire* when they hear his name, but if you look through any book on radio and television history, you find him on at least one-hundred different shows and that's only scratching the surface.

JANET: As you say, he was on everything. I must tell you, I have a tape with Frank Sinatra and Benny Goodman. I was Teenage Tina. The music was absolutely marvelous. Frank was in great voice and all the kids in the audience were screaming. It was a live show and Marvin Miller was the announcer, advertising Old Gold cigarettes. That sort of takes you back.

JASON: At least a few years. There were and are so many of these cartoons that you were involved in, but for the vast majority of them we're talking about one production team, Bill Hanna and Joe Barbera. Tell me how they got started in their specialty, animation.

JANET: They were both at MGM many years ago where my husband, Bob Lee, got to know Joe especially. They decided to go off on their own. They did *Tom and Jerry*, which really made them somewhat famous. I think they were still with MGM when they did those. They achieved much of their fame in those years and then started their own studio. You should see their facility today. When I first started working on *The Jetsons*, it was a tiny place. We used to do some of the recording in a little studio on Sunset Boulevard. They didn't have enough room to do that kind of recording session. It has grown so much. Now they're adding a huge new complex on Ventura Boulevard in the Valley.

JASON: A world built by little people and animals on a screen. You mentioned *Granny Sweet* and *Precious Pup*. Weren't they part of the *Atom Ant–Secret Squirrel* show?

JANET: No, that was just called *Precious Pup*.

JASON: But wasn't it part of a combination of cartoons put together, similar to how they did *Quick Draw McGraw* and so forth?

JANET: They did that later. You're really up on cartoon history.

JASON: Thank you, Janet. I always try to be prepared. I think they combined *Precious Pup* and *Squidlly-Didlly* and *Hillbilly Bears* and some others.

JANET: They did combine several of them together. I remember my agent negotiating that. At first, they were separate series. Howie Morris played *Atom Ant.*

JASON: Of all the voices you've done, and I think I know what your answer will be, which one was your favorite?

JANET: Of course you do. It has to be Judy Jetson. I feel so free doing Judy. She was my first character and I feel such a kinship to her. She's still going strong. I also loved doing some of the far-out things that I've done. I did *Beauty and the Beast* for Ruby-Spears. I played Beauty. It was a beautiful script, so well written that the actors had a chance to do a little acting and emoting. I also got to play one of their wicked sisters and an old crone. I loved doing Beauty because she was so sweet and had such innocence.

JASON: There's so much more we could talk about, but the clock on the wall says no. I don't want to slight your radio and TV careers, but this was about Saturday Morning Queens and you can assume that throne.

****

It is a fantasy world where Janet Waldo spends her working days, and as of this writing, she is still at it. Not one of us can honestly say that we never got a good laugh from a cartoon at some time in our lives. We should be grateful to people like Janet for lifting us out of our everyday turmoil, at least for a few minutes at a time.

I still speak with her regularly and I am pleased to report that she is one of those people who never ages. She still sparkles.

ACT IV:
SCENE TWO
MAN OF 1000 VOICES

Anyone who is at all aware of the performing arts knows right off that the Man of 1000 Voices is none other than Mel Blanc.

On the evening of January 26, 1961, we came very close to losing that kind gentleman and all of his incredible voices in the blink of an eye. Mel had recently acquired an Aston Martin Mark III, a fine driving machine. He was headed for home along Sunset Boulevard when he slowed to less than thirty miles per hour as he entered what was known as Deadman's Curve, a treacherous stretch of road that had claimed six lives during the previous years and was responsible for thirty major mishaps over that same period of time. Driving very cautiously, he was suddenly and without any warning, smacked head on by a much larger, much heavier Oldsmobile 98.

The steering had failed the driver of the Olds and it was out of control. Mel's little vehicle collapsed around him and enclosed him like a tomb. When police arrived on the scene, their first impression was that it was hopeless. They called for additional equipment in order to extricate him and avoid further damage. When they finally got him out and checked his wallet for some kind of identification, they got a shock. One of his rescuers blurted out, *Holy cow, it's Bugs Bunny!* He was taken to UCLA Medical Center with little hope of survival. He was severely concussed and nearly every bone was broken. He had sustained thirty-seven fractures in his right arm alone.

News reports were grim. A *Los Angeles Examiner* headline stated that he was near death. *The Honolulu Herald* proclaimed him already gone, but he survived thanks to some fantastic medical care and the never-ending faith of his wife, Estelle and his son Noel. He spent many months in a full body cast that engulfed all of him except his left arm. It was not until 1964 that he was able to walk without assistance. A positive about the whole event is that his voice box was not damaged.

I spoke with Mel on July 10, 1986.

****

JASON: Let's see what's up with Mel Blanc.

MEL: Eh (chomp, chomp, chomp), what's up Jason?

JASON: Well, what do you know? It's Bugs Bunny. Mel, I know you began on radio playing real people then somewhere along the way you drifted into doing animals and a variety of odd characters and sounds.

MEL: When I was a youngster in grammar school, I always wanted to be in Vaudeville, so-called Vaudeville there. I used to entertain the other kids at assemblies, mostly with dialect stories. I used to learn these dialects and talk to the kids in grammar school. They would laugh and the teachers would laugh. Then the teachers would give me lousy marks. That's more or less the history of my start. When I was in high school, I was hired by Portland, Oregon's KGW that had a program called *Hoot Owls*. On *Hoot Owls*, I was asked to sing a song. I did "Juanita," not the beautiful "Juanita" you may think about. This was "Wanna eata–wanna eata." It's a very cute sequence that says, *They say that nanny goats eat tomato cans and such. My girl eats a lot of things that a nanny goat won't touch.* Those were some of the lyrics. Then I was made a member of the gray team of Hoot Owls, a charitable organization. That was my start on radio.

JASON: Then you were doing a combination of voices right from the beginning?

MEL: Mostly in dialects. I used to learn each type of dialect. I'll give you a little example. I wanted to learn the Japanese dialect, so I went to one of those produce markets that sold fruit and vegetables. I saw a little Japanese man there so I pointed to a head of lettuce. I said, "What do you call this?" He said, "Ah, thassa hedda reddus." I said, "What?" He said, "Hedda reddus." I said, "Oh, it's the same as this?" And I pointed to a cabbage. He said, "Oh no, entirely different. Thassa hedda cabbash." That was one way I picked up dialects. It was very successful for me and I used to tell these crazy stories, dialect stories, on radio. People just loved them.

JASON: I remember a character you played that wasn't in dialect. He was a guy with a problem. He couldn't smile. He showed up on *The Burns and Allen Show*.

MEL: That was the Happy Postman. They wanted a postman and they said, "Think of a voice you can use for a postman who might deliver the mail late sometimes." I thought of a guy I used to know who talked that way. I said, dejectedly, "Here's your mail Mrs. Burns. Remember, keep smiling."

JASON: A little later, you began a long run with Jack Benny. You did a lot of things on his show. You played his violin teacher, Professor LeBlanc, the P.A. announcer at the train station, Jack's old Maxwell, but my favorite was a little Mexican guy named Sy.

MEL: It was a cute sequence. I'd walk up to Jack and he'd say—

****

JACK: Want to shake hands?

MEL: Si.

JACK: Can I consider you my friend?

MEL: Si.

JACK: Will you always help me?

MEL: Si. Before you leave, I'd like you to meet my six-year-old son, Tomas. He's learning to be a magician. He does a wonderful act with his sister.

JACK: Hello Tomas.

MEL: (*as Tomas*) Si.

JACK: So, you're a magician, Tomas?

MEL: Si.

JACK: You have an act?

MEL: Si.

JACK: With your sister?

MEL: Si.

JACK: What's her name?

MEL: Sue.

JACK: Sue?

MEL: Si.

JACK: What do you do in your act?

MEL: Saw.

JACK: Saw?

MEL: Si.

JACK: What do you saw?

MEL: Sue.

JACK: Sue?

MEL: Si.

JACK: Now wait a minute! Someone put you up to this. Who was it?

MEL: (*as Sy*) Me.

JACK: You?

MEL: Si.

JACK: Who are you?

MEL: Sy.

JACK: Sy?

MEL: Si.

JACK: Now cut that out.

****

MEL: Jack just loved it. He used to break up every time we did it.

JASON: On an earlier radio show from the thirties, *Tommy Riggs and Betty Lou*, you played Rover, the dog. Was that your first radio animal part on the radio?

MEL: I think it was, yes. Tommy Riggs and Betty Lou were good friends of mine. I worked on almost every one of their shows, doing different voices of characters.

JASON: You're not slighting Betty Lou with that statement because she was a ventriloquist dummy.

MEL: But I got to think of her as a real person.

JASON: At about the same time you worked with Joe Penner.

MEL: I tried to get an audition with Joe. His producer kept saying, "No, I'm sorry, we have all the voices we need." I kept asking him and asking him. Finally he called and said, "We're giving you guys, who think you're funny, a chance to be funny before Mr. Penner." I said, "Great!" So I did a little spot for Joe. He got such a kick out of it. He came to me and said, "Why didn't you come to me sooner? I could have used you." I said, "Well, I just didn't have a chance. Your producer just didn't have an audition for me." I worked with Joe for some time. He was a wonderful guy. That was my first network program.

JASON: Again, around the same time, you were with Abbott and Costello.

MEL: I did the Scotsman who always came over to see them. He was more or less the housekeeper. Someone would ring the bell and he would say, "Get your finger off the button. You're using up the electricity." I did various other voices on *Abbott and Costello* and I worked a lot with Judy Canova. I did a lot of radio work, practically every big show in the business.

JASON: Do you remember a show that was similar to *It Pays to be Ignorant* called *Nitwit Court?* I have a reason for asking.

MEL: I remember it. I was on it several times.

JASON: You were listed among the credits. My reason for bringing it up is because Ransom Sherman was the host. Everyone tells me he was a real comedian's comedian, but he never quite made it to the top.

MEL: He was a wonderful guy. I worked with him and loved it. We did quite well together. He had me do some crazy stuff. I was doing some kind of crazy thing where I kept winning prizes. I'd say to Ransom, "Look, I want to go home, it's getting late." He'd say, "No, no, you won these prizes. You have to work them off." He kept me going all night. He was a very good comedian in my estimation.

JASON: Another man on that show was Arthur Q. Bryan.

MEL: Of course. He later became the voice of Elmer Fudd. He passed away about thirty years ago and they came to me and asked if I'd like to do Elmer. I told them that I don't like to copy people. They told me that Arthur had been gone for some time and Elmer was already in animation. They had to have someone to do his voice. I said, in Elmer's voice, "All right, I'll do a voice for Elmer, but I don't know if it will work out—OK?" They said, "That's him!" I've been doing it ever since.

JASON: Elmer was my wife's favorite Warner Bros. character. Before we move on to cartoons, let's talk about some of the funny ladies you worked with on radio. You mentioned Judy Canova. There was also Bea Benaderet.

MEL: She was a wonderful comedienne too. She and Elvia Allman worked in tandem on the Benny show.

JASON: The two switchboard operators.

MEL: Right. I can't think of too many other women who were comediennes outside of Veola Vonn. It's hard to name the different characters, but Bea Benaderet was a terrific woman—Elvia Allman was along with her too. There weren't many women I was associated with on radio.

JASON: A couple of others were Verna Felton and Sara Berner. Then there was Jane Morgan, who worked with Eve Arden for quite a long time. While we're on the subject of funny ladies, let's hear from Judy Canova and her Mexican handyman, Pedro played by you.

****

MEL: Pardon me for speaking in your face, senorita.

JUDY: Oh Pedro, excited about all those baby things I got for you?

MEL: Si senorita. I got some of those disposable diapers. We almost lost the baby because I followed the directions.

JUDY: Why Pedro? What did it say?

MEL: When you have taken the diaper off the baby, throw it away.

JUDY: Did you feed him anything, Pedro?

MEL: Oh, Si. We had lunch together, scrambled eggs with Tabasco sauce.

JUDY: Pedro! How could you feed an infant scrambled eggs and Tabasco sauce?

MEL: It was easy. I just put a big hole in the nipple.

JUDY: At least, when he was finished, did you burp him?

MEL: I didn't have to. He burped himself. When he finished I picked him up and threw him over my shoulder. It's a lucky thing someone was there to catch him.

****

JASON: Your association with Bea Benaderet lasted many years.

MEL: We even worked together on *The Flintstones*. She was Betty Rubble and I was the voice of Barney. They wanted me to copy somebody. I said, "No, I'll give you what I think is an original voice." They liked that best so I kept on doing it. Bea had to leave the show later for her own show, *Petticoat Junction*. She worked on that for some time and then she passed away.

JASON: There was a short-lived show that you did with Cliff Arquette back in 1946. The character you did was August Moon, who sounded a lot like Porky Pig.

MEL: Cliff was a sensational guy, a very, very funny guy. The character was called Mooney for short. He was always running his fingers through the rice bin. He always said, "I love to run my fingers through the rice bin."

JASON: Just one more thing about radio. You seem to have a penchant for Mexican characters, Sy for Jack, Pedro for Judy and then on *The Cisco Kid* you were Pancho.

MEL: Si, Pancho. They more or less matriculated. I'd change the voice a bit for each one. Another one was Speedy Gonzales—"Ondele, ondele." He talked pretty fast. Incidentally, that won a prize in the cartoon world. It was initially from a dirty joke that I did.

JASON: Since you keep going there, I guess it's time to talk cartoons. Tell me more about Bugs Bunny.

MEL: Bugs worked for almost every different studio during World War II. He was called Sad Sack. He'd tell guys what to do, but he would always tell them wrong and someone would come in and correct him. Like on the rear gun he would say, "Well, you take the rear gun here and you hold it—no, no,—you hold it up here and then you aim it—no, wait a second. You turn it around here and then you aim it…" I used to give crazy directions. Then someone would come in and straighten me out. Actually, just from looking at the cartoon, three men went up in a plane as rear gunners and claimed they got two positives and one probable just from watching the program.

JASON: As you said, you worked for studios other than Warner's.

MEL: I did Sad Sack for Disney and I spent some time with Walter Lantz. Warner's let me do Sad Sack for Disney because it was for the war effort.

JASON: In more recent times you've been spending a lot of time at Hanna-Barbera.

MEL: Yes, I have. I do Barney Rubble and then on the *Jetsons* I do George's boss, Cosmo Spacely who always screams, "**Jetson, you're fired!**" There are so many voices I've done through the years, Yosemite Sam, Pepé Le Pew, Henery Hawk, Foghorn Leghorn and on and on. Those were just a few. I can't think of them all.

JASON: Interestingly enough, one of those shows was *Tom and Jerry*, which was mostly non-vocal.

MEL: I did two of those for Chuck Jones, who was one of the instigators of characters of *Tom and Jerry*. They didn't seem to have to have voices. I did just the two. That was all.

JASON: On the screen and on TV, it seemed that you did mostly animals. One of my favorites was Wile E. Coyote, the eternal loser. Do you ever have trouble finding your own voice when you get home after a long day at the cartoon factory?

MEL: No, but there is one voice that makes me a little tired, Yosemite Sam. They told me he was just two feet tall with a big red mustache and a couple of guns, a real cowboy. They said to give him a voice that would make him notable on the screen. I gave him this one. "My name's Yosemite Sam, the roughest, toughest cowboy that ever shot a Gumdrop." I can't do too much of him in one session.

JASON: Some of them were soft spoken like Tweety Bird and others were real loud mouths like Sylvester. Those were both yours, weren't they?

MEL: First, they'd show me a still picture of a character. Then they showed me a storyboard (what the character was going to do in the cartoon). From this, I would have to create a voice. When they showed me Sylvester and Tweety, Tweety was a little baby character, so I gave him a baby voice. On the other hand, Sylvester was a big sloppy cat, so I gave him a sloppy voice.

JASON: Through the years, a lot of years, there have been a steady stream of new characters coming out of your voice box.

MEL: As I said, I'd see the picture and create a voice. So far, I've been pretty fortunate in picking the right one almost every time. I don't know of any that have failed except one: Bugs Bunny, when he first started. He had long teeth sticking out in front, "So I made him talk like this (*lisping*)." They couldn't figure out what the heck I was saying. I just took the thing away and told them to make his teeth shorter so I could talk like a real rabbit. That's what they did and I changed my voice accordingly.

JASON: You told me that Warner's does all of their animation in-house. I know that most of the studios don't do it that way anymore.

MEL: Warner Bros. is perhaps the only one that still does full animation. Let me tell you the reason for that. Each frame is drawn. Each one is done individually because they know that when they complete the story it will be sold to television, which pays big money for it. I'll give you an example of how it used to be. They used to give a picture, free of charge, to any theatre that would hire a Warner Bros. picture. They would give it to them free even though it cost them $50,000 to make it. The reason for the $50,000 was that they had one hundred and twenty-five people working for nine months to make one six and a half minute cartoon. Nowadays the price to make that same cartoon would be close to a million dollars. That shows you the increase for artistry in animation.

JASON: That makes it an expensive promo.

MEL: They couldn't continue to do it.

JASON: That must be the reason we don't see cartoons in the movie houses anymore.

MEL: That's one of the reasons. Another one is that they have double features and don't have the time for them anymore. I've been told they're coming back. They'll have a little cartoon to introduce the main feature. I've done several holiday specials for TV. Those are actually one and a half hour shows shown on prime time. Animation is one thing that television pays big money for. Even though it costs Warner's an awful lot to make those pictures, they know they can get more than their money back selling to the networks.

JASON: There is a lot of cartoon programming on these days on Saturday mornings and throughout the day, a lot of animated people. They don't seem to have the same fluidity. They don't have the professional look of those from the past.

MEL: That's very true. There's a great deal of difference between limited animation and full animation. Warner Bros. will never do anything but full animation. That's why their pictures are so good. You can see every movement, every little thing. The animator has a mirror in front of him and a blank picture of whatever character he's doing. He watches in the mirror and if Bugs would say, "Eh–what's–up–doc," he follows the lip movement and draws it in. That's why it comes out so perfectly with every single movement that he makes. His lips are actually Bugs' lips in the cartoon. That's what you call full animation. The other way, you see a guy, he turns his head a little, and maybe his eyes blink. That's limited animation. They do maybe one in ten frames. Warner's is the only studio that sticks to full animation.

JASON: You can certainly see the difference. Do you ever get tired of doing this kind of work?

MEL: No, I love it. People often ask me what I want to be when I grow up. I always say I just want to continue doing what I'm doing because I'm having so much fun. I don't think I can get any higher in this field.

JASON: Before we wrap up tell me, which is your favorite character, either live or animated.

MEL: (*in voice*) "I think Bugs Bunny is my favorite, doc. He's done so much for me. I have his picture on every one of my shirts, and I have a lot of shirts." I always have his picture on them because people recognize his voice quicker than any of my other characters.

****

Without question, Bugs has done a great deal for Mel. In fact, there are those who swear Bugs may have saved his life. After the accident at Deadman's Curve, he was in a deep coma for one and a half months until a resourceful medical man, Dr. Conway, came up with a new approach. He noticed that the television in the room was turned on and what was playing was a cartoon with the sound turned down. As we often see in the comic pages, a light bulb flashed in his head and he said "Why not?" The good doctor went to Mel's bedside and said, "How are you, Bugs?" Mel's eyes flickered and a feeble Bugs voice said, "Just fine, doc. How are you?" From that day on, his slow tedious recovery began.

He was never forgotten by his many friends, but a special accolade is in order for Jack Benny. He was in the room every Monday when he was in town. Even when he was far away, he made it a point to call at least once every week. He also sent many humorous wires. In one of them, he told Mel he was fired because he should have known better than to drive that piece of road.

In his later years, we heard and saw Mel Blanc doing many commercials that he and his son Noel produced. MB Associates was an agency created by Mel and an ex-Warner Bros. producer, Johnny Burton. It was initially set up one day before the near fatal crash and therefore remained only a good plan for a while. In 1962, Burton dropped out, saying that he could not handle the workload. At that time, Noel came onboard as the new Corporate President with his father as Chairman of the Board. Business soon rose a healthy 25%. For a long time, Mel had been thinking that advertising needed an injection of humor, something unheard of at the time. Within five years, they had hired thirty-seven writers and were billing over $500,000 per annum. They have won more than two hundred and forty awards nationally and internationally for their impressive efforts.

Among those commercials were, Porky Pig for Paper Mate, Bugs Bunny and Mel for American Express and of course, the Frito Bandito.

One parting note: before his death in 1989, Mel convinced Noel to try some of his 1000 voices. As it turned out, Noel did so well that his dad commented, "He's so good I should sue him!"

Photo Gallery

Overture

Jack Benny in 1913 with his first piano playing partner,
Cora Salisbury

OVERTURE

George Burns with one of his many early partners

SILENTS PLEASE!

One of a very few available photos of True Boardman
(CBS)

SILENTS PLEASE!

A very young True Boardman in his role as Michael O'Halloran
(Wikipedia)

JACK, GEORGE AND GRACIE

Jack didn't keep all his cash in his vault!
(Special Collections in Mass Media & Culture, University of Maryland)

JACK, GEORGE
AND GRACIE

Mr. Benny with his manager and agent Irving Fein at a benefit concert in Nashville
(Nashville Public Library—Special Collections, Nashville Banner newspaper Archive, photo by Owen Cartwright)

GEORGE AND GRACIE

Gracie Allen, George Burns & Mel Blanc
(NBC)

GEORGE AND GRACIE

The Burns' in their natural habitat
(CBS)

GEORGE AND JACK

Jack Benny, Mary Livingstone, George Burns and Gracie Allen
(NBC)

GEORGE AND JACK

George recovering from heart surgery with Jack just two weeks before Jack passed away
(CBS)

Swing It!

Dick Jurgens, relaxing between sets.
(Special Collections in Mass Media and Culture, University of Maryland)

SWING IT!

Eddy Howard, crooner deluxe

THE MUSIC MAN

Frank DeVol as Doc Joslyn in a scene with Bambi Hamilton for the pilot of Camp Runamuck—1965
(NBC)

THE MUSIC MAN

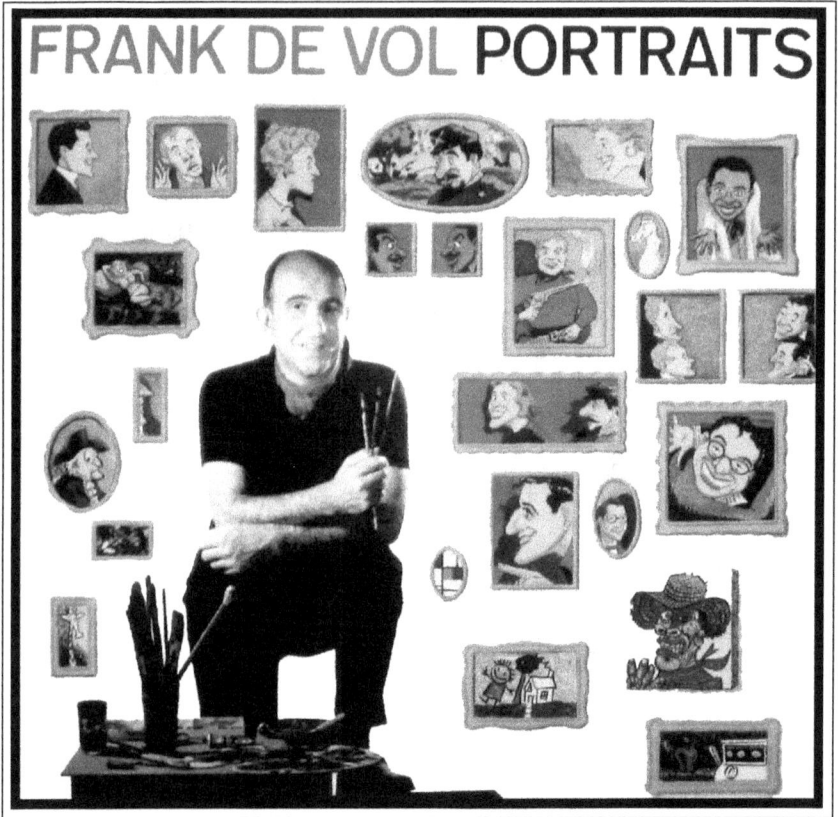

Frank was a musical artist of the first dimension.
(Bing Images)

LIVELY LADY!

This is one of the few times Lina Romay ever sat still
(Bill Arbresch, Jr. Collection)

LIVELY LADY!

Lina doing her thing with Cugie and Miguelito Valdés
(Columbia Pictures)

The Maestro

Leonard Bernstein in his favorite Gustav Mahler sweatshirt during a rehearsal in Avery Fisher Hall–1967
(New York Philharmonic Archives)

THE MAESTRO

Leonard Bernstein with Dimitri Mitropoulos—circa 1960's
(New York Philharmonic Archives)

MORE THAN JUDY

JOSIE
AND THE PUSSYCATS

JUDY
JETSON

PENELOPE
PITSTOP

To Tom —
Congratulations
on your new book
I'm sure it's
"Out of this world"
"Spacefully" —
Judy Jetson"
Janet Waldo

JANET WALDO

FRED FLINTSTONES
MOTHER-IN-LAW

GRANNY
SWEET

Janet Waldo surrounded by a few of her favorite characters.
(Janet Waldo Lee Collection)

MAN OF 1000 VOICES

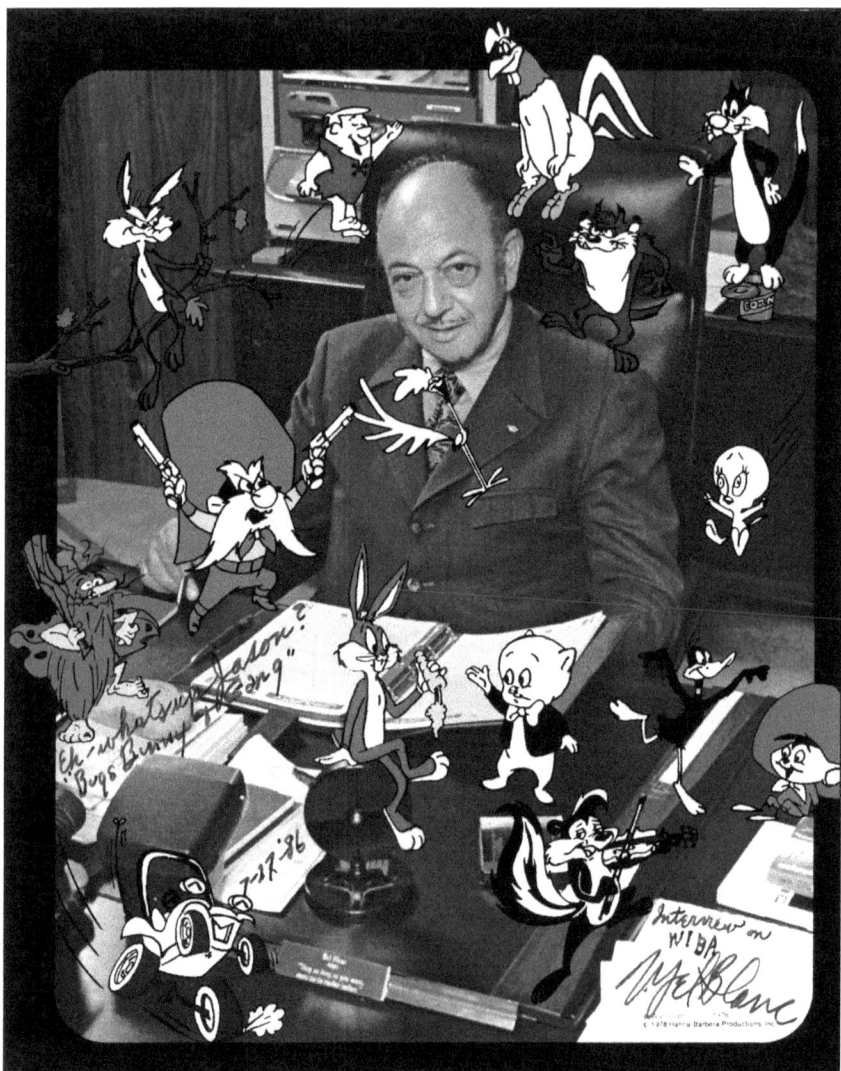

Mel Blanc with Bugs Bunny and many more
(Mel Blanc Collection)

FINALLY, AN OSCAR

Ralph Bellamy in a scene from *Picture Snatcher*—1933
(Warner Brothers)

FINALLY, AN OSCAR

Ralph Bellamy in a scene from *Picture Snatcher*—1933
(Warner Brothers)

Randolph Scott and Ralph in *Coast Guard*—1939
(Columbia Pictures)

FASCINATING LADY

Evelyn Keyes (left) in her role of Suellen in *Gone with the Wind*—1939
(MGM)

She may have been allergic to horses, but here is Evelyn on a different mount for *Around the World in Eighty Days*—1956
(United Artists)

THE ENIGMA

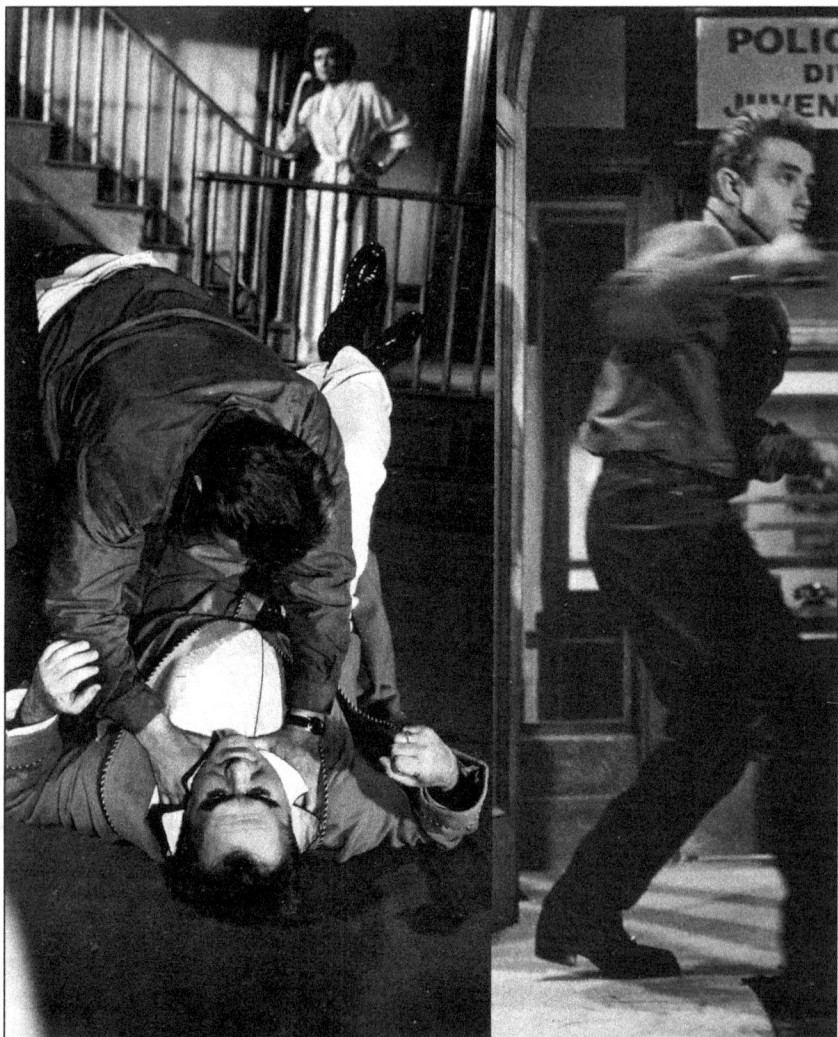

James Dean and Jim Backus not getting along in *Rebel Without a Cause*—**1955**
(Warner Brothers)

Dean looking over his not too good car in *Giant*—1956
(Warner Brothers)

BROADWAY WAS THEIR BEAT

Jerome Lawrence and Robert E. Lee in 1986
(Janet Waldo Lee Collection)

Jerry and Bob in an earlier time
(Janet Waldo Lee Collection)

Man of Mystery

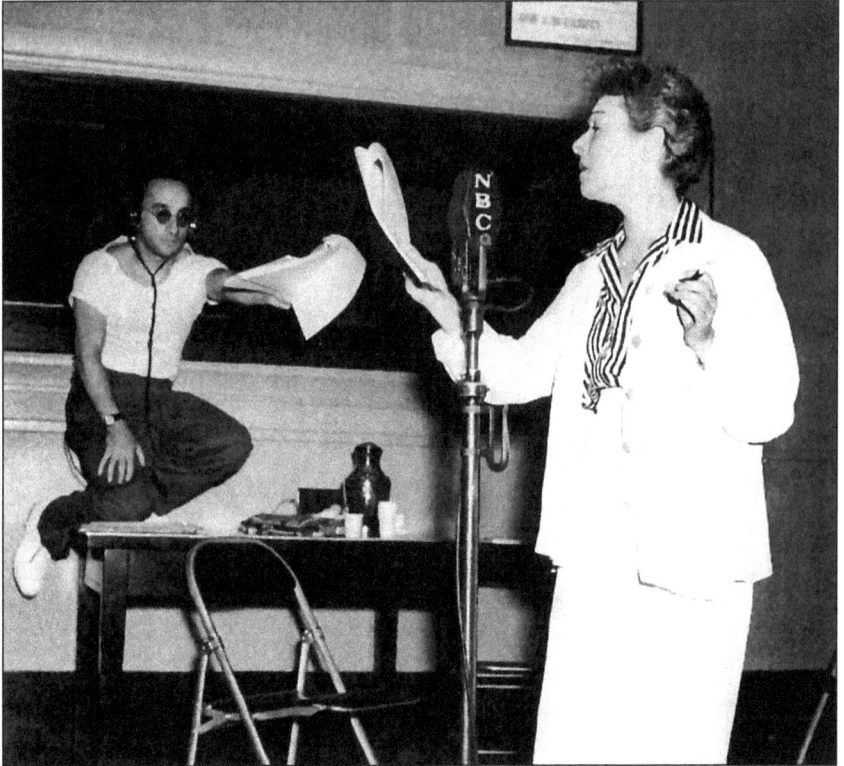

Arch Oboler directing one of his favorite people—Alla Nazimova
(NBC)

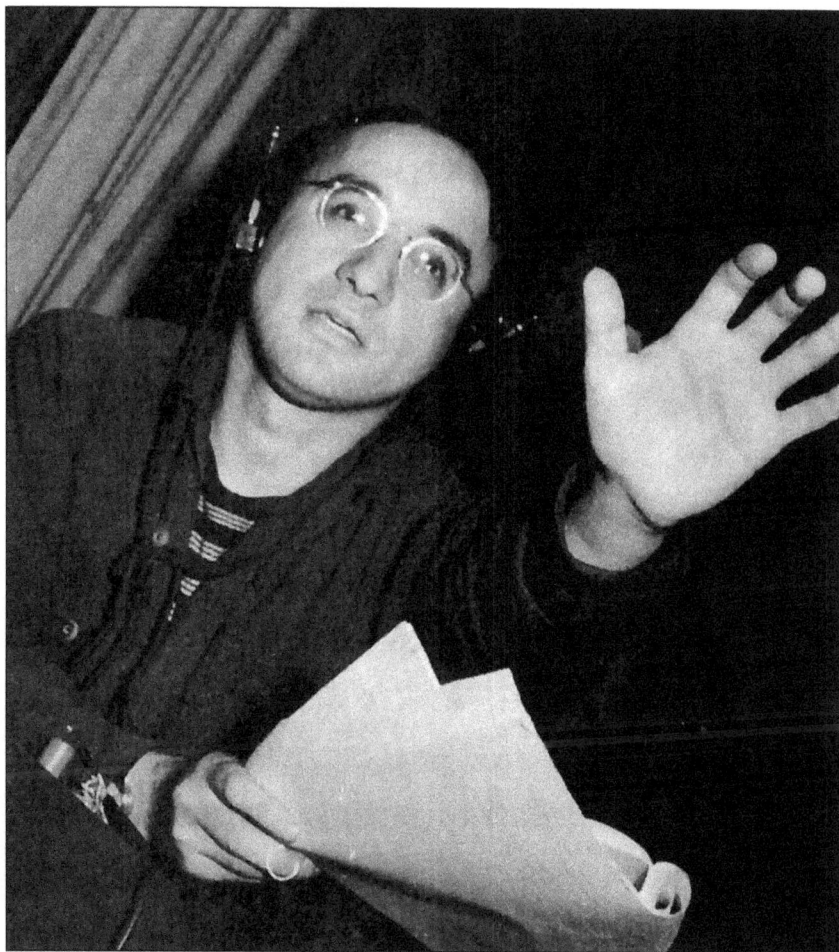

Arch Oboler-writer-director-doing what came naturally
(NBC)

THE CLASSISIST

John Houseman with his long-time co-worker, Jean Rosenthal
(WPA Photos)

John receiving his 1974 Oscar from Cybill Shepherd for Best Supporting actor in *Paper Chase*
(Academy Award Archives)

DRAMA–ADVENTURE–HUMOR

Elliott Lewis seated between Bill Robson and Barton Yarborough, going over a script for Hawk Larabee
(CBS)

The Gang's all here! Norman Corwin, Chester Markle, Elliott Lewis, Arch Oboler and a small furry friend
(Sears Radio Theatre—1979)

IMPORTANCE

William N. Robson at work during a Columbia Workshop broadcast (CBS)

Bill Robson checking the script for *Man Behind the Gun* with Nathan Van Cleave and Frank Lovejoy.
(CBS)

THE MASTER

Norman Corwin-the master at work in the control room
(CBS)

Norman contemplating one of his many scripts
(CBS)

THE AUTHOR

The author, Jason Hill, in his own control room
(Capital Times—1984)

ACT V:
A DAY AT THE MOVIES

We all like a good picture show. Movies are a good way to leave reality behind for a couple of hours and slip into other worlds—some gratifying, some hilarious, some strange or downright terrifying. Whatever your particular taste, I think at least one of the people in this Act will fit in somewhere along the way. All three were dramatic actors, but it would be hard to find three performers that are more diverse.

Two of them enjoyed long careers on the silver screen, while the third was a shooting star, who left a short, but distinguished impact on the Hollywood archives.

ACT V:
SCENE ONE
FINALLY, AN OSCAR!

With so many directions to choose from in the world of motion pictures, it was a bit challenging to make the right selections. The options were many. I decided to begin with one of the most versatile old pros of both the audio and the visual art forms. His film career alone spanned fifty-nine years, but he also did much more before and during that time span.

My first guest from the movie world was a man who was very gracious in the giving of his time–Mr. Ralph Bellamy.

We spoke for a long time on August 8, 1987.

****

JASON: Before we get started, Ralph, I hear that we have a couple of things in common. I grew up in Chicago and for the last several years, I have been living and working in Madison, Wisconsin. I know that both of those cities are important to you as well.

RALPH: They are indeed. I was born in Chicago, out on the south side near the university and Midway Airport. I was born on Monroe Street, lived on Kimbark Avenue and then we moved to Wilmette. Later on, when I began my professional life, my second acting job was at the old Orpheum Theatre in Madison. So, I have a big Midwest history, not only in those two towns, but many others in the Midwest.

JASON: I want to ask a question that I've never asked anyone else because I've never had the opportunity to talk with anyone else who has done as many movies as you have. Some of them were bunched together. How do you approach memorizing several scripts at the same time and manage to keep them separate?

RALPH: Well, you don't do many at the same time, they follow each other. Let's put it this way. When sound came into pictures was when I came into pictures, in 1930, around the end of 1930. They found that a lot of silent picture people couldn't learn lines or their voices weren't right so they went to the nearest source, which was the theatre. I was part of that group. We all came out at the same time. That included Freddie March, Clark Gable, Jimmy Cagney, Pat O'Brien and so forth, a lot of us who had theatre backgrounds. Referring again to Madison, where as I said, I had my second job as part of a stock company, A lot of people confuse stock companies with what is known today as Summer Stock and there is absolutely no resemblance. The old stock companies existed in almost every city, of fifty thousand or more, in the United States. A company would come into a city. It would consist of eleven to thirteen people; leading man, leading woman, second businessman, second businesswoman, juvenile, ingénue, character man, character woman, comedian, director and general businessman. We would do a different play each week for a period of from fifteen to thirty-five weeks, playing each night plus matinees—eight or more performances a week, no days off, and every day rehearsing for next week's play. So you were always learning one, rehearsing one and playing one. That was the best background for learning and acquiring and putting to use the written lines.

Does that briefly answer your question?

JASON: That answers it, but it still leaves me dismayed as to how anyone can keep that much dialogue in their memory, particularly on the stage. Those performances are done straight through while, on a movie set, it's broken up, scene by scene.

RALPH: Well, you just do it. You have to do it.

JASON: You were working on stage quite a few years before you got into films.

RALPH: This is my sixty-fifth year as an actor.

JASON: And you are still very active.

RALPH: Yes, I stay active.

JASON: You were in *Winds of War*. Now they're doing the sequel, *War and Remembrance*. You are in that one as well?

RALPH: Yes indeed. I just finished *War and Remembrance* six weeks ago after two years in production around the world at the unheard of cost of $140,000,000. It's in several episodes, about twenty-seven hours.

JASON: We'll come back to that later. We'll get into the Franklin Delano Roosevelt aspect of your career. You played him several times. Going way back, the first movie you made must have been *Secret Six* with Carole Lombard, Jean Harlow and Wallace Beery.

RALPH: It was quite a cast. It was Clark Gable's first picture at MGM. Johnny Mack Brown was the leading man. There were quite a few prominent people.

It was finished by the end of 1930 and released in '31.

JASON: When you talk about prominent people, you've worked with just about all of them.

RALPH: Pretty much. In those earlier days, we all came from working on the stage. Everybody knew everybody in the picture business. It was a small town back then, even after that through the forties. When you went to work, you knew everybody on the set.

JASON: Similar to the way radio was during its golden era.

RALPH: Very much the same thing.

JASON: There were a lot of crossovers and doubles on the radio. They could do that because we couldn't see them. You did considerable radio work. You had a couple of series plus many guest spots.

RALPH: I guess I was on every prominent radio show and every prominent television show when that came on.

JASON: On television, you did *Man Against Crime* and some other series, continuing runs.

RALPH: *Man Against Crime* could have been, I'm pretty sure it was the first private eye series on the air and close to the first series of any kind on the air. The studios in New York, where it was made, were not equipped for TV. They had been experimenting on the second floor at Grand Central Station, that's where they did *Man Against Crime* live and then later on film.

JASON: When you went to film, which I assume was around 1949 you were probably using a two-camera system, which tended to be tricky.

RALPH: No, one camera. That was the oldest studio in the United States. It was built by Thomas Edison. I hesitate to say the year, but it was the first one, at Decatur and Webster Avenues.

JASON: If you were to go through your list of film credits, and there were over a hundred of them, which would you say were your favorite roles?

RALPH: Oh Jason, I've been asked that question so many times, but I always find it difficult to answer. There was a wide variety. There were one hundred and three feature films beginning with *The Secret Six*. I worked with a lot of people. I had a lot of fun on all of them. *The Narrow Corner*, and *This Man Is Mine* with Irene Dunne, *Boy Meets Girl* and *Carefree* with Astaire and Rogers, *Lady in a Jam*, again with Irene Dunne, *The Awful Truth*, for which I got an Academy Award nomination, *Hands Across the Table* with Lombard and another one with her, *Fools for Scandal*. I did *His Girl Friday, Court Martial of Billy Mitchell, Dive Bomber, Trading Places* and I guess as everybody knows, *Rosemary's Baby*. There was something in every one of them. I enjoy working. I enjoyed working on most of them. I can't say all of them. There are some I'd like to forget.

JASON: You were somewhat typecast for a long time. You were the other guy who never won the girl.

RALPH: That seems to be the impression that's around. I've heard it before. I guess, to a certain extent that was true. Those were mostly lesser pictures, B pictures.

The ones I mentioned, those were all big pictures and were not that type. They were varied characterizations. I suppose, to a certain extent, people who have followed pictures for a long period of time, over the span of my participation, are justified in making that kind of characterization.

JASON: The only reason I brought it up is because it is a misconception. You've done just about every sort of dramatic or comedy role. One of the things that I thoroughly enjoyed was a series of films, and there were only four of them. It was the *Ellery Queen* series.

RALPH: That was interesting. In preparation for those, I went to New York for several weeks and spent a lot of time, mostly at night, in the squad rooms around town–daytime too. I became very familiar with the people in the police department, their customs and practices. Combining that with the play, *Detective Story*, which I did later, I got to know almost everybody on the force in one way or another and was made an honorary member of several of their organizations.

JASON: For television, were all your shows shot in New York or just *Man Against Crime*?

RALPH: No, just that one.

JASON: There was quite a time lapse between that and *Eleventh Hour*.

RALPH: That's right. That was the next one, but it wasn't too successful.

JASON: *Survivors*?

RALPH: That wasn't too successful either, but there was
          another one before *Survivors*. *Survivors* just cost
          too much money. That was the only trouble with
          that. I thought it had a good chance.

JASON: Around that time, you did another one, *Most
          Deadly Game*.

RALPH: That's the one I couldn't remember.

JASON: And more recently, you did *Hunter*. Am I wrong
          in assuming that it wasn't the one that is currently
          running?

RALPH: No, it wasn't the one from now. That was ten or
          fifteen years ago. I was the host.

JASON: It was an anthology?

RALPH: Yes, it was, and again, it was not too successful. It
          only lasted ten or twelve weeks, if that.

JASON: There are some interesting movies on your list.
          You mentioned *Rosemary's Baby*, but you were also
          in one called *Ghost of Frankenstein*, which sounds
          like something that would not fit into your ball-
          park, but it proves your versatility.

RALPH: I did a couple of those Frankenstein-type things.
          The other one was *Wolf Man*. Actually, both of
          those have become cult classics.

JASON: Many people remember you best for a role you
          played on stage for some time and then later on
          film. It was a role that you've done in other films as
          well. I'm speaking of Franklin Delano Roosevelt in
          Sunrise at Campobello and then again in *Winds of
          War* and very recently, *War and Remembrance*.

RALPH: Yes. I'm doing him in *War and Remembrance* and that will be the last time I'll do FDR. There's a danger in this business, particularly in film, of being categorized, stigmatized and attached to one part. I figure I've done him enough. Only three times, but that's enough. I absolutely loved playing FDR. I knew him during his White House period. I knew most of the family except his daughter. I enjoyed every bit of it, but now I've done that. I'm going to leave it alone.

JASON: It was a role you could play with a minimum of make-up.

RALPH: I didn't use any on the stage. I just made my eyebrows a little heavier, his were quite heavy. That's all I did on stage. We used a little more than that in pictures, not to look like him because I look nothing like him. The performance of FDR, to my way of thinking, was one of physical characteristics. His gestures were all broad. That was due to his confinement to a wheel chair, the tilted chin, the same reason. He was seated while most of the time, the people he was talking to were standing, which caused him to have to raise his chin. It became a habit. I didn't try to imitate him except in three or four instances, phrases that were familiar to the public that they could have heard directly from his lips. In the main, it was a visual impression more than the voice and sound. That was what the story was, his battle with his infirmity. I did a lot of research on that at the Institute for the Crippled and Disabled in New York. I worked with a young fellow who had a similar infliction as FDR. For quite a while, before rehearsal, I would work out with him. That's the kind of research you do for a part.

JASON:	I find intriguing gaps in your resume, but they're not really gaps. For example, between 1942 and 1960, you did very few films, but it wasn't really a gap because you were devoting most of your time to the theatre.

RALPH:	I worked all of that time on the stage. It began when I went to New York after having started in pictures. One day I was visiting with a friend of mine from Warner Bros., Mark Hellinger, who was producing there. It was just a social call. His phone rang. He excused himself. I was left facing him across his desk. There was a script facing me on the desk with the cast exposed on the first page, which I proceeded to look over. It described each character by name and traits. About half way down it named a character, a charming, but eccentric fellow from the southwest, a typical Ralph Bellamy part. Right then and there, while Mark was still on the phone I said to myself, *I'm going to New York to get back in the theatre and try to fill this if that's what it is.* I had done *The Awful Truth, His Girl Friday, Brother Orchid* and *Trade Winds,* all of which were eccentric characters. So I went to New York and did a play for two years. I came back to Hollywood for a year, then went back east to do *State of the Union,* for which I got a Pulitzer. That was followed by *Detective Story* and *Sunrise at Campobello.* I've been in California ever since.

JASON:	You did something else that kept you pretty busy between 1952 and 1964. You were president of Actors Equity.

RALPH:	Right, twelve years.

JASON:	That had to be a bit tedious because people in your business are not always content.

RALPH: We went through the McCarthy era and that was, oh well, you know. Let me just say, it wasn't the happiest kind of job and the hours were unnamed. Sometimes, in the middle of the night, calls would come in from some disturbance out on the road or wherever. I can think of a couple of those years it cost me some money and it was an unpaid job.

JASON: You talk about the McCarthy era. That was a terrible time to be the point man for Equity. You were bucking the *Counterattack* people and many others who were making it hard on nearly everyone at the time.

RALPH: Absolutely right.

JASON: Something very nice happened to you recently; you finally got your Oscar.

RALPH: That was this year. It came as a complete surprise, one of the nicest, proudest things that ever happened to me. It was not for a specific performance. It was an award from the Academy, from my peers in all branches of the business. I said at the time, if I remember correctly, that it was the greatest award that could be given to an actor.

JASON: I believe that to be true. It was for the culmination of all the work you've done throughout the years, a Lifetime Achievement Award. That says a bundle.

RALPH: Aside from that, I'm still looking for a great part in a great picture.

JASON: That's why people in your business can never really retire. There's always that un-mined nugget out there just waiting to be found.

RALPH: Yes, nothing specific, just what I said, a great part in a great picture. I never aspired to any particular person or characterization or play. All actors are always looking for a great part in a great picture. I'll know it when I see it.

JASON: I noticed you said *when* I see it, not *if* I see it. That's telling. Is there anything else new that you want to add?

RALPH: I might have a radio show. I did a pilot that's now being circulated. It's like some of the television shows, sort of like *Dynasty*. I don't know yet what will happen with it. It could be interesting. I haven't done radio for years.

JASON: Radio is trying to have a small resurgence these days.

RALPH: I was just about to say that.

JASON: Several people I've recently spoken with are doing radio. Two of them were always 'radio first' people, Bob Elliott and Ray Goulding. The other one was Steve Allen. He's come full circle and is doing full time radio now. He likes it better than any other medium and he's done them all. I'd like to see radio come back, but I know that it won't. It's still the most creative field in the industry.

RALPH: Also in my opinion. Radio has been neglected for years. A lot of people do a lot of driving, locally and long distance. They only have their radios for company and they don't have much selection. That's not criticism of today's programming, but frankly, they're all the same. You certainly get popular music all over the dial, but no drama shows like we used to have.

JASON: As recently as the early eighties, they were still trying with CBS Mystery Theatre and a few others but they couldn't sell them.

RALPH: Couldn't get sponsors.

****

After running away from home at the age of fifteen, he joined his first road show to do what he had always wanted to do. By 1927, he had his own stock company. He was then twenty-three years old. At twenty-seven he landed his first movie role in the aforementioned *Secret Six*. At eighty-six, he did the last of his one hundred and four films, *Pretty Woman* with Julia Roberts and Richard Gere.

Stage, radio, motion pictures and television were all big parts of Ralph Bellamy's prolific career. He left no stone unturned. Another thing he did along the way was to be one of the founders of the *Screen Actors Guild* to protect himself and his peers. Until then, civil rights, royalties and even some credits were unheard of for those in the thespian arts.

In 1991, he was gone, but the memories linger on, and yes, he did finally get his Oscar.

ACT V:
SCENE TWO
FASCINATING LADY

Did you ever begin a day intending to do one thing and end that same day going in an entirely different direction, with very pleasing results? That is exactly what happened to me one day in 1986.

After going above and beyond my usual sources of information, I was rewarded with the phone number for Artie Shaw, a very private person. I wanted to interview him, but I knew from the start that my chances were slim to none. He was a man who had opted to drop out of the public eye several years before for his own reasons, but it was worth a try. Much to my surprise, it wasn't Mr. Shaw who picked up the phone. It was someone else who had been on my radar for a future conversation.

The party I spoke with that day and several times since was none other than Artie's last ex-wife, Evelyn Keyes, who just happened to be there that day. She said, "Oh please, don't you want to do me?" Then she gave me her own private number and I called her back the next day at her home. The end result was a long talk with a delightful lady. Her life was anything, but mundane and she had no qualms about discussing it.

After extensive editing, here is how that conversation aired on *Life in the Past Lane* on February 18, 1986.

****

JASON: Evelyn, much of what we'll discuss today comes
          right out of your autobiography, *Scarlett O'Hara's
          Younger Sister: My Lively Life In And Out Of*

Hollywood. It's a book that has been in my own personal library for some time. We'll begin at the beginning. You grew up in Atlanta, but you were born in Texas.

EVELYN: I was born in Port Arthur, Texas. My father died when I was about eighteen months old and my mother went back to where her mother was, where she had come from. That's how I happened to grow up in Atlanta. I was a southern belle at that time, Jason.

JASON: And that created some problems for you when you got to Hollywood.

EVELYN: Yes it did. Cecil DeMille signed me to a personal contract. That's how it began. The first thing he said to me was, "You don't want to play southern girls all your life, do you?" I hadn't thought about it one way or another. I said, "No, no, no sir. I don't." He said, "We'll start giving you diction lessons immediately." That's what happened. Every day I went to coaching and got rid of my drawl, as you can hear. They had a cult showing of all his films at the county museum. I went. I was curious because I was a teenager and really, for the first two years I didn't get on film. He was a godlike figure. He had a beautiful speaking voice and beautiful diction. I can see now why he wanted me to lose any kind of accent. He liked beautiful speech. Wasn't I lucky? I feel I was lucky to have had that beginning.

JASON: You were only in Hollywood three months when he signed you at Paramount.

EVELYN: Something like that. I was under personal contract to him. I was the only one he signed in ten years.

He didn't make a test or anything. I just went right to school.

JASON: According to his own biography, he signed less than thirty people to personal contracts throughout his long career. You must have been something special.

EVELYN: You see, DeMille was on the radio at that time. Radio was the big thing. He had the *Lux Radio Theatre* on Monday nights. All of America listened to that. He had all the stars, so you can imagine how thrilling it was for me to have had him start my career.

JASON: *Lux* was a story in itself. On the air, he got credit for production and direction, but he never produced or directed any of them.

EVELYN: No, he was an actor like everyone else.

JASON: It was a good chance to hear his voice.

EVELYN: And wasn't it beautiful?

JASON: Your first film was the *Buccaneer* with Fredric March. You had, what, three lines?

EVELYN: That was sort of a screen test. That was the first time I was seen on film. That's how DeMille did his screen tests. It would be in mob scenes, but I did have some lines with Fredric March. I was then on film. I'd never been on a movie set, so the whole thing was new to me. I was quite nervous, you have to know. I was scared to death the whole time. I figured later, that if I could take that particular day, anything would be all right. There were about two hundred extras on the set. The makeup man came over to put lipstick on me. Whatever they wanted, I let them do. I'd never been there, so I didn't know the procedure. DeMille was way up on the boom with the cameraman. Through his megaphone, in front of all those people, he said to me, "Don't worry about your looks. Learn to act. The looks will take care of themselves." I shrank like Alice in Wonderland. I felt about two inches high. I was humiliated.

JASON: He was pretty good at doing that to people.

EVELYN: He did it to all the girls. He had a woman cutter and he wanted some particular piece of film. She didn't understand exactly what piece he wanted so she brought several big reels of film. He couldn't find it right away so he started ripping off film until he had a huge pile on the floor. That poor woman had to pick it all up. Nobody came to help her. It only occurred to me recently that I hadn't gone to help her either. One was so intimidated by the man. That was her turn to be humiliated. It was awful.

JASON: I wonder if anyone would have been allowed to help her.

EVELYN: That's my feeling. If they had gone to her aid, they would have been traitors to him.

JASON: The only other production you did for DeMille, where you had a speaking part, was in *Union Pacific*.

EVELYN: That was the other one. Those were the only two pictures he made while I was there.

JASON: And you had one line, "Help, help, the Indians are attacking the railroad," or something like that.

EVELYN: Big part, huh? They had a dramatic coach. They also had a little theatre where the young contract players could act. We wouldn't do whole plays, just scenes from them. I remember doing one with Tony Quinn, *Waiting for Lefty*—the Odets classic.

JASON: There was a movie in which you had a chance for a sizable role in at Paramount, *Say it in French*. You got sick at the time and had to be replaced.

EVELYN: That's right. I got ill. I haven't been ill since. I've had superb health. Yes, I'd forgotten that.

JASON: Then, not too much later the big one came along. David O. Selznick contacted you. I understand that you were one of the many actresses considered for the lead in *Gone with the Wind*.

EVELYN: Oh no! I never even thought that way. I didn't know enough. I was borrowed from DeMille. I was still under contract to him. I was on loan to Selznick. I'd only had acting lessons with DeMille. That wasn't enough to be able to handle a role like Scarlett. I never considered it.

JASON: But you did get a good role, the name of your book, *Scarlett O'Hara's Younger Sister...*, Suellen.

EVELYN: My publisher called it that. I wanted to call it *A Good Man is Hard to Find*. I think you know why.

JASON: I won't get into that on the air, but anyone interested can pick up the book and find out why. Suellen brought you back to Atlanta in triumph.

EVELYN: Oh yes it did. The whole town turned out, bands on every corner, people dressed up as Confederate soldiers. My name was never alone. It was always "Atlanta's Own Evelyn Keyes." It was like that was my full name. I was the only one in the picture from there. It was quite something.

JASON: Quite an event for a young lady of eighteen.

EVELYN: Yes, quite an event. It was indeed.

JASON: David O. Selznick and his wife, Jennifer Jones, became your close friends in the ensuing years.

EVELYN: I must say, I had a good time with them. I enjoyed being around them. David was a big game player. They had a big house way up on top of a hill. Naturally, they had a swimming pool and a tennis court. I was a big tennis player then. He lived such a zestful life. He'd charter a boat and we'd all sail off to Catalina or somewhere. It was fun. It wasn't like he played all the time, in fact, he worked all the time. I think he wore himself out. He died rather young.

JASON: He made some true classics. A little after that, you found yourself at Columbia.

EVELYN: It took DeMille forever to prepare a picture. He took his time. He was so big on small details. He wanted to keep me on for a third year without a salary raise. My agent thought I could do better, and that I ought to break away. DeMille never gave me a real part. I wasn't getting anywhere with him, so we nixed his deal and went out into the world of Hollywood to see what I could do. That's how I got to Columbia.

JASON: You were at Columbia for eleven years. You did a bunch of pictures including some very good ones and some that weren't so good, but that's par for the course. One that I remember well was recently remade. It was *Here Comes Mr. Jordan* with Robert Montgomery. The original still shows up occasionally on late night TV reruns.

EVELYN: Has it held up? I haven't seen it in forever.

JASON: It holds up very well. You can't ruin good work. You had some problems with Montgomery while you were making it.

EVELYN: He was rather difficult. I had started going around with Charles Vidor, a director at Columbia, whom I later married. Charles hadn't gotten his divorce at that time. Montgomery took it upon himself to criticize me. I didn't know that man. I never met him before in my life. He told me I shouldn't date a man who was still married to someone else. I told him it was none of his damned business. I'd gotten a little stronger by that time from the shy little creature I'd been. He didn't like that. He made something out of nothing.

JASON: There were other top drawer movies you made at Columbia.

EVELYN: *Jolson Story!*

JASON: Right, with Larry Parks. Larry was one of the many victims of the House Un-American Activities Committee.

EVELYN: They ruined his career. He was going great guns until then.

JASON: That ended his career altogether.

EVELYN: He was nominated for an Academy Award for *Jolson Story*.

JASON: Another good one was *One Thousand and One Nights* with Cornell Wilde and Phil Silvers.

EVELYN: They did very well with that picture. They made pots of money. I played the Genie. Cornell was Aladdin and Phil was his right hand man. It was a comedy made from the *Arabian Nights*.

JASON: Another one with Larry Parks, *The Renegades*.

EVELYN: Ah, the Westerns.

JASON: You didn't get along too well with horses, did you?

EVELYN: I was allergic. I still am. If I go to the races, I have to sit up high. If I walk through a horse barn, I start sneezing. When it all started, I'd have to sit around with ice bags so my eyes wouldn't swell. I did one with Charles Vidor, the husband I mentioned, called *The Desperadoes*. We went to Kanab, Utah to shoot it. Someone who was recently in Kanab, Utah told me my picture is still on a wall there.

JASON: Sneezing?

EVELYN: You'd think so, wouldn't you?

JASON: I know you couldn't pick your roles in the old studio system. You were unfortunate enough to have been in a flick with Ann Miller and Keenan Wynn. It was a remake of *Front Page*. For some unknown reason it was dubbed *The Thrill of Brazil*.

EVELYN: First of all, that title...it was awful.

JASON: It doesn't say anything to me.

EVELYN: For me either and I was in it. I think it was about a newspaper reporter. It was a musical, you know. I mean, there were dance numbers all over the place. Figure that one out. I cannot remember the story. I think it was a mess.

JASON: Something you had to do in several movies was to birth a baby in grungy places.

EVELYN: Out in the wilderness, snow covering everything, then in an abandoned gold mine with all the grit.

JASON: *The Prowler* was possibly the best one you made, at least in your own mind. Isn't that true?

EVELYN: Yes. It was a well-made movie. Joe Losey made it.

JASON: And that was his last before, once again, HUAC (House Un-American Activities Committee) stepped in. The last I heard, he was still doing films in London.

EVELYN: Where he died last year.

JASON: Sorry, I didn't know that.

EVELYN: He never came back. He was very content over there. Dalton Trumbo wrote *The Prowler*, only I didn't know it at the time because he too was blacklisted. Some other name was on the screen. I didn't know it until many years later and you know what a fine writer he was. It's no wonder *The Prowler* did so well.

JASON: Did you see a recent Woody Allen movie called *The Front*? It's an excellent lesson for anyone who is not familiar with blacklisting and its devastating effects on so many lives. He was a front for four blacklisted writers. Since he couldn't write himself, some humorous situations arose. Putting the humor aside, it brought the main subject into clear focus.

EVELYN: Yes, I know about that film. Writers had to use a front because they couldn't get hired. They had families to support.

JASON: You made a couple of films at Universal with one of my favorite actors, a man who, due to a medical error, died much too young. He was Jeff Chandler.

EVELYN: Oh, Jeff! Wasn't that awful?

JASON: I remember him from his radio days as well as from the screen. He was on *Our Miss Brooks* for years. He was Mr. Boynton. When I talked with Eve Arden, she spoke at length about him. He must have been a really nice person.

EVELYN: A nice man, a likable bird.

JASON: You did *Smuggler's Island* with Jeff. You were on a set with an island and an ocean that was six feet deep. Only Hollywood could do that.

EVELYN: On the Universal back lot. It's still there. They now have tours of the lot. Not too long ago I was doing a Spielberg thing on that lot, *Amazing Stories* with Eddie Bracken, when a tour came through. In the old days, nobody could get on a movie set, but now you see people everywhere being guided through. I have to tell you a funny story. Eddie and I were playing ghosts and we were inept ghosts. We were living up in the attic and we wanted to scare someone in the house, so we watched a horror show and tried to follow suit. What we had to do was put on makeup, black and white, like a devil mask. So there were Eddie Bracken and Evelyn Keyes in this wild makeup, with wigs that were purple. As we stood there, the tour went by. They knew they weren't supposed to walk any place that they hadn't been allowed or look where they weren't supposed to. They didn't even notice two strangely made up people standing there. They didn't even look at us.

JASON: That says a lot about how jaded we've become. You worked at other studios as time went by. You did some work at Twentieth Century Fox. One of them was *The Seven Year Itch* with Tom Ewell and Marilyn Monroe and then you vanished from the scene for a few years.

EVELYN: That's when I took off with Artie Shaw and went to Spain to live happily ever after in a castle overlooking the Mediterranean, so much for foreverness. Here I am, right where I started.

JASON: John Huston was your husband for several years.

EVELYN: Four to be exact.

JASON: There were some really funny things that happened while you were with John, although they may not have seemed funny at the time. There was one incident in particular when he brought home a chimp.

EVELYN: That was pretty funny at the time. He was giving a party. Knowing that he loved animals, Jennifer Jones brought him a chimpanzee. I got to the party rather late. By that time, it was pretty drunk out there. The band was playing and people were feeling no pain. The poor chimpanzee, who had probably never been away from her compound before, wrapped herself around John. So there was the picture, my husband John, with a little chimpanzee hanging on to him. Finally, at two or three in the morning, it was time to go home. The trainer came to get the chimp, but she wouldn't let go of John, so he said we'd have to take her home with us. Being used to that sort of thing, I said okay. So I'm driving home and there's John in the back seat with the chimp wrapped around him. The trainer was following us in his truck. We got to our apartment in town (we lived in the Valley, but we also rented an apartment in town). We were working, so it was too far to go all the way home. Mind you, this was a rather elegant apartment. It had white silk chairs and velvet drapes, rather well done. We got out. The animal trainer brought in the chimpanzee's cage and set it down in the living room. He put the chimp back in her cage. The minute the trainer was out the door, the chimp looked at the bars and then looked at John. She took the bars in her hands and ripped them, one to the left, one to the right, climbed out and jumped back on John. John said, "She'll be all right. We'll just go to bed. She'll sleep somewhere." I preferred not to sleep with a chimpanzee. I called my friend, Paulette Goddard, who lived above us and said, "Can I come up there? There's a chimpanzee down here." She said sure, so I went up. I came back in the morning. Fortunately, John had closed the door to the bedroom because when I opened it there was total chaos in there. The chimp had not slept. She had swung on the drapes. They were down. The lamps were over. The drawers were open. Shirts and underwear and ties were everywhere, not to mention chimp excrement. It was utter chaos, you wouldn't believe. She was pretending to be asleep over in the corner. When she saw me, she got up and went back to John. It was like I was the 'other' woman. I woke John with a fury. I said, "Look what you've done! Look at this mess!" He looked and started to laugh. Then I saw that it was funny and I started to laugh. The two of us sat there in that hellhole of a mess laughing until tears rolled down our cheeks. The chimp just watched us. It was a ridiculous scene.

JASON: I laughed too when I read the story, but then, I wasn't there. I just had to get it on tape.

****

Life was not always kind to Evelyn Keyes, although, by her own admission, she was not entirely blameless for that fact. She died in 2008 at the age of ninety-one as a result of uterine cancer and Alzheimer's disease.

Until then, she lived life to its fullest, in spite of many disappointments along the way. I have to toast anyone who can come out on top no matter what roadblocks get in the way.

I spoke with her several times after our initial contact, each time a joy.

Thank you, Evelyn, for letting me share in your life story.

ACT V:
SCENE THREE
THE ENIGMA

A riddle within a puzzle within a total mystery——that was James Dean. He was a hard man to know. If one managed to get close to him, chances were, before long, he would turn on him or her. He had a similar dilemma within himself, trying to find his identity. He was never quite sure who or what he was, or why. Unfortunately, he did not have time to find his true persona. His violent, tragic death in 1955 found him much too soon. If you were to speak with ten different people, you would get ten different views of him. James Dean was, without a doubt, a talent on the screen, and that is really, what we ought to look into. His career was brief, but he left behind three enduring films.

At the time of his death, he had been chosen for two additional leading roles. The first was as William Bonney in *The Left Handed Gun* and the other was as Rocky Graziano in *Somebody Up There Likes Me*. Both parts were assumed by Paul Newman, who did them proud. Dean was eagerly anticipating *The Left Handed Gun* because Billy the Kid was one of his personal heroes. He felt that nobody ever got the Bonney story quite right and that he was falsely portrayed by most historians.

Among his living idols were Marlon Brando and James Whitmore. He tried hard to mimic Brando's sullen image and Whitmore helped him with his acting technique.

For obvious reasons, it was impossible to talk directly with Mr. Dean so I had to take a different track. I contacted Bill Dakota, from the James Dean Memorial Foundation, and also two well-known co-stars from two of his three feature films.

First, from September 17, 1986, here is Bill Dakota.

****

BILL: He was born in Marion, Indiana. His mother got sick and died when he was eight or nine years old. His father was a dentist and decided to move to Santa Monica, leaving Jimmy to be raised by his aunt and uncle, Ortense and Marcus Winslow. He went to school in Fairmont, Indiana. He wanted to be an actor so he ended up in New York. He did a few live television guest shots, *Studio One, Playhouse 90* and so on. Then Elia Kazan brought him out here to do *East of Eden*. That's a little over simplified, but that's the gist of it.

JASON: Is it true that his screen image, in many ways, was very close to his true personality?

BILL: People I've talked to say no. He wasn't anything like that. His fans wished he was like the character he played in *Rebel Without a Cause*. He was a very lonely person.

JASON: I've been told by others that he had a lot of personality problems and was a very reticent guy.

BILL: I don't know about problems, but he was a loner. He had several groups of friends around town, none of them close. He would be talking with someone for a couple of hours, get on his motorcycle and go across town to talk to someone else who would be a different kind of person, sort of his secret little world. He might be at Googie's Restaurant, which used to be on Sunset, sort of a hangout for young actors. He'd be there with Maila Nurmi, who played Vampira in *The Vampira Show*, then leave and ride down Sunset Boulevard to

Santa Monica. He was pretty active, always on the go. He always tried to be around photographers. There are so many pictures of James Dean around. Considering how long he was there, it's incredible.

JASON: Maybe it had to do with the fact that he wouldn't conform to the Hollywood style. That didn't go down well with some of the people who wrote about him.

BILL: At the time, he was always in blue jeans. When people went to premieres, they always wore tuxedos or gowns. Jimmy was the first to say he wouldn't dress up, although he did dress up for one opening that he attended with Terry Moore. That was all studio arranged. In those days, with people under contract to a studio, it was a whole different animal than it is today. If your studio said, "Jump," you said, "How high?" Now everybody is independent. There are very few contract players. They don't have the protection the studios used to give them. If someone got into trouble, arrested or something, the studios would step in with their attorneys and try to hush it up. Nowadays actors have to look after themselves.

JASON: It's a reversal of the way radio operated. In the early days talent was at the mercy of the producers. Then later, nearly everyone was under exclusive contract to a particular show.

BILL: I don't know where it will lead. If you put Burt Reynolds in a picture and he demands a salary of five million dollars, you have to fill out the cast with unknowns. There would be nothing left in the budget to do anything else. The industry is in pretty bad shape. It was better when they could make a picture for a couple of million and have ten or twelve stars in it. In those days, you could go to a movie theatre and know everybody on the screen. It felt almost like family. Now you get one star and a bunch of people you never heard of. Half of them never get another chance. They're learning gradually that you don't always have to have a big name if the story is good. *E.T. the Extra-Terrestrial* was a high grossing film. There were no big names in that one. All of the big funding is going to end soon. It has to.

JASON: There really is no star system anymore. There are very few we can identify as **The Star,** like we could in the forties and fifties.

BILL: Sometimes they act like they don't want publicity, but if there's a camera around, so are they, posing. Back in the fifties, there were all sorts of movie magazines. There used to be twenty or twenty-five of them. The studios used to feed them all kinds of pictures and stories, some of them were even true. Then the contract system stopped and so did all the publicity.

JASON: Let's get back to James Dean. Since we were talking about the star system, I have to bring up *East of Eden*, the first film in which he received credit. There were many quality actors in that one, Raymond Massey, Julie Harris, Jo Van Fleet, and Burl Ives, all big names.

BILL: A pathetic example from *East of Eden* was Richard Davalos, who played Dean's older brother. That was his first film too. He did a splendid job. People were so overwhelmed by Dean's death, that about a year later, when the movie was released, they forgot about Davalos. He's still around, but he disappeared for ten years. I think there might have been more of a career for him too.

JASON: What do you think is the secret of the mystique of James Dean? Why has it lasted so long?

BILL: His sudden death was untimely, but in a sense, timely. It created an idol that has lived for thirty-one years. There are new fans today. Kids in their early teens are writing to me to ask for pictures and to find out how many books there are about him. It's sort of frightening in a way. I was an eighteen-year-old kid when he died. These people are going through the same feelings thirty-one years later. You have to wonder what it is. I guess his characters on the screen are holding up today. He's still reaching the teenagers.

JASON: He really didn't do that much, just three feature films. There are many people who did a whole lot more and yet, they aren't remembered at all.

BILL: Look at Steve McQueen. He was getting big roles and big salaries for a long time, but you never hear much buzz about him now. I remember back in '55 when the accident happened, *Giant* was held back a year before they released it because the publicity was building. Every magazine had a story about James Dean because they knew it would sell. People wanted to know more about this kid who died at twenty-four and just completed his third picture. It wasn't all studio hype. It came from his fans and continued to build. The studio wasn't about to spend money when a natural phenomenon was taking place.

JASON: In fact, *East of Eden* was the only one released before he died.

BILL: That's true, but *Rebel* was out very soon after. I was working for Butterfield Theatres in Michigan. About two weeks after he died, we ran *Rebel Without a Cause*. It was a two thousand-seat theatre, a big theatre. If anything ran over a week in those days, it was unheard of. It would have had to be a blockbuster. It turned out that *Rebel* ran for three weeks. Each week picked up from the previous week. People were coming back two and three times to see it. That had never happened before. I was the doorman in the afternoon, taking tickets. I would go home, pack a lunch, and then go back in the evening to see it myself.

JASON: Do you think that part of it is the way he died?

BILL: Not the accident itself. I think so many people identified with the character he played in *Rebel*. They always said about James Dean, "Older women wanted to mother him and the young girls wanted to be his sister." He sort of represented what we were going through at the time. No one had done that before on the screen. Then Elvis came along the following year. That helped to get the image going because he was supposed to be a rebel. Magazines tried to compare Elvis with Jimmy, but they were two entirely different types.

JASON: Two different worlds. An interesting thing that we should note is that one of the most important scenes in *Rebel* was the chicken scene with two cars racing each other, bent on destruction. In a way, in a very remote way, that was how Dean met his end in the desert.

BILL: I've been out to the spot where the accident happened. That's a straight highway in a pretty remote area. I don't know how the road was in those days, but it looks like it would have been easy to open up. I don't think that Porsche could do even a hundred on the straightaway and at the time, he was still breaking it in. There was a crossing road and this guy just pulled out. He made a turn into the road in front of Jimmy. The Porsche was silver and the sun was going down. This guy was just blinded by the sun. He didn't see the Porsche when he pulled out and Dean simply slammed into him. I don't think he was a reckless driver, but he did love to race. It was just one of those things. Rolf Wutherich, the mechanic who was riding with him, was later killed in an accident in Germany. It's just fate, I guess.

JASON: As you said, *Rebel* was released shortly after the accident, but they held back Giant for another year. He portrayed a slightly different image in that one, while still retaining a good deal of his edge.

BILL: Many think that *Giant* was his best acting role. They also say that they liked him as the young Jett Rink, but that they didn't age him too well. I thought he did a heck of a job. It was a good picture. It still holds up well. When doing the banquet scene near the end, he was supposed to be drunk. He got mad at the director, George Stevens, and mumbled his lines. They had to redub that part. Since Jimmy died in the meantime he couldn't re-loop it himself. Nick Adams, who was Jimmy's roommate, did it. That's Nick's voice at the banquet scene. You can't tell the difference.

JASON: One thing all three of those pictures had in common was great background musical scores. Dimitri Tiomkin did *Giant*. The other two were the work of Leonard Rosenman, whose style was similar to Tiomkin's.

BILL: Rosenman was a friend of Dean's. He knew him in New York, so Jimmy got him the jobs of doing the music for *East of Eden* and *Rebel Without a Cause*. He's still doing a lot of sound track work. You recognize his style right away.

JASON: It was great exposure for him. The score from *East* is unforgettable, once you've heard it.

BILL: It was so strange. I was at the memorial and as I got back into my car, the radio was playing the main theme from *East of Eden*. It was a verse I'd never heard before. His fans think that when something like that happens, it's a sign from Jimmy.

JASON: Everything is an omen in Southern California.

BILL: I guess. It's just part of the fantasy here.

****

It is time to bring in a couple of James Dean's co-stars. First, Burl Ives, an Oscar winner himself for *Big Country*. He worked with Dean in *East of Eden*.

****

BURL: There was a part of that film where Raymond Massey asked Dean to read the scripture. Now, Massey was a fine gentleman from the old school. When I say old school, I mean 'old school.' He was an aristocrat from Canada. He had the finest education. He was a wonderful man. James Dean was out of his quality, part of this generation that was kicking up its heels. It was an immovable object hitting up against a flashy satellite. So Kazan, who was a great director, said to me, "Do you think I could get Massey angry?" I said, "I suppose you could." He said, "How would I do it?" I said, "You have two elements there. You don't have to do very much to get it started." Jimmy Dean pretended to be completely undisciplined, but he wasn't. That was part of the rebel influence in his life, the thing that he created around himself. So what happened was, Kazan went to Dean and said, "Now I want you, when he asks you to read from the Bible, I want you to needle him. See if you can get him mad, but don't tell him." So James Dean started playing the scene and he used all of the seven words we're not supposed to say, all of them, while he was reading. I thought Massey would blow up. You could see him fuming. Elia Kazan shot his picture while he was hearing the taboo words. Finally, Massey stood up and said, "I shall go no further with this scene!" It was terrible. He made a speech and walked off the set. He muttered, "Language like that in front of ladies and gentlemen..." He walked off, but Kazan had his scene.

JASON: I remember that scene well. Dean would read a verse and then say, with a vengeance, "Selah." You could see Massey getting madder and madder. Now I know it was more than just acting.

BURL: Oh yes, Dean was picking on him.

****

In case you do not remember it, here is how that scene played out after some redubbing. James Dean is Cal, Richard Davalos is Aaron and Raymond Massey is their father.

****

MASSEY: Perhaps you had better read from here on, Cal.

DAVALOS: I'll read it, dad.

MASSEY: No, it's for Cal to read. Start from the fifth verse, verse five.

DEAN: I acknowledge my sin to thee. I will confess my transgression unto the Lord and thou forgiveth the iniquity of my sins. Selah! Six!

MASSEY: Go on. I suggest you read a little slower, Cal. You don't have to read the verse numbers.

DEAN: This shalt I repent that is repellant to thee. As surely as the floods and breakwaters, they shall not come nigh unto him. **Selah! Seven!**

MASSEY: Not the numbers, Cal.

DEAN: Thou art my hiding place. Thou shalt preserve me from trouble. Thou shalt encompass me with songs of deliverance. **Selah! Eight!**

MASSEY: You have no repentance! You're bad! Fully through, bad!

DEAN: You're right. I am bad. I've been that for a long time.

MASSEY: I spoke in anger.

DEAN: Well, it's true. Aaron is the good one.

****

Now, here is Jim Backus who was Dean's father in *Rebel Without a Cause.*

****

JIM: Just a word about *Rebel*. You hear a lot of stories
            about how hard it was to work with James Dean,
            mostly from people who never met him. I can say
            from my own experience that he may have been
            different, but he knew what he was doing. He
            would go off by himself while everyone was waiting
            to shoot a scene. Of course, that would infuriate
            people who were trying to stay within budget. He
            would sit alone and organize his mind around the
            character he was playing. Delays on a set are costly,
            but when Jimmy would come back, the scene
            would be shot with just one take, saving money.

JASON: In one scene, you were violently thrown off the
            steps by Dean.

JIM: And he was also the one who caught me. If he
            hadn't, I would have had some broken bones. He
            wasn't gentle.

JASON: In the final analysis, what would you say about
            him?

JIM: He was a talent. He knew what he was doing and
            how to do it.

JASON: If he was still around, knowing what you know,
            would you want to work with him again?

JIM: Probably not. He could be hazardous to your
            health.

JASON: One of the eerie things about *Rebel* is that all three
            of the leading actors, James Dean, Natalie Wood
            and Sal Mineo met with violent deaths.

JIM: There was also Nick Adams. He died in not the most common situation. It's amazing how many of the people are gone. The director, Nick Ray, the head cameraman, the list goes on. It's a little spooky.

****

Here is a small snippet from *Rebel Without a Cause*. It is the scene where Jim was tossed down the stairs.

****

DEAN: I think you can't just go around doing things, pretending to be tough.

JIM: That's right.

DEAN: If you look a certain way, you can't —

JIM: That's right. You're absolutely right.

DEAN: (*very loud*) **You're not listening to me!** You're involved in this just like I am. I'm going to the police ...

JIM: Did anyone see you there? Did anyone see your license plate?

DEAN: **I don't know! I don't know!**

JIM: I don't want you going to the police. There were other people. I don't want you to get involved.

DEAN: I am involved! **We're all involved!**

****

To complete the cycle of three, here is a bit from *Giant* starring Rock Hudson as Bick Benedict, Liz Taylor as his wife and James Dean as Jett Rink. The first of Jett's oil wells has just come in.

****

ROCK: Hello Jett, what do you want?

DEAN: My well came in Bick. Ha, ha, ha.

ROCK: Fine.

LIZ: That's wonderful Jett.

DEAN: Everybody thought it was a duster. Well, I'm here to tell you it ain't. It's here and there ain't a dang thing you gonna do about it. My well came in big, so big, Bick, and there's more down there and there's bigger wells. I'm rich, Bick. I'm a richy. I'm a rich boy, me. I'm gonna have more money than you ever thought you could have, you and all the rest of you sons of Benedicts. (*Jett leaves*)

ROCK: We should have shot that fellow a long time ago. Now he's too rich to kill.

****

Before leaving the Dean scene, there is one more short story which I would like to relate. Earlier, we spoke of strange signs and omens. Draw your own conclusions from this:

On September 23, 1955, James Dean met Alec Guinness at a restaurant in Hollywood. He asked Alec to go outside with him to see his new Porsche Spyder, which he was very proud of. Guinness looked it over and found it very foreboding. He said, "If you get in that car you'll be dead in it by this time next week." On September 30th, Jimmy was removed from the wreck and taken to Robles War Memorial Hospital, where he was pronounced dead on arrival.

Think about it!!!

ACT VI:
THE PLAY IS THE THING

To successfully perform a play, many things are required before the actors ever reach the stage. You must have lighting technicians. You must have costume designers. You must have a producer and a director and most importantly, you must have a writer, whose agile use of verbiage can bring it all together. Without a good writer, you have nothing, nothing at all. The possibilities for imaginative programming arise initially from those marvelously talented wordsmiths, who can take a single idea and turn it into a full-blown production on the boards or over the airwaves.

Here, I present the spoken words and opinions of four of the best qualified practitioners from the field of theatre and the theatre of the mind (radio). All four have much to say beyond the words they have written and produced. You may not recognize their names, but you should be acquainted with their work.

ACT VI:
SCENE ONE
BROADWAY WAS
THEIR BEAT

Drama can be presented in many ways, in many forms and on many venues. It is written in many nations, in many languages and translated, to allow the material to cross borders not always easily crossed. In this way, drama, and comedy as well, can do what no team of diplomats seem to be able to accomplish with their sometimes stumbling trial and error.

The first two gentlemen featured in Act VI of this journey through the archives of show business, were proponents of that sort of international diplomacy. They were very political in a general sense without getting directly involved in any nation's politics. They were an international embassy for peace among the diverse people of the world. As you will find out, they also had serious funny bones.

On April 29, 1987 I had a three-way exchange with Jerome Lawrence and Robert E. Lee.

****

JASON: Today we have two gentlemen from Ohio, whose careers have overlapped to such an extent that they're almost inseparable when it concerns their credits and their personal lives. Please meet Jerome Lawrence and Robert E. Lee, usually referred to simply as Lawrence and Lee.

BOB: This is Bob, Robert E. Lee.

JERRY: And this is Jerry, Jerome Lawrence.

BOB: My wife, Janet Waldo, was worried about my being Robert E. Lee. She said, "Can't you at least lose the E?" I said, "Look, one of the biggest problems in life is remembering people's names." Jason Hill is easy to remember. Some names are more difficult, but you can't forget Robert E. Lee. I decided, as a courtesy to my friends, to keep the full generalship, epaulettes and all.

JERRY: Occasionally we've tried to make it Lee and Lawrence instead of Lawrence and Lee, but nobody knew who we were. Saying Lee and Lawrence is like saying Roebuck and Sears.

BOB: Whatever happened to Roebuck? By the way, Jason, we're very glad to be back among our Mid-Western friends.

JERRY: Also back on radio, which is our favorite medium.

JASON: You both have extensive radio backgrounds. Let's turn on the way-back machine. You're both from Ohio and you both attended big ten schools.

JERRY: Interestingly enough, we never knew each other in Ohio. Bob was born in Elyria and I came from Cleveland. I went to Ohio State. Bob went to Ohio Wesleyan and then briefly to Northwestern. We were just a few miles apart. We knew all about each other because we both worked at the same radio stations in Ohio, but we never met there. It wasn't until just after the war broke out, in January of '42, that we met in New York, downstairs at CBS. We spotted each other across a crowded restaurant so we had lunch.

BOB: We've been having lunch ever since.

JERRY: On a fluke, we decided to write some scripts together. We had a little spare time, so we started writing commercial scripts together. By another fluke, six or seven of them got on the air that same week. *Variety* had a big headline: "Lawrence and Lee take over radio."

BOB: I should explain. I was an announcer there for several years. Then I found out I could make more money typing than talking, so I started to type.

JASON: Jerry, I believe you started out as an actor.

JERRY: Yes, and as a director. I did a lot of summer theatre things on the *borsht circuit* and acted all through college, but I realized, that when you're a writer, you get to play all the parts.

BOB: I was a director at Young and Rubicam for a number of years before I met Jerry.

JASON: And the ad agencies, like Young and Rubicam, were so tied in with radio in those days, that they were an integral part of the radio systems.

BOB: That's true. You know, what we forget, is how short a time radio flourished. It was really only during the thirties that radio dominated the media. In that decade, we had Norman Corwin and Arch Oboler and so many of those playwrights, Arthur Miller, Robert Anderson ...

JERRY: Early on, when all those playwrights' biographies were written up, they never mentioned radio because everybody thought that if you were a radio writer, you were a soap opera writer. They forgot the really great dramas. Now, looking back into your *Life in the Past Lane*, radio at its best was truly golden. It was the theatre of imagination. Do you know the story, Jason, of the little boy who got measles and couldn't watch television? He had to be in a dark room with no light at all. His parents got tapes of a bunch of great radio shows including one of ours and Norman Corwin's *My Client, Curly* and other things. After he could watch TV again he said, "No, I want to keep listening to radio. I like it because the pictures are so much better."

BOB: We probably did the last radio show, *The Railroad Hour.*

JASON: Speaking of *The Railroad Hour*, I understand that that complete library is now at the Lincoln Center.

BOB: I've got to tell you, Jason, we barely rescued those from oblivion. You have no idea how few copies there were of those radio broadcasts at the time they were made. There was always next week's show, so the past ones were ignored, but there was usually an air-check acetate made.

JERRY: Remember, they were all live. All network was live.

BOB: Let me explain, audience, Jason did one introduction of us and then he said, "Wait a minute. Let me try that again."

JASON: Thanks a lot. Now I have no secrets.

BOB: Sorry, I'm telling stories behind your back, but you couldn't have done that in the old radio days. I remember once I did a show with Herbert Marshall. He was a wonderful actor, but he made about fifty mistakes in the course of the show and we couldn't go back. It was live. If you made a mistake, it was forever. It went out to five million homes. I went down to see Bart and he looked a little abashed. He said, "I ruined your program." I said, "I didn't know you were human."

JASON: The other thing was that, if anyone made a mistake on live radio, they waited for the roof to fall in because they knew something terrible was about to happen.

BOB: It was much the same in early television. Somebody would suddenly walk across in front of the camera and there was nothing to be done about it. It was wonderful. What was wonderful about it was that it was **NOW**. That wonderful presence of the moment is gone from television. So much of the time, we are seeing reruns. That's why the news is one of the best things on television.

JASON: Since we're talking about radio, there was something very important that both of you were involved in. In fact, you were two of its founders, along with Tom Lewis. That was Armed Forces Radio. The name Lewis also brings to mind another man you worked closely with on the project, Elliott Lewis.

JERRY: Elliott was not only an executive and a great technical wizard, but he was also a fine actor. We were pleased to direct him and Howard Duff and all the other great radio actors. There was a whole school of them who were brilliant.

BOB: People were drafted into the Armed Forces Radio Services. For example, the entire Casa Loma Orchestra was blown apart by the draft. They all ended up being part of Meredith Willson's orchestra for Armed Forces Radio.

JERRY: We were pleased to go with True Boardman and Tom Lewis, along with Loretta Young who was married to Tom, to go to Washington before the Pentagon was built, to help to start Armed Forces Radio. We were in uniform. We were just expert consultants to the Secretary of War. It turned into the world's largest network. When I went overseas to North Africa and Italy, right up to the front lines, I realized how important it was. It was the only piece of home the troops got. True, Rich Hill and I went to North Africa. He was a Colonel and I was a Sergeant, but no rank was ever pulled.

BOB: I was a Private, eventually Private First Class. I was directing and a Major was conducting the orchestra. People would come out from Washington and ask why these Privates were giving orders to Majors and Colonels. They could not understand it. We couldn't understand it either. We thought we should be Colonels too. We were Ohio Colonels, not Kentucky Colonels.

JASON: Many of the programs that had been on radio in past years were saved from the scrap heap by the transcription service that AFR had available. Howard Duff was one of the people who worked on that project, Elliott too.

BOB: All true. A lot of those things were saved by being stolen. We would do a show that we were quite proud of and …

JERRY: We got a test pressing that would have been thrown away.

BOB: Well Jerry, I'm trying to make it more dramatic. All right, we borrowed them covertly.

JERRY: Some of those are now also at the Lincoln Center.

BOB: Tape had not yet been invented. Some of those things, those acetate records, those huge sixteen-inch acetate records, were on a glass base. Aluminum was too valuable for making airplanes. Many of the records were broken and lost forever.

JERRY: A lot of them were deliberately lost. They were worried after the war. Some lowbrow Colonels would come in and destroy the records because they were worried about copyrights and union commitments, things like that. Fortunately, a lot of us saved them.

JASON: Many of those early shows were lost because no one thought they'd be of any value later on, which was certainly not the case. I went to several of the stations in Chicago a long time ago and found boxes of old material they were planning to get rid of, including old transcriptions. That's one reason I have many old shows that might have been only historical memories.

BOB: That's wonderful. We have two major collections. One is at Ohio State, their theatrical research institute, which we were honored to have named after us.

JERRY: The Lawrence and Lee Theatrical Research Institute.

BOB: Which is the best theatre library in the world. Before they built this one, they had collected, over the years, 450,000 frames of microfilm of set designs and costume designs and director's prompt-books. Pretty soon, you're all going to be able to tune in on it if you want to see what Molière wore as an actor playing "Cartouche" at the *Commedie Française* way back in the sixteenth century. Anyhow, we got into the theatre and were quite successful. We had a number of well-received plays. We had some flops too, but we wrote the flops to make it look more difficult to write the hits.

JASON: You have a few credits on your list of Broadway plays that I don't recognize at all. Maybe they fall into that last category.

BOB: Jason, we don't consider them flops. The only people who considered them flops were the audiences and the critics. We loved them all. Curiously enough, one of the most produced plays is *The Night Thoreau Spent in Jail.*

JERRY: Which has had more performances than all of our other plays put together, all over the world. Our plays have been translated into thirty-three languages, most recently into Chinese. But *Thoreau* was never produced on Broadway.

BOB: It played in Leningrad. The only thing is, because we have done so much theatre, people disassociate us from radio. I feel bad about that. I feel that the opportunity to try out new things was possible on radio, and it only cost a few thousand dollars to put on a radio show. We're doing a television show this summer about the Constitution. It will cost four million dollars.

JASON: That's a drop in the bucket these days. If you want to talk about budgets, we should go back to Armed

Forces Radio. There you had million dollar stars working gratis.

JERRY: There were some hidden gems on AFR that nobody ever heard of, like *Yarns for Yanks*, where we had Benchley come in or Groucho Marx or Spencer Tracy or Pat O'Brien. All of the great stars who weren't appropriate for *Command Performance* or *Mail Call* or *Jubilee*, or any of the others. All the great actresses were there as well: Loretta Young, Ingrid Bergman and many more. They would read poetry or stories or encore acts like Corwin's *Words Without Music*. There were some wonderful programs. I used to listen to them in all kinds of forsaken places, in Algiers, in Casablanca, and at the front lines in Italy. That Fifth Army mobile radio station parked outside Florence was a godsend for those troops. They were playing all those records and all those programs we wrote, so I could hear Bob's announcer voice on some of them.

JASON: The technology is different now, but the whole thing still goes on today for all of the troops, wherever they may be. We still have Armed Forces Radio and Armed Forces Television.

BOB: Oddly enough, television is ungainly. It's too bulky. To tote cameras around requires a crew of thirty, but with radio, you can sneak in a microphone and catch marvelous moments that would otherwise be lost.

JASON: But once a program is made, it's so easy to uplink to a satellite and send it almost anywhere.

BOB: And the word. They say a picture is worth a thousand words, but sometimes the right word, in the right place, at the right time, is worth a thousand pictures.

JERRY: Bob and I both teach. Bob's a professor at UCLA and I'm at the graduate school at USC. We're sad that our student playwrights will never have a chance to work on the big dramatic shows on radio.

BOB: I worked on *The March of Time.* Our reader was Westbrook Van Voorhis, who was seven feet tall. News was constantly coming in. I was assistant producer on the program.

JERRY: Live! On air!

BOB: Once in a while, I used to stand under Van's arm and rewrite the script just ahead of where he was reading to keep it up to date.

JERRY: Especially in the early days of the war.

BOB: I had to teach the entire *March of Time* group the national anthem of China. We have had a number of contacts with the Chinese lately. All of the sudden, one day that song came back to me and I started to sing it. All of the Chinese started to sing along with me. They couldn't understand how an American could know all the words of their national anthem in Chinese, but it was because I had worked on radio.

JASON: You both did a lot of touring the world and did a lot of lectures. I'm thinking of one in particular at the Gorki Writers School in Leningrad, where you also taught.

JERRY: Yes we did. A wonderful thing happened there. Nixon was in the White House at the time and he was on his way to the Soviet Union. We said, "Look, we want you to be nice to him despite this fact. We want to explain to you what the American system of government is like. We live in California and we have privileges and rights. We voted against him seven times-for senate, for governor, for vice president and several times for president." A major in uniform, who was also a writing student said, "That's not possible!" He didn't believe it was possible that we were coming over on a State Department visit and talking about how we voted against our president.

BOB: But we did add that he had one of the toughest jobs in the world.

JERRY: That's what democracy is all about.

BOB: I'd like to say that we've had quite a few contacts with Chinese and Soviet writers. We had a conference with these people and spent several days with them. Suddenly we began to read each other's eyes and each other's minds and pay less attention to translators. It is culture. It is contact of culture and the voice of the face of art. Art is going to triumph over governments. When we were in the Soviet Union, the Cultural Attaché at the embassy asked if we could introduce him to Abramov. He was the head of the Moscow Art Theatre.

JERRY: The embassy people had never met him.

BOB: The night before we left Moscow, almost the entire Moscow Theatre contingent visited the American embassy. They held a party in our honor after we had been there a month. We can live together. We must live together!

JERRY: If we don't, we'll all die together.

JASON: If everybody could communicate internationally as well as they do in the arts and sciences, a lot of things could be so different.

BOB: We must be able to communicate. We must tear down the Tower of Babel. Radio and the word is how we're going to do it. That's how we're going to save ourselves. That's the only way we can remain friends.

JERRY: See, Jason, we're not only speaking of life in the past lane. We hope there's some future ahead too. I think that radio and theatre and films are a way to do it.

BOB: I'm not sure about the past, present and future. Of course, the present doesn't exist because it immediately becomes the past. The future is imagined. We live in the future lane. I think if we're going to live and we're going to communicate and perform the functions that we want to perform as human beings, we have to live in the future lane as well as the past lane.

JASON: That's why the past lane is so important. History does repeat itself in cycles. Unless we understand the past, we will never know what the future may hold.

BOB: Santayana made the most famous statement.

JERRY: "Those who do not remember the past are condemned to repeat it." That's very, very important to keep in mind. We want you to watch for three things that are forthcoming. One is called *Whisper in the Mind*. This is a play we wrote with Norman Cousins, a good friend. His theory about laughter is that it is internal jogging, which we ascribe to.

It's about Mesmer, who stumbles onto hypnotism, and about the fact that Benjamin Franklin was in Paris at the time and was head of a committee investigating it. It's a very exciting play. It's already been translated into Chinese, Russian, French and Lithuanian, but there hasn't been an English production yet. We hope there will be either here or in England in the fall.

BOB: If you'd like a Lithuanian production in Wisconsin, we can arrange it.

JERRY: Tell Jason about the second project, *Now is the Time*.

BOB: *Now Is the Time* is about the Constitution.

JERRY: It's a contemporary play about the Constitution for the two hundredth anniversary.

BOB: We decided that for the two hundredth anniversary, there were going to be a great deal of silk stockings and powdered wigs and quill pens, but we wanted to do a story on how the constitution works today.

JERRY: And the dangers, if there's another constitutional convention. All the nuts would come loose.

BOB: Kate Hepburn will probably be in that.

JERRY: The third project is called *Barbara*. It's a musical version of *Major Barbara*, Shaw's play. We've written the book. Henry Mancini did the music and Leslie Bricusse did the lyrics. We hope that will be on in 1988. It's very timely because it's about the elements of the evangelical Salvation Army religion.

BOB: It's also about the problem of selling arms and the non-productivity of killing. Maybe a lot of people were very talented and made a lot of money in radio, television, theatre and films, more than we have. Our main concern is the human race in the future. It is in writing things that will make our world better and life richer for everyone. That's our aim. The people you talked with about Armed Forces Radio had to have, during that time, the same dedication. We must not lose that dedication, Jason. We've got to hang on to it and be dedicated to the future as well as the past lane. We will keep on! We're going to raise hell!

JERRY: And, I hope, a little heaven too.

JASON: I'm sure you both know what Eleanor Roosevelt once said, "Yesterday is history, tomorrow is a mystery and today is a gift. That's why they call it the present."

BOB AND JERRY: AMEN!

****

During this discussion with Jerry and Bob, heavy emphasis was put on their radio background, but do not forget, they have also collaborated on more than forty plays produced on Broadway and elsewhere around the world. We all remember *Inherit the Wind* (the story of the Scopes Monkey Trial), *Auntie Mame* and later, the musical version simply titled *Mame*.

Sadly, both of these theatrical giants are gone now, Bob in 1994 and Jerry, ten years later in 2004.

Their works live on.

ACT VI:
SCENE TWO
MAN OF MYSTERY

What can I say about this man? He was probably the most prolific writer during the heydays of radio, but his talent went far beyond just radio. He wrote for the stage, for television and for motion pictures, not to mention several books. He never tooted his own horn. He just kept coming up with new material, over eight hundred and fifty plays of one sort or another.

He was never thought of by others in neutral terms. Many loved him, while others had no use for him, but one thing is certain, no one thought of him as vanilla. He was a deep thinker, very set in his opinions. More often than not his views were right on target.

He was Arch Oboler. Here is a portion of what he had to say to me on September 6. 1986.

****

JASON: Tell me a little about your early days in Chicago and what led to your first radio production, *Futuristics.*

ARCH: When you talk about Chicago, the first thing that comes to my mind is nickel O'Henry Bars. That must tell you how long ago it was. I used to sit in the waiting room at NBC at the Merchandise Mart, waiting for someone to read my plays. Not having much money, I would always carry along a nickel O'Henry Bar. I didn't want to miss the people who were running the NBC facility at the time, which was the fountainhead of dramatic production in those days.

JASON: Chicago was the center of all radio then.

ARCH: It certainly was. I had been out of Chicago then. It was home and it was the roosting ground, but that didn't change the fact that nothing was happening for me. It didn't happen until they opened a place in New York called Radio City, that very tall building that the Rockefellers put up. Someone in Chicago remembered that, when it came to dedication, there was a guy named Oboler, a rather unkempt child, who brought in a play called *Futuristics*, which concerned itself with the future. They said why not get in touch with him and buy his play. So they did. It was a glorious moment when they called up on the phone and said they were going to buy my play. When I finally asked for how much I was told it would be seventy-five dollars. I was taken aback even in my joy by the fact that I had spent three months writing that play. Seventy-five dollars didn't seem quite enough. Of course, that's all I got and I was happy to get it.

JASON: You had written somewhere in the neighborhood of fifty or sixty plays before that, that they read and didn't like, or just didn't want to use at that point in time.

ARCH: You're very bright to remember that, because later on, when they thought I was being very prolific, they didn't know I was reaching down into my trunk and getting out those old plays that I had written a long time before that they hadn't even read. The network theory at the time was that they weren't ready for idea plays. They wanted pure

entertainment. If I would write pure entertainment, they would broadcast it. That's how
Lights Out came to be. That series was kind of
revolutionary at the time. It got into the very bones
and marrow of the listener. I took the program,
which had been started by a very charming man
named Wyllis Cooper. He had wearied of it. I took
the program because I had nothing else going for
me, nothing at all. Although it was horror and
terror, I realized that, at that hour, which was after
eleven, none of the Vice Presidents would be
awake. I could do what I wanted and they wouldn't
know about it. Of course, there were a few
exceptions; they heard a few they didn't like. I
must tell you this one. We were talking about
Futuristics. No one had bothered to read the script,
which is hard to believe these days. They had that
department, but everyone thought that someone
else had read it, so it just went on the air unread.
No one had noticed that among my sketches of the
world of the future, was a little section where a
man was smoking the last cigarette on earth. He
was smoking the very last permitted cigarette.
One of the sponsors on the network and on that
program was a large cigarette company. When they
heard that, the fat was in the fire. Why didn't I get
fired? Well, they were a little kind to this Oboler
character, who would accept seventy-five dollars for
a broadcast. They thought that if I was courageous
enough or insane enough to do that kind of thing,
maybe I could set a few sparks going out there so
they let me alone until the next time. The next
time was my first *Lights Out* program. Did I write
a nice quiet little horror story, little men arriving
from Mars or a small child with a big head? Oh no,
I was writing about human beings here on earth. I
did a play about a family standing over an open
grave for the last rites for their sixteen-year-old

daughter. I went into the mind of each person around the grave, each one, in turn, telling what they were thinking about, ranging from the great grief of her parents to small children being puzzled and indifferent. One thing I forgot. In writing the play, my device was that the sixteen-year-old girl being lowered into the grave was not dead. She was in a cataleptic spin. She had awakened and she knew what was happening. She was crying out, "Please don't! I'm alive! Don't cover me!" At the end, one hears the dirt falling in. I forgot, in the excitement of the technique, that there were thousands of people who had lost their loved ones, perhaps just the day before. You can imagine the impact on them, listening to this tremendously realistic program, far more realistic than anything you could do on television. On TV you see it happening and you say, "Oh well." You know they're going to get up out of the grave and walk away. This was on the medium of radio. In your mind, it was happening. It was real. The network got 50,000 letters of protest, 50 thousand. It grew me up to the responsibility of what one does on the medium. One of the letters was written on a piece of paper, obviously tear stained. It simply said, "I lost my sixteen-year-old daughter yesterday." I'll never forget that.

JASON: The style that you used in most of your writing, stream of consciousness, made it sound all the more real. You were there. There was no other way it could be.

ARCH: You are absolutely right. Up to that time, I say this immodestly, the dramatic writing on radio was an imitation of a conglomeration of motion pictures and the theatre. It really had no art of its own. It appeared to me, when I started to write for it, that it was a new form. It was getting into places that no other means of communication had ever reached. So I got into the minds of the listeners. I got into them all right.

JASON: Yes, you did get into our minds, no two ways about it. Here's a short piece from a later production that again, took place in a cemetery. It was called *Poltergeist*.

****

KAY: What a place to pick flowers!

EDNA: Ooooooooooo!

KAY: What did you scream for?

EDNA: You danced on a grave! I saw you! I saw you do it!

KAY: For heaven's sake, control yourself.

EDNA: Oh Kay, I'm so sorry for you! You danced on a grave
.
KAY: Stop talking like that. Sure, I danced on a grave. It was perfectly accidental. What of it?

EDNA: The poltergeist!

KAY: The what? What are you talking about? What's that word you used?

EDNA: Poltergeist. Oh Kay, what have you done?

KAY: Stupid, vicious little fool, if you don't stop talking that way I'm going to slap your face. What's the matter with you? I didn't do anything.

EDNA: You danced on a grave! You danced on a grave!

KAY: Be sensible. We walked on graves. It was only accidental. I had no intention of desecrating.

EDNA: It doesn't matter, I tell you. It doesn't matter! The poltergeist, he'll come. I know he will.

KAY: What are you talking about? What's a poltergeist?

EDNA: It's an omen. If you walk on a grave, if you dance on a grave, he'll come.

KAY: What is a poltergeist?

EDNA: An evil spirit. He comes out of a grave and it kills and destroys. It'll kill us all! It'll kill you, but it won't kill me! (*Edna runs away*)

JANE: I'll catch her.

KAY: Edna, don't run away! Nothing will hurt you! Oh Edna, look out!

EDNA: (*screams*)

KAY: Jane, Jane, what happened?

JANE: That stone, it hit Edna!

KAY: Edna, Edna, open your eyes.

JANE: Blood, blood all over her face!

KAY: Who threw that stone? Who threw it?

JANE: I don't know. It came from the graveyard.

****

JASON:	Isn't it true that people, Clarence Menser was one, didn't give the public enough credit for what they could absorb?
ARCH:	Clarence Menser was a combination of a good businessman and a very, very astute technician. He was a fine technical man. He taught me something that I wish some of the television workers would know—the people behind the control boards. That is, that what works in the studio, is not necessarily what is good out of state because there is a great loss over the wire popping up to the satellite and back. It may sound real and articulate in the studio, but many times, by the time it reached Podunk, Iowa or Azusa, California, it's not quite that clear. He made me take recordings all along the line on the network. I listened to them and some of the things I heard clearly in the studio were not quite so good. So I learned how to have the actors use the microphones more proficiently. I learned that from Clarence.
JASON:	Your use of sound effects, what you did with them, was something to be heard. One that comes to mind was a man turning himself inside out.
ARCH:	That really was something and it was fun. One wonders how a man turning himself inside out can be fun. I can only say that I'm talking technically. It turned out to be, that if you turned a wet glove slowly inside out, it sounded exactly like what I wanted the listener to believe in their own mind. In the end, when the final person turned inside out, it was silent. Then in the silence, you heard one plop, one drop of blood. It was terrific.

JASON: The point being–that each of us would see something different. That's why it was so effective.

ARCH: That's why my monsters worked better on the radio than in motion pictures. I'm not speaking about a medium I know nothing about. I worked with Mr. Zanuck and many others. I sat at their feet—learning how to direct and so on. So I know motion pictures, but they can't begin to compare with the effect you can get on radio.

JASON: Let's hear from one of those radio monsters. This is from your play called *The Hungry One*.

****

RALPH: Look, it's forming into something. It's forming into a head. How can it be, Dianne? Flesh in a meteorite growing, growing into a head.

HEAD: (*mumbles*)

RALPH: It's speaking.

HEAD: Yessss, speaking.

RALPH: You hear and understand me?

HEAD: (*low growling laugh*)

DIANNE: It's laughing.

HEAD: (*low bass voice*). I laugh at the fear and wonder in your simple little faces.

RALPH: Who are you? What are you?

HEAD: If I told you, would your little earth mind understand?

DIANNE:	Earth? Ralph, what does it mean? What?
RALPH:	Yes, tell us, whatever you are. Tell us what you are.
HEAD:	What you on earth will soon have as your masters.
RALPH:	Wait, I must know more. You, thing, what can I call you? Tell me what you mean, masters?
HEAD:	Only you, little man, do not think that a new creation has reached the ultimate.
DIANNE:	Grey flesh–talking? I'm getting out.
HEAD:	You will stay.
DIANNE:	I can't move.
RALPH:	Nor can I.
HEAD:	You cannot move.
RALPH:	Who are you? Tell us who you are.
HEAD:	You saw how I came.
RALPH:	A tiny bit of protoplasm in that meteorite.
HEAD:	I willed myself to reach your earth.
RALPH:	You came in that?—Through space?
HEAD:	Through space beyond your furthest conception, you earthling. I am the first to succeed.

****

| JASON: | That was a typical Arch Oboler monster, but not |

all of them were from outer space. Sometimes they were normal people who were changed by circumstances beyond their control. Here's one from a play called *Mungahra.*

****

ALEC: Well, Sheldon, my friend, tell them to fatten up the fatted calf. I'm coming home rich. Alec Riverton won't have to take their infernal snobbery. He struck it rich out here and he's coming back to buy the town and everybody in it.

SHELDON: Liar! Liar! You may be rich, but you're still a tramp. You're nothing, nothing! Four years in hell and you're nothing! That's it, laugh. Keep laughing. Alec Riverton have you heard? He's back in town. He's always broke, broke! (*Door opens*) Mungahra, didn't I tell you to stay out? Out of here! Get out!

MUNGAHRA: Boss man, look. Me find. Me. Mungahra find.

SHELDON: Give it to me.

MUNGAHRA: No. Me find. Me!

SHELDON: Diamond as big as your hand!

MUNGAHRA: Me take stone to Queenland. Buy two, three wife. Me, Mungahra.

****

ARCH: I've always felt the person you hate most becomes that monster. He doesn't have to have a thousand fingers or slimy feet or an unformed head. He's the husband you divorced. He's the boss who fired you when you needed money. He's the banker who wouldn't give you a loan. Those are the monsters in our lives. Those are the ones we see as the most vindictive.

JASON: We were all our own special effects people with radio. I remember listening to some of those shows under the blankets late at night, when no one knew I was awake. I'm sure a lot of kids growing up in the thirties and forties did the same.

ARCH: Bill Cosby used that very theme in one of his nightclub routines. You must remember "Chicken Heart?"

JASON: Of course I do. I have a copy of that program as well as Cosby's routine.

ARCH: I'm very pleased that after all these years some of those plays are available again and they're being played on the air. I've done nothing with them until recently. Some of them have never been rebroadcast in all that time. I wrote 850 plays.

JASON: I think you wrote more than anyone else I know of, some of them very serious things.

ARCH: After *Lights Out*, I did get kind of serious. I found eleven broadcasts that I had completely forgotten in my old files out here in the country. I'm on the top of the Santa Monica Mountains. When I moved in, my closest neighbor was five miles away. Now they're only one mile away.

JASON: They're moving in on you.

ARCH: Yep, getting crowded.

JASON: The thing about a lot of your work is that it seems

to have been somewhat prophetic, stories like "Rocket from Manhattan."

ARCH: You do know my plays. I made a stage play of that one. It was on Broadway and the critics said it was too science-fictiony–couldn't happen. A year and a day after that, the Russians sent up their first Sputnik. The basis of the play—this rocket returning from the moon to land on a space station, hasn't happened yet. The crux of the play—an atomic war has broken out and there is no place for them to land. I hope I'm a poor prophet.

JASON: That's exactly what you said on the radio version.

ARCH: Did I really? My, my, I repeat myself.

JASON: Here is your statement right out of the original broadcast.

****

Prophecy is an easy thing, for rarely is the prophet brought to judgment. Tonight I bring you a false prophecy. A play set at this hour, one minute after ten, Eastern Peace Time, but the years have moved forward to the number of fifty-five. The place of the story is a great rocket speeding away from the moon–yes, away, for the first trip to the moon has finally taken place and a triumphant airship is now rapidly returning to the mother earth. Here then is a story of a tomorrow fifty-five years hence, September 20th in the year of our Lord–two thousand, onboard a rocket ship. A play that is, I sincerely hope, a false prophecy.

****

ARCH: You know, these days we've all gotten a shade older, a tiny bit wiser, but one wonders whether, from the standpoint of consciousness, if that has happened. Are we all still thinking that Santa Claus and the Tooth Fairy will take care of everything?

JASON: You did some comedy along the way. One short routine comes to mind. It was on the Bergen/McCarthy show. Want to talk about that one?

ARCH: You mean with Don Ameche and Mae West?

JASON: Bingo!

ARCH: That came about because my agent came to me pleading that I revise someone else's play that was to go on *The Chase and Sanborn Hour* the following Sunday. I told him I didn't write that sort of thing, but he said a writer is a writer. I said I would do it on condition that I'd be permitted to use the original source of the play, which was the story of Adam and Eve. I could go to the Bible. That was agreed upon. I started on Wednesday. It had to be done by Friday. Friday I turned it in. They rehearsed it on Friday and Saturday. I never went near the place. On Sunday, it was broadcast and there was a tremendous explosion because Miss West was very near sighted. In those days actresses didn't like to wear glasses, so she didn't wear hers during rehearsals, but when she got on the air, she simply had to wear them. She didn't know the script. She came on stage waving her glasses, put them on and actually saw the words for the first time. The result was a great number of ooooos and aaaahs and pauses that were not your or my ooooos and aaaahs. They were the sensual type that she used when she appeared in movies in those early days with Cary Grant, *et al.* If, at a party, one takes a telephone book and says we're going to make something erotic of it, it can be done. That's exactly what happened with my skit right out of the Bible.

****

MAE: Listen, tall, tan and has none, it's time I told you a thing or two. Ever since creation, I've done nothing but play double solitaire. It's disgusting. It's got me down.

DON: We've got a nice place here.

MAE: That's the trouble. It's too nice.

DON: I'm not complaining.

MAE: I want something to happen, a little excitement, a little adventure. A girl's got to have a little fun once in a while. There's no future under a fig tree.

DON: Come on woman, be like me. Why don't you relax and take it easy?

MAE: Because I'm a lady with big ideas.

DON: What kind of ideas?

MAE: Oooooh, you have no idea. First of all, I've got to get a chance to expand my personality.

DON: Well, go on, expand.

MAE: I will—out there.

DON:	Out there? You mean beyond the gates of the Garden of Eden?
MAE:	Now you're talking.
DON:	But, who knows what's out there?
MAE:	Mmmmmmm, let's find out.
DON:	Oh, no, no, no. We still have a lease on this place.
MAE:	You mean a lease is a thing that's holding me back from developing my personality?
DON:	A lease is a lease. Anyway, we've got a nice place here, temperature's perfect–sun always shining, nothing but heavy dew once in a while.
MAE:	Aaaahh, what are you, the Chamber of Commerce?
DON:	Go away and let me sleep.
MAE:	Listen, long, lazy and lukewarm. You think I want to stay in this place all my life?
DON:	I do. I gave you one of my ribs.
MAE:	Yeah, it was one of your floating ribs. A couple of months of peace and security and a woman's bored all the way down to the bottom of her marriage certificate.
DON:	Then what do you want, trouble?
MAE:	If trouble is something that makes you catch your breath. If trouble is something that makes your blood run through your veins like seltzer water, uuuummmmm, Adam, my man, give me trouble.

****

ARCH: There was such a response from the Bible belt that the network was losing sponsors, so they banned her from the air. She had been paid $10,000. It was her first broadcast. That was like being paid $60,000 or $70,000 for a program now, one five-minute skit. So she was barred. They didn't do anything to me. To read the script, it was perfectly safe. It was right out of Genesis.

JASON: When I spoke with Alan Young, he mentioned that Mae West had been a guest on one of his shows. I thought her ban was for life.

ARCH: No, even with life imprisonment there are always mitigating factors. She was off the air for a number of years though, until it was forgotten in certain circles, so they put her back on. If they could make a dollar out of Mae West, their memories were short. By then the advertisers and the networks didn't care.

JASON: It seems so harmless in today's market, but back then—things were different.

ARCH: So harmless. In those days, Miss West couldn't ooooh or aaaah.

JASON: I know that you worked with Rudy Vallee and that you did some *First Nighter* and *Grand Hotel* shows, but I think you would probably rather talk about some of your more serious opuses. Things like *Plays for Americans* or *Free World Theatre*.

ARCH: Let me say, that as time goes along, one learns one's craft. Before I ever went to *Lights Out*—between *Futuristics* and *Lights Out*, because of my persistence, I got to do a few shows for Don Ameche on *First Nighter* and *Grand Hotel.* I was grateful for that because I had had no on-the-scene training with actors and what have you. What that enabled me to do was to realize the limitation of the number of people you could use on one mike boom, how to use sound effects and so on. It was sort of a training ground. I was grateful again to Clarence Menser. I must tell you how I got on those series. I was in New York and *Lights Out* was interesting, but I'd done all that, so I got together with a group of actors and, with my last few dollars, I rented a recording machine. That wasn't the little tape recorders of now. It was a machine that made records, sixteen inches in diameter. I was the engineer and director and mixer and what have you. I wrote a play and we got together in my small rented apartment. The next morning I took the big record and another machine I rented to play it back on. I brought it into NBC and the office of Louis Titterton, who was a literary genius, and I don't use that term sardonically. He was an outstanding man. I played it for him. He didn't say a word. He just got up, took the record and walked out. An hour and a half later, he came back. I was still sitting there. He said, "I've seen the people upstairs. You're going to start a series of plays called *Arch Oboler's Plays* next week at eight-thirty in the evening." Prime time! It was like a dream come true. It was like fairyland. That's what started it. So, one a week, I wrote them. I could write on any subject I wanted. I went from a woman who wanted to abort her child to one titled "Profits Unlimited," where I dared to question the private enterprise system, whether or whether not it was the best way to live and organize one's society. I was in a world of capitalism and I wrote a play that questioned whether all the facets were as kosher as they appeared to be at the time. They let me have my head.

JASON: You did some very innovative work on the *Everyman's Theatre* series. One was with the NBC symphony orchestra in the studio to help you delve into musical history. It was about the life of Pyotr Tchaikovsky and starred Alla Nazimova.

ARCH: That was a nice time, a very nice time. I wrote an hour play. NBC had never had a play that went for an hour. They gave me, for musical background, Arturo Toscanini's symphony in Studio 8-B. It was a live broadcast. It was magic that night. I cannot find the broadcast. It disappeared. It was stolen out of my files. Someone, somewhere out there has it and I'd sure like to have a copy. What happened was that NBC started to make a recording for Victor Records, but something went wrong with the recording machine and the technician didn't have two machines going, one for protection, so we never got it. The only living copy, I repeat, was in my files. How it could disappear from my personal files, I do not know. Somebody must have loved it and just slipped it out one day when we had company.

JASON: Didn't you redo it later for *Everyman's Theatre*?

ARCH: Yes, but it was a shorter version, a thirty minute version.

JASON: You worked with Alla Nazimova quite a bit after that.

ARCH: It's amazing that you remember her name. Very few people have a breath of memory about her. She was one of the world's best actresses. This was a woman who came out of Russia and became one of the truly outstanding artists on the stage in Europe, Asia and America. She also did silent movies. She was very well known in silent movies–before our time. She was a very old lady when they called me up and I didn't know who she was. I didn't know where she was. They called me and gave me her name, said she'd love to do radio, had never done radio. I madly went through all the reference books to find out who she was. She was like the Helen Hayes of her time. You know how quickly reputations are forgotten. She did a fantastic broadcast. I'll tell you a story that's never been told. During rehearsal, sitting around, I died a thousand deaths. She was from the theatre and she was projecting all over the map. I'm afraid I reacted visibly, not vocally. She saw that. After rehearsal, she called me aside and said, "Arch, dear boy, I could tell you were not happy. You saw all the other radio actors, how good they were. They'll never get any better after they rehearse. I will get better." And let me tell you, by the time she got on the air, she was superb. She knew the technique. She knew that the microphone was as exposed to the performers as to the ear of the listener. Even if the smallest nuance was wrong, it came through like a heart wrench. She played the fabulous woman who sponsored Tchaikovsky.

JASON: I would imagine that a stage actress would have to do some of the visual things in order for the audio impressions to come across to the listeners.

ARCH: That's true. Most of them had a great deal of trouble, but she was bright. There were some fine, moneyed actors from motion pictures who were no good at all on radio. I remember sending a man named Walter Pidgeon home one time. We were doing a charity broadcast of one of my plays. I couldn't stand it. He didn't understand what I was talking about at rehearsal. His agent and the studio were terribly unhappy. I pointed out to them that inside the thirty minutes of the broadcast, people would hear Mr. Pidgeon and resent him. I would do him an injustice to let him go on. My other run-in was with Judy Garland. She was always late. I don't like people coming in late for a broadcast. We were all too immersed in what we were doing and the fact that she had other interests made no difference to me. I remember how Mr. Mayer, who was running Metro, couldn't understand how dared I. I told him how dared I. I respected her and her ability and I respected the medium. I wanted the best from all of it.

JASON: There were also many radio performers who couldn't make the transition to film. They just didn't come across the same when they were used to using only their voices to give life to a script.

ARCH: There was a certain amount of unhappiness about that. Some of them were not recognized until they were beyond the years when they should have been recognized. The finest radio actress I ever used was a girl named Mercedes McCambridge. She didn't get into motion pictures until she was past the bloom of youth, as the expression goes. She was an awfully pretty Irish gal when I met her. She won an Academy Award later, but that was a bit late. She had so much more to give in her earlier years.

JASON: You are the sixth person in a row that I have interviewed, who, without any coaching, has brought up Mercedes McCambridge. She seems to always come into the conversation, whether I'm talking with someone from the genre of comedy or drama or direction or writing. She came from the same area as you and I. I believe she was born in Joliet, Illinois.

ARCH: Yes, she too sat in the waiting room at NBC at the Merchandise Mart. That's how I knew her. But there were many girls, men too, who didn't make it. There was a gal named Ann Shepherd on the stage in Chicago. She was a tremendous hit on the stage and she was great on radio, but she never made it in motion pictures. There was a sort of schism during those years when motion picture people thought that radio and television people were beneath them. Many times, I had to hide the fact that I was out of radio when I was trying to do pictures.

JASON: Radio was, by far, the most creative medium.

ARCH: It took time for people to realize that, that it was a special art form. As we talk, I have my own mind's eye picture of the people who are listening, as they have of me. I have not had any recent pictures in the papers, particularly since three generations have gone by. In the minds of those listening, one could conjure up images or get very romantic. That's never been true of any other medium.

JASON: The last thing Bill Robson said to me recently, before he said goodbye, was that radio will never again be what it once was.

ARCH: No, no. How shall I put it? None of us are the same today as we will be tomorrow. Even the cellular structures within us change. What impinges on us changes. Going beyond that to the larger areas of the world, it's obvious that nothing is the same, nothing at all. I'm not sad about radio because I think it's still a good medium. I defy anybody to listen to those programs that we've been talking about and not get the reaction I wanted from them. The same motivation, the same magic, appears. You, in your position, know that the basic thing is the word. It starts with the word. I'm a playwright. It starts there for me. The words are there no matter what the medium. No matter how much time intervenes for the listener or reader, the reaction is still there. We pick up a book of the best of Hemmingway and we react to it just as people did when he first wrote it.

JASON: The printed word works as well as the spoken word, sometimes even better.

ARCH: You read and the pictures form in your mind.

JASON: What do you think about the fact that some of those shows are being replayed on the air today?

ARCH: It's fine to put some on the air, but they put on the bodies being turned inside out and bones being cracked. My theory is that, once you break a bone you can't do it again. The effect is gone. I wish I could tell that to some of the people doing horror things like *Chain Saw Massacre*—motion pictures like that. They think that if they do one horrific thing, they have to top it with something even more horrific. It's not true at all. What's horrible to people is something they live with and know about. I know that your listeners would be much more horrified if they were in bed and heard something moving under it, unknown, than they'd ever be by a horrible thing living in a swamp and waving a machete or a chain saw.

JASON: Whoa! Time to change the subject! What are you up to these days, Arch?

ARCH: I just finished writing a book and I'm working on a play that has nothing to do with horror.

JASON: A great deal of your work had nothing to do with horror or science fiction, probably the best of it did not.

ARCH: The genre of science fiction has been pretty much prostituted. There's too much nonsense. There are only a few writing good material and the world of books on horror is mostly overdone. People are writing too much. They're reaching to the bottom of their trunks for an old book to keep their output up. The only reason I'm doing something different is because I've had this idea for a long time. So, life goes on. One enjoys and one laughs and one sleeps, and one lives.

****

This interview with Arch Oboler was one of, if not the last on air conversation he granted during his lifetime. On September 2, 1986, we spoke for hours. On March 19, 1987, at the age of only seventy-nine, his heart gave out. With him went his marvelous talent for the macabre, his ability to use dramatic effects and, some might say, his prophetic skills.

His Frank Lloyd Wright home, Eagle Feather, built to Arch's own specifications, still juts out from the peak of a Santa Monica mountain overlooking a frightening abyss. His home was very appropriate, when you consider the thrust of so much of his work.

We will never see the equal of Arch Oboler.

ACT VI:
SCENE THREE
THE CLASSISIST

When thinking about stage classics, one name usually jumps to the head of the class. That name would be William Shakespeare. Obviously, I could not talk to old Will (that would have been a good trick). However, I did spend time with one of his modern proponents. A man, you could say, had much ado about everything Shakespearean and much, much more. He was a man who explored the impossible in the world of drama. He was not afraid to tackle projects where others feared to tread and turn them into successful entities, sometimes against heavy odds. Unless you are deeply immersed in the history of experimental theatre, you may not realize the depth and breadth of his abilities. As a writer, producer, director, teacher, and in his later years an actor, he probed all the possibilities of his perspectives.

We all know him for those years after his seventieth birthday, when he was very visible on television and on the silver screen.

He was John Houseman. The date was October 9. 1986.

****

JASON: We are honored today by the presence of a distinguished master of the classical theatre, Mr. John Houseman. John, before we talk about your many show business credentials, tell me a little about your roots. I know you were born in Bucharest.

JOHN: I have no Romanian ancestry at all. My father was a Frenchman who happened to be in business, in our family business, at a branch in Romania. He'd been sent out there to look after the Romanian branch and I happened to be born while he was there. My very early education was in Paris. My parents continued to live in Paris most of my early life. Then I was sent to continue my education in England.

JASON: Eventually you found yourself in this country in the grain business.

JOHN: That was the family business. After a great deal of visitation, I followed the family business for about eight years. I practiced it mostly in this country. I was quite successful at it. I became a little over confident. I went into business on my own. We hit the big grain crash in 1929 and I went bankrupt. As a result of that, I went into what, in my heart, I really wanted to do, which was the theatre.

JASON: And you began as a writer?

JOHN: It was the only way I could make any kind of a living, as a writer, adapter and translator. Then, in due course, I discovered my true talents lay in production and direction. That's what I've done ever since.

JASON: Before we go farther, let me just explain that your career has been so long and so unique that it's difficult to do an in depth interview in limited time so what I'd like to do is to focus on your most recent book, *The Entertainers and the Entertained*. I've read most of it, plus I have your three volume memoires.

JOHN: The new book is sort of an appendix to the autobiography. It's all articles that I wrote over the past forty-five years, a lot of them for *Harpers Magazine*, some for *The New York Times*, and several other publications. They mostly relate to the same events as I mentioned in the memoires, but in some cases, they are sort of special attitude toward the problems.

JASON: It's a quick synopsis of your career in many ways.

JOHN: That's right.

JASON: Let's go back to the Federal Theatre—the WPA project. You really began there. You worked with Orson Welles.

JOHN: I worked with Orson for about five and a half years. Our official partnership lasted about that long.

JASON: This led into many other areas. Tell me about the Project 891 show you did, called *The Cradle Will Rock*.

JOHN: That was like everything we did. We were unpredictable and we were not necessarily consistent. We started up in Harlem with the Negro Theatre Unit then we moved downtown where we had our classical theatre. But of course, since we were head strong, crazy young men the program we did was not so consistent. The first thing we did was a nineteenth century French farce, which was a classic in a way. The next thing we did was a great play by Christopher Marlowe called *Faustus* and the third thing we did was not classical at all. It was a contemporary work by a young American composer named Marc Blitzstein. He called it a labor opera and he named it *The Cradle Will Rock*.

JASON: You had a few problems with that show.

JOHN: It was a matter of timing. I've never tired of telling
people that neither Welles nor I were politically
minded. Naturally, we had our political feelings,
but our programming did not follow our political
inclinations. This piece was chosen by us simply
because it seemed to be a wonderful musical with
contemporary implications. We did it simply for its
artistic quality. It happened to coincide with a time
when there were tremendous labor problems, labor
unrest and violence, which was the spring of 1937.
Suddenly, this piece, which we considered merely
an artistic interest, became a political hot potato.
We found ourselves in the middle. We behaved
rather obstinately and rather arbitrarily. The
Federal Theatre suggested that we postpone the
piece and not open it until there was less electricity
in the air. We were very headstrong, so we said
we'd open it regardless of government or no government sponsorship. And we did. We opened to
an empty theatre with Marc Blitzstein at the piano
and the rest of the cast actually scattered around
the house, around the theatre, all parts of the theatre,
because they'd been forbidden by the authorities
and their union to appear on stage.

JASON: It is an amazing story how the opening night
audience followed from the Maxine Elliott Theatre,
where you were prevented from entering, all the
way to the Venice Theatre where the performance
eventually took place.

JOHN: It was unique in theatre history. The audience
actually walked twenty-two blocks from our own
theatre to this big empty theatre on 59th Street. As
they walked, they gathered more people. They
started out about eight hundred strong and ended

up with almost three thousand.

JASON: Was that the first chance you had to work with
           Jean Rosenthal?

JOHN: No, no, no. Jeannie was actually working for the
           WPA at the time. She had just come out of Yale
           and was to work as an assistant to Abe Feder. I
           took her out of WPA and sent her on tour with
           Leslie Howard's *Hamlet,* which I directed. Then
           she came back into the project right afterward.
           She became technical director and lighting director
           of the new Mercury Theatre, which Orson and I
           founded.

JASON: You worked with her for many years.

JOHN: Many, many years. I worked with her, not regularly,
           but off and on every few years. Our final
           collaboration was with the American Shakespeare
           Festival at Stratford, Connecticut, where again she
           was technical and lighting director for the four
           years I was there.

JASON: I know a story about Jean Rosenthal and her wan-
           derings with a piano on the night *Cradle* opened.
           Care to elaborate?

JOHN: It's a long story. Jean was an apprentice and a sort
           of gofer with the Federal Theatre. She was around
           all of the time and we trusted her. On the famous
           night that I described, we had to find a piano
           because the empty theatre did not contain a piano.
           So I sent her out to buy a piano, which in the
           Depression you could do for ten bucks, and also
           get hold of a truck to haul it in. She did all that
           and then asked what she should do with it. We
           told her to keep driving around until we told her

where to take it. At the time, we were still not sure what theatre we were going to be able to use. Finally, we got permission to use the Venice, so Jean dropped the piano and sighed. That was the piano that Marc Blitzstein used that night.

JASON: That little ride lasted quite a while.

JOHN: She was riding around for about two and a half hours.

JASON: What was the reason for your transition from the Federal Theatre to your own entity, the Mercury Theatre?

JOHN: As a result of our defiance of the authorities, Orson and I were fired by the Federal Theatre. Within two weeks, we'd created our own theatre, which was the Mercury. I never made any secret of the fact that, in my opinion, we would never have started the Mercury Theatre had it not been for our two and a half or three years experience with the Federal Theatre. Our program for the first season at the Mercury, our triumphal season, was very close to the season we had projected for the classical theatre at the Federal. We took a lot of people with us. We took a lot of technicians and a few actors from the project to the Mercury.

JASON: Some pretty big names came out of the Federal project.

JOHN: Well, yes. You see, the Federal Theatre had very intelligent and very constructive provisions. You could hire ten percent of your personnel, not from the relief roles. They received exactly the same remuneration as the relief people, but they did not have to qualify as relief people. So some of the people like Joseph Cotten, Arlene Francis, Orson himself, of course, and other people who worked with us at the Federal came over and joined us at the Mercury. We were very poor, very young and we didn't really pay them much more than they got on the relief roles, but they wanted to join us so they came.

JASON: One of those people was a man who recently passed away—Martin Gabel.

JOHN: He was indeed. He played Cassius in *Julius Caesar* and Danton in *Danton's Death*. He was a case in point. Martin was earning quite a lot of money on radio at the time, but he had a passion for the theatre, so we invited him to join us and he did.

JASON: When you produced your first *Mercury Theatre on the Air* for radio, he was the star in *Dracula*. Then, of course, there was Orson. He was quite a piece of work on days when a program was scheduled. A few hours before a broadcast it always looked like nothing would go right.

JOHN: That was chronic with Orson's shows. It was fairly chronic with radio in general. There were usually enormous confusions and improvisations right up to the last moment.

JASON: When talking about the *Mercury Theatre on the Air*, it is inevitable that we get into *War of the Worlds*. If I'm not mistaken, that was a last minute selection.

JOHN: Yes, those shows took about ten days to two weeks to write, but nothing was ever planned very far in advance. We felt there was a need to do a science fiction program, so we did.

JASON: And we know what the results were. Were there any long-term problems created by that perform-ance other than what we can readily read?

JOHN: Well, no. There was a very large national panic. A few people were inconvenienced. There were, I believe, some miscarriages, some broken limbs, people rushing out into the street, but in fact, when the two million dollars of lawsuits were untangled and settled, there were no damages paid for that show.

JASON: One reason it was so effective had to do with the fact that news was still in its early stages when it came to remote broadcasts.

JOHN: As a result of the Munich crisis, the American public had shifted its prime concern for news from the newspapers to the radio box. They found that radio was giving them news faster and more graphically than the papers the next morning. As a result, the credibility of *War of the Worlds* was considerably higher than it might have been six months earlier.

JASON: Howard Koch wrote the script, but you had your share of input as well.

JOHN: I was the general editor of the series, so naturally I had a lot to do with all of the shows.

JASON: While Orson was in the theatre digging huge holes in the stage.

JOHN: He was very elaborate, quite wonderful, but not very successful in the production of *Danton's Death*. I've always maintained that the direction of a show, the effectiveness of a show, had a lot to do with Orson's particular form of courage and music. He pushed further beyond the limits that anyone else would dare to push.

JASON: After the Mercury Theatre, you were involved in many things. During the war, you were with the Office of Information, the *Voice of America*. What did that entail?

JOHN: Contrary to what one would think, a nation that depended so much for years on advertising did not have any overseas propaganda or news service at all until the middle of 1941. Then they began, with the certainty that there would be a war, to plan an organization. When Pearl Harbor came to pass, although we had no government broadcasts of our own, we were ready to start. A lot of us were summoned from various parts of the country and set to creating the *Voice of America*. Our first show was in German on February 16, 1942. Within three months, we had a thousand shows a day going all over the world, each in its appropriate language.

JASON: You had already been in Hollywood by then.

JOHN: I spent a year with David Selznick.

JASON: Over time, you were deeply involved in some film classics.

JOHN: That came later. That was after the war. That ran from about '45 until 1956. Those were my really fruitful years as a movie producer.

JASON: From Shakespeare you did *Julius Caesar* with Orson in blue serge.

JOHN: That was in the theatre. When we did the movie, we actually did it in togas. We still did it very modern. Joe Mankiewicz directed it. The experience was very modern, but we did do it in Roman costumes. The show you are talking about was in 1937. That was at the Mercury, Orson's very famous production.

JASON: I know. Sorry. I'm jumping around a little, but he did do that one in a blue serge suit.

JOHN: Correct. Everyone was in modern clothes.

JASON: At the Mercury, you had some problems with special effects because of the small stage.

JOHN: The real problem was that, Orson, having done a lot of radio, got some of his radio friends to prepare these elaborate sound patterns. With the inferior equipment we used in the theatre in those days it never worked. We threw them all out.

JASON: Now let's get into the movie version of *Julius Caesar*. You had an impressive cast including someone a lot of people had reservations about, Marlon Brando, who proved them wrong.

JOHN: He was wonderful. He was absolutely wonderful. I never had any doubt. I heard him do a poetic play and I knew his speech was perfect. I never doubted, but everyone around Hollywood was skeptical indeed. They didn't know what they were talking about.

JASON: Just on the face of it, to throw him in with James Mason, John Gielgud and Louis Calhern doesn't sound plausible.

JOHN: It may not have sounded right, but it sure was right.

JASON: You did *Julius Caesar* at the Mercury and on film, but when you got to Stratford, it wasn't included in the repertoire.

JOHN: It had been done the year before I got to Stratford. It was the first show ever done at the American Shakespeare Festival Theatre. For many reasons, including the fact that the theatre wasn't ready, plus the whole thing was not carefully enough planned, it was a critical failure. Besides, I'd done it with Orson at the Mercury and I did the movie. I didn't want to do it a third time. It was done later when other management took over.

JASON: The first season at Stratford had no connection to you at all. Isn't that right?

JOHN: Nothing to do with it, nothing at all.

JASON: But you were appointed artistic director for the second season.

JOHN: They called and asked me. I had a very remarkable contract at MGM, which permitted me to take a year off any time I wanted. So I did take a year off to run the 1956 Stratford season. Then, because things in Hollywood changed, the management at MGM changed, and because I was having such an exciting time trying to create a National Repertory Company, I stayed four years.

JASON: You were appointed to that position by Lawrence Langner?

JOHN: He was one of three. Lincoln Kirstein was involved

along with Joseph Verner and Lawrence Langner. Lawrence was somewhat opposed to my taking over the position and the authority I insisted on having, but the other two insisted.

JASON: You knew Lawrence and Lincoln long before that.

JOHN: Yes. I had worked for the Theatre Guild. I've known Lincoln since he came to town.

JASON: There were so many motion pictures that you had a hand in. We can't possibly mention them all, but there was one I particularly enjoyed. That one was *Lust for Life* with Kirk Douglas. I don't know how well it did at the box office, but I liked it very much.

JOHN: It was very successful. It was a wonderful movie. I was very proud of it. Vincente Minnelli directed it. It was beautifully directed. We spent a lot of time and money going to all the right places where van Gogh had lived and worked.

JASON: The book was written by Irving Stone, who had a very rambling style. Was that a problem?

JOHN: The truth is Metro owned that book for ten years before I got near the place. It's a perfectly researched book. However; on that particular story, the material is so rich and so true. It all comes from the letters van Gogh and his brother Theo exchanged over the years. There were other letters too, including some from other painters. It wasn't difficult to get the right slant on the story.

JASON: Irving Stone was very careful with his research.

JOHN: Very good on research. When we did the movie, Norman Corwin did the screen treatment.

JASON: We both know what kind of writer Norm is. Aside from all your credits for film and radio, I believe the theatre is still your first love.

JOHN: It has to be because it is the core of all theatrical enterprises. All of the others are ultimately, no matter how far they go technologically, still ultimately related to the theatre.

JASON: But radio is the theatre of the mind.

JOHN: Radio was a wonderful medium. It's a very sad story that radio has disappeared. As a dramatic medium, it was very imaginative, very interesting.

JASON: When it came to drama on television, a whole new set of problems arose.

JOHN: Television is derived from its father and mother, which are radio and the theatre. It's somewhere between. It's a very distinguished, interesting medium of its own. Some of the stuff you can do on radio is undoable on television, including *War of the Worlds.*

JASON: A lot of early television was theatrical. You garnered a couple of Emmys for the likes of *Playhouse 90.*

JOHN: *Playhouse 90* was live until its last year. They were exciting. Sometimes they were flawed, but the spirit and the intelligence and the energy underlying those shows was extraordinary.

JASON: When did you get into the acting business?

JOHN: Not until I was seventy years old.

JASON: Your first substantive role must have been Professor Kingsfield in *The Paper Chase.*

JOHN: I had done some small parts in other films about ten years earlier, but that was as a joke on a friend of mine.

JASON: You must have done something right. They gave you an Oscar for *Paper Chase.*

JOHN: It turned out quite well.

JASON: *Paper Chase* became, and still is, quite a story. It became a long running series on television.

JOHN: It's still around. We made fifty-seven in all. We made twenty for CBS and thirty-seven for Showtime. They are being shown right now.

JASON: There have been so many television shows that were buried before they had a chance, due to poor scheduling. That's a game the networks play all the time. Aren't you still doing more of them for Showtime?

JOHN: We just did the last seven this spring. For the time being, we're not making any more. Eventually, who knows, we might do more.

JASON: Maybe it's a little too intellectual when you consider the audience the networks target.

JOHN: I don't think it's intellectual. It's literate and intelligent, but that doesn't make it intellectual in the pejorative sense. It's being seen all over the world. It's very successful. On the BBC in England, it's the most successful dramatic show. It's shown right now in sixty-one counties. I did quite a bit of television. I've done some movies. I do commercials. I amuse myself in various ways.

JASON: Who can forget your commercials, especially the ones for Smith-Barney?

JOHN: We just finished making three more of them. I enjoy making them.

JASON: I mentioned earlier your Academy Award for *Paper Chase*. You were also nominated for an Emmy and an Ace Award for the television version. More recently, you got a Golden Globe nomination for your portrayal of Aaron Jastrow in *Winds of War*, a mini-series based on a book by Herman Wouk.

JOHN: It was a nice part. I saw it again the other day when they reran it. People often ask me which, of all the things I have done, I like the best. My answer is, none. I really liked them all. It's been an enormously fortunate life. I've had the luck to be very long lived. I have very good health and energy. The thing that I'm proud of is the aggregate of what it all amounts to.

****

Not many months after this interview on October 31, 1988, fifty-five years to the day after his somewhat notorious *War of the Worlds* broadcast, John Houseman succumbed to spinal cancer. He left behind an unending trail of achievement after achievement after achievement.

As a teacher, he was instrumental in the launching of many careers. Among those beneficiaries were Kevin Kline, Patti LuPone and David Ogden Stiers. They and many others were products of Mr. Houseman's acting company, which came out of his years at the

Julliard Drama Division, something he founded and nurtured through its infancy.

In order to more fully comprehend the integrity of this media giant, I highly recommend reading his final book, written in 1988. In his own words, it tells the entire tale of his life, cradle to grave. The title is *Unfinished Business: Memoirs 1902-1988*. It is a well-documented fact that much of what he started, with high hopes, remains unfinished.

ACT VII:
FAR MORE THAN
SUSPENSE

This is a tale of two multi-faceted mammoths of radio. Each was a longtime producer/director of *Suspense*, a classic radio show that appeared on the air over nine hundred and forty times between 1942 and 1962. They did not work in tandem on that show. Each was the man in command for a long stretch, but at different times.

However, this is not about *Suspense*, in spite of the fact that they did each speak briefly about the subject. No, this is about the massive body of work of each in other areas. Their careers took very different tracks, but both became radio giants along the way. They did have a few shows in common. They both did *Columbia Workshop*. Both were involved with *Hawk Larabee*. Both also worked in *Fall of the City*, from opposite sides of the microphone. One other common thread, they both worked for government agencies, but not the same one.

Act VII:
Scene One
Drama–Adventure–Humor

Not all stars get to see their name up in lights and not many ever get the recognition they so richly deserve. That does not mean that the glitter surrounding them is diminished. Talent will show its face, whether we hear the name connected to that person or not.

This man was one of those unsung heroes of the airwaves. His acting roles were legion in a time when credit was rarely given. His writings for radio and in print were ingenious. His sense of presence, when producing or directing, was unmistakable. His research was thorough and faultless. Before any of his work appeared on the air for our entertainment and scrutiny, he made sure it was as perfect as he could make it.

He managed to enjoy it all as he progressed through his career. His name was Elliott Lewis. We conversed on October 16. 1986.

****

JASON: Some actors are producers. Most directors are writers. Not too many can fit comfortably into all four of those categories as well as Elliott Lewis. Elliott, you've had quite a career. You've covered all the bases, but I believe you began as an actor.

ELLIOTT: Actually, I think my first paying job was as an actor, but I had started as a writer. I guess it was the right time and I was in the right place, so I got acting jobs. I had so many acting jobs that I didn't have time to do as much writing as I wanted to do. Somehow, because I was acting in odd shows, and also a writer, I was doing a lot of editing on those shows. I went from there to directing and producing on those shows so everything kind of tracked as you might expect it to track.

JASON: Where did you actually get your start on radio?

ELLIOTT: I was born in New York, Mount Vernon, New York. I came out here to go to college. I was going to Los Angeles City College. They were starting a class in radio. I had room on my schedule so I took the class. One day, when I was not in class, a man named True Boardman, who had graduated from City College, and who was an actor, writer, director and producer, came down and spoke to the radio class and invited them all to come down to the station where he worked, KHJ. KHJ at that time was the CBS outlet on the West Coast. It was part of the Don Lee Network. He invited all the kids in the class to come down and audition. They did and I was told about it. So I called True and said that I was sorry I hadn't been there, could I also come down? He said sure. So I went down and a couple of other kids and I got jobs as actors on some of the shows they were doing. I think the first one I worked on was a benefit for the Red Cross. From there I picked up other jobs and started working enough so that I dropped out of school and kept working.

JASON: One of those early shows must have been *Knickerbocker Playhouse* with Marvin Miller.

ELLIOTT: The ones I'm talking about were around 1936. Was *Knickerbocker* before the war?

JASON: About 1940 or '41.

ELLIOTT: Right, just before the war. I was working on a show
called *Silver Theatre* out here, a Sunday dramatic
anthology with guest stars. Conrad Nagel was the
host. Once again, Boardman did the show. He was
the story editor. He was in charge of the scripts. A
man called Glenhall Taylor was the producer and
director of the show. They both worked for Young
& Rubicam. In those days, the advertising agencies
had control of the shows. They did the production.
The network simply supplied the time and
then billed the agencies for it. The agency, in
turn, called the sponsor, which in this case was
International Silver Company, which is why it was
called *Silver Theatre*. They were planning to do a
show called *Knickerbocker Playhouse* and were
looking for a star, co-star actually. Betty Lou
Gerson, who lived in Chicago, was going to be the
lady star and they needed a man star. They heard
me on *Silver Theatre* and came out here to talk to
me. I auditioned for them. Here's a funny story.
We were doing a *Silver Theatre* and our star was
Rosalind Russell. In the middle of the *Silver
Theatre* rehearsal, I got word that in a studio
across the alley, the people from Chicago were
waiting and wanted to know if I could get away
for a few minutes and come over to audition. I
didn't have anyone to audition with and I didn't
have any material. Roz Russell said she'd go over
with me and we could do the scene we'd been
rehearsing. She said they wouldn't recognize her.
She was in rehearsal clothes. She told me to introduce
her as Miss Brown. So the two of us walked across
the alleyway to the studio and did the scene. I
introduced Miss Brown. They didn't have any idea
who she was. We finished and went back to work.
My agent called me that night and told me they

wanted me to come to Chicago and do the show. That's how I got that job. I worked in Chicago during the summer of '39. When I was driving home from Chicago that Labor Day, the series having concluded, the news on the radio was the invasion of Poland. That's how I can pretty well date it. Not long after I got back, the excitement on the radio was Orson Welles' Martian broadcast.

JASON: Howard Koch's *War of the Worlds.*

ELLIOTT: Right, marvelous show. It always puzzled me that there was so much excitement because if the Martians had landed in New Jersey, how come it was only on CBS? You would have thought that NBC, who had Edgar Bergen on at the time, would have broken in to say that the Martians had invaded. But no, it was only on one station.

JASON: I never thought of that angle. I talked with John Houseman a few weeks ago about the same subject. He seemed to think that it was because remote coverage of the news was a pretty new thing at the time. Obviously, it wouldn't work today.

ELLIOTT: Absolutely right. Today, the first thing out would be the helicopters to make a report back immediately. At that time, if the broadcast was legitimate, if it was really something that was going on, everybody would have picked it up. It wouldn't have just been on CBS. It was so well done. It was such a brilliant production. It was a great idea to start with—to do that story and to do it, not just as a broadcast, but as a part of another broadcast that was being interrupted, to give you this hot news thing. Good show.

JASON: I was one of the victims that night. I heard the original broadcast. I know it worked in my family, at least for a while.

ELLIOTT: Oh yeah! I don't think there's any question that it worked. As somebody in the business, I had to look at it a little askance. Listening to actors that you know and Bernie Herrmann doing the music, with all that stuff going on, you had to be suspicious. They were doing a brilliant job. They were a good group, as were all of the radio people in those days, just before we got into World War II. Radio was busy and active and growing. I remember a special broadcast about that time. They were going to do *The Fall of the City*, Archibald MacLeish's brilliant book. They had done it once in New York City and staged it for radio in the armory. Now they were going to do it again out here. This was a half-hour radio broadcast, live. I think it was done under the umbrella title, *Columbia Workshop*. There were three directors, Bill Robson, Irving Reis and I can't remember who the third man was. They got the Coliseum, the Los Angeles Coliseum. They had aircraft and motor vehicles detoured, so they wouldn't interfere with the broadcast. I remember I had two lines. For my first line, I was seated three quarters of the way up in the stands. I had to read the first line and then come running down the Coliseum steps, without breaking my neck, to do the second line eighty per cent closer to the microphones, which were down near field level. Those kinds of broadcasts were, well, you wish those days weren't gone. Those were fun.

JASON: The *Fall of the City* used those three directors for entirely different purposes. They had one directing the crowd, which was like one single voice, and one for the sound effects. The third was for the dramatic part of the show, the actors.

ELLIOTT: Exactly. I seem to remember that somebody was in a portable booth. I have a feeling it was Irving Reis. He was kind of *Director Prima*, running the whole thing, and Robson handled the crowd. Who was the third director?

JASON: I know the New York group. Wasn't it the same there?

ELLIOTT: I don't know. I didn't realize until we were in rehearsal, that they had done it in New York. I think it was Irving who mentioned it. I know he was in New York. I would imagine Robson was too. I don't think he had moved out here yet.

JASON: I want to say Norman Corwin, but I know that was before most of his time.

ELLIOTT: '39? I thought he was active then. No, I guess that was mostly after the war. Corwin was there, because I was in his *On a Note of Triumph*, which he did on V-E Day with Martin Gabel. When we did it, it was such a success that we did it again, live. The first one was at CBS. Then we did the whole thing over the following Sunday on NBC. I think the recording that's still around was taken from the CBS broadcast.

JASON: That was a true classic. The copy I have, I got directly from Norman, so I don't know where it originated.

ELLIOTT: All of the Corwin things were tremendous experiences, just to be able to work with him. Recently, Sears and CBS had a notion to bring back radio. They asked me to have a hand in it and try to do an original one-hour show, five days a week, an anthology. I agreed to try and I got Fletcher Markle to help me. Norman did one of those shows. He wrote a special show and came in to direct it. He had a wonderful time.

JASON: Was that *Zero Hour*? I always get that and the *Sears Theatre* mixed up.

ELLIOTT: No, *Zero Hour* was a thing I started with a guy named Jay Kholos. He was going to syndicate it. What we would do, was to take a mystery novel, a published book, break it into five half-hours, so it would run a week. We'd record three half-hours one day and the last two half-hours the next day, giving us the rest of the week to edit and polish it, but there was so little money that there was nothing we could do with it. I quit after a number of weeks. He picked it up and tried to continue it with another staff and another crew. I think he did pretty well. I really don't know. I have a feeling he may have taken a bath because he didn't have the broadcast facilities that we had on the Sears-CBS thing. Then when Sears dropped out and CBS dropped out, Mutual picked it up and we did it as the *Mutual Theatre* for, I don't know how many weeks. Every hour was different stuff.

JASON: Dick Crenna was in one of them.

ELLIOTT: Crenna did one of the *Zero Hours*. He also did one of the Sears-CBS things. I remember—because I wrote it.

JASON: And Vincent Price as well.

ELLIOTT: Vincent was the host on the mysteries, and Lorne

Greene on the Westerns. Andy Griffith was the host on the comedies. For the adventures, we had three hosts. We started with Widmark, then Howard Duff came in, and then Leonard Nimoy, because Howie had to do a picture or something. The trick was that for each of these series, we were actually doing five series. We had to have, before we started, six scripts ready for each series because we had to record the host before we could record the shows, so we knew pretty well, what he was going to say and how. We couldn't begin the show without him. It was quite a task. At first, Nelson Riddle did original music for every single one of those shows. He'd get the material. We'd leave a space on the tape where there would be music or a bridge, anything like that. Then Nelson would listen to the tape, time things and then come in and talk to me or Fletcher, depending on which one of us had depicted the show. We'd figure out what type of music we were thinking about because he was limited by budget to three or four men, the instrumentalists, men or women. It was a device I had used on a radio show when radio kind of folded dramatically, a show called *Crime Classics*. I did the same thing with Bernard Herrmann. We didn't have budget for a live orchestra, so what they wanted to do was to use recorded tracks from one of the libraries. I suggested that for the same price, we could have an orchestra of three or four instruments, since there was no thematic material. The show was an anthology that took place in different countries at different times in history. You could change the grouping each week and it would be a benefit to the show. They told me to get together with Bernie and the two of us could figure it out. So we did and Bernie wrote all of the scores for a year and a half of *Crime Classics*. He would do a string quartette, he'd do four trombones, he'd do a studio full of timpanists. He had a ball doing it. We all had fun. Keeping that in mind, when we were doing the budget for the Sears-CBS thing, I mentioned it. They said Nelson Riddle was available. Nelson and I met. I played a couple of those for him and we talked and he did it. How he did it, I don't know. I know he was ill by the time he finished because he was working day and night. There was no way out of it. We weren't simply doing bridges. On a radio show, you have to underscore narration, all that kind of stuff.

JASON: You brought up *Crime Classics*, which you produced and directed and often wrote. Those stories came mostly from your own personal crime library.

ELLIOTT: I love books and I had been getting book catalogs from places in New York and London and everywhere else. I had been doing *Suspense* and one of the first things I wrote when I was a kid was *The Whistler*, which was a mystery, suspense kind of show. I'd pick up these books, looking for stories and I'd find old cases, some old crimes. I had quite a decent library. Mort Fine and David Friedkin did most of the writing for *Crime Classics*. The three of us were able to go through this material and really skip around and get all kinds of stuff. We got some pretty good stuff. We gave Bernie Herrmann some time because, if he was going to do the assassination of Abraham Lincoln, it would be a different orchestra than if it was an Earl, killing his mother or a murder case in the twenties in America. I had developed quite a library. Unfortunately, we got caught in the early sixties in the Bel Air fire and the whole thing burned up. I had the only copies of some of that stuff. When we got finished, we swore that we would never buy another book, but twelve years later, we moved to Malibu because the ride got to be too much. Again later, when we left Malibu, we needed a moving van just for the books we had accumulated. Now we sit on a hill overlooking the city and as I talk to you from the room that I use as my writing office, I am surrounded by books again. It was a terrible thing to have happen, but, God forbid, if it ever happens to you, you will be amazed how quickly the wound heals and you start replacing stuff, or your friends find a copy of something they know you had loved, and make it a gift to you.

JASON: I'd be lost without my books. Nobody should be without them. Let's go back to your acting days on radio. When you were in Chicago, you did more than just *Knickerbocker.* I'm thinking of a show called *This is Judy Jones*, a soap opera.

ELLIOTT: I was in Chicago just that one summer, but while I was there, since *Knickerbocker* only took me a day and a half and it was on the weekend, the agency involved also had a soap opera. I can't remember the name of it but it wasn't *Judy Jones*. I got a part in it. It was more to keep me occupied than anything else.

JASON: When considering soaps and Chicago, we could list them all day and never come up with the right one.

ELLIOTT: If my wife was here, she'd know immediately. She had played one of the parts in it when it was in Cincinnati. When we first met, she always accused me of stealing her job by forcing the show to move from Cincinnati just to give me something to do during the week.

JASON: *Ma Perkins* started in Cincinnati.

ELLIOTT: A lot of those things did. Mary Jane worked on all of them.

JASON: On "The Nation's Station," WLW.

ELLIOTT: I'd love to visit there. I've never been there.

JASON: Apparently, you were wrapped up in mysteries from very early on. You've done quite a few mystery shows. You were on *Nero Wolfe* for one, and *Casebook of Gregory Hood*, where you followed Gale Gordon.

ELLIOTT: That's right. That was the most embarrassing thing that ever happened to either one of us. Gale had been doing the show and they hired me because the client didn't like Gale. I don't know why. I'm sure it was something stupid. They assured me that they had spoken to Gale and that he understood and everything was taken care of. I walked into the studio for rehearsal and there sat Gale. We were old friends. What they had nicely done was not to tell him what was going on. They let me tell him that I was the new Gregory Hood. You know Tony Boucher? I was just reading the Sunday paper, the *L.A. Times*. They had an article about the Bouchercon, a yearly meeting of mystery writers, publishers and fans. This year I think it was in Baltimore. Anthony Boucher was a writer and also a critic of mysteries for *The New York Times*, among others. Tony was one of the brains behind *Gregory Hood*, one of its creators.

JASON: He was one of the actors too.

ELLIOTT: He was? I didn't know that, maybe in Gale's time. I think the co-creator was Denis Green, a big, tall Englishman.

JASON: Who had played Sherlock Holmes at one time.

ELLIOTT: He did *Nero Wolfe* too when I was acting.

JASON: You were with an old silent movie actor on that one, Francis X. Bushman.

ELLIOTT: Right. Frank was Nero and I was Archie. I think it was the most fun I ever had as an actor. I don't particularly like acting, never have. I prefer writing, but that was fun and I was working with nice people. I think there must have been five hundred guys who played Archie and at least three hundred and seventy-five who played Nero over the years. They just tried it again on television a couple of years ago.

JASON: Sydney Greenstreet was one of the many who played Nero Wolfe.

ELLIOTT: I didn't realize that.

JASON: There was a comedy role you played on radio for a long time. I think most people would remember you as Frankie Remley.

ELLIOTT: Nine years I did that endeavor. Remley was fun and I was working with the best of people, Phil Harris and Alice Faye. Ray Singer and Dick Chevillat were writing it. Good writers. It was a very pleasant experience.

JASON: Walter Tetley was there and Gale Gordon.

ELLIOTT: Gale and Walter and an actor named Bob North, who was Phil's brother, Willie. One of the kids on the show, who played Phyllis, called me up a couple of years ago. She was in town. She lives somewhere up in the state of Washington. It must have been while the Sears-CBS thing was going on. She was in town to see her mother and she heard about the show. She wanted to know if she could come over and act in it, pick up a dollar and a half or whatever, but mostly just to have some fun.

JASON: Frank Remley was Phil's guitarist in his band. Is it true that he was the one who suggested that you play him on the show?

ELLIOTT: I think so. They went on the air with Frankie playing Frankie. The character had pretty well developed on the Benny Show, but he'd never spoken. They talked about this bum, this guitar player who didn't know music. He was a bum, a friendly lovable bum, a left-handed guitar player. So when Phil and Alice started their own show, naturally they were going to use Remley. He would speak. On their first show, Remley played himself. I was doing another show at NBC at the time. When they finished Phil's show, which I had not heard, the gang came out and Phil saw me in the hall. I said hello and asked him how it went. He said he and Remley had been talking and it just hadn't worked out with Frankie doing it. Frank didn't want to do it anymore because it embarrassed him. He didn't know what he was doing and he wasn't getting laughs. He had suggested that maybe I could make-believe I was him. Phil asked me if I'd do it the next week and if it went OK, we'd see what would happen. So I did and we ran nine years, nice job.

JASON: It was a major role. Quite a few of the shows that I have are mostly Phil and Remley.

ELLIOTT: That was the set up. Fortunately, Phil is married to a gracious, lovely, friendly, warm, no-ego lady named Alice Faye. Alice knew immediately what the joke would be on almost every show. She said to Phil, "One thing I don't want you to do is the following. I have to go to the hairdressers or the market, whatever, and I want to make sure that's taken care of." The body of the show is Frankie and Phil getting involved in what she said she didn't want us to do.

JASON: How about a small sample?

****

REMLEY: Hi Curly.

PHIL: It's you!

REMLEY: Yeah, it's me. I just dropped in to say hello.

PHIL: Yeah, but it means a lot more than just hello to me right now. A real friend seems to know when to show up, doesn't he?

REMLEY: If you say so.

PHIL: There's a silent bond between us, Remley. You didn't know I needed you and yet you're here. Why? Why?

REMLEY: The poolroom was closed. I had nowhere to go. Hey, Curly, what's bothering you?

PHIL: Little Phyllis has a boy friend and she won't even bring him to meet me.

REMLEY: Philly's got a boy friend? That should make you proud.

PHIL: Well, it does, but I'd be prouder if I could meet my son-in-law.

REMLEY: Don't rush it. Phyllis will introduce you to him eventually. You know, you're not the kind of guy anyone can meet too suddenly.

****

ELLIOTT: The last quarter of the show and the last scenes are the face-off with Alice, where she can't believe what happened while we're trying to get out of it. She never once in the nine years said, "Wait a minute! Why don't I have more to do?" Which was a little unusual because, of the whole bunch, she was the big star. I think the show got on the air more because of Alice than anyone else.

JASON: She was a big movie box office star at that time.

ELLIOTT: Biggest star Fox had, biggest for a long time.

JASON: In 1948, you were with another big box office star, although she was a little older at that time, on *Junior Miss*.

ELLIOTT: That was funny. I played her father. I was about nine years older than she was

JASON: You followed Gale Gordon on that one too.

ELLIOTT: Was that with Shirley?

JASON: Right, Shirley Temple.

ELLIOTT: Did they do *Junior Miss* ahead of that, with Shirley?

JASON: She was one of the people who played Judy Grimes on that show.

ELLIOTT: I remember doing Shirley Temple's father for a short run, the summer before I went into the army. It was a Thursday night show. I have a clear memory of doing that show, going home, packing my bags and going into the army that Saturday. That had to be 1940 or 1941.

JASON: The show ran much before 1948.

ELLIOTT: Yes. I did it that one summer when it first started. Maybe I was rehired later. I got out of the army in '46. I couldn't get a job. Then Ozzie Nelson put me to work. I called him and told him I was out of the army and couldn't get a job. Nobody knew who I was. He said, "What are you doing Friday?" I said, "Nothing." He said, "Come on over in the morning."

JASON: From all I've heard he was a very fine gentleman.

ELLIOTT: A wonderful man. Of all the people who aren't with us anymore, I miss Ozzie as much as anybody.

JASON: I understand he was exactly the same in real life as he was on his show.

ELLIOTT: Really! He was so funny. He was so good at so many things. He was such a dear man, such a good man, such a decent man.

JASON: Let's switch back to Norman Corwin for a minute. He did a series called *26 by Corwin*. You were on one of them called "The Undecided Molecule," with a very strange cast. Groucho Marx was on it as were Robert Benchley, Vincent Price and

Keenan Wynn. You played the vice president in charge of psycho-chemistry.

ELLIOTT: I got called at the last minute. I don't remember whoever was playing it, but whoever it was, through no fault of his own, wasn't doing what Norman wanted or expected. I got a phone call from Norman at noon or one o'clock saying, "I'm having a little problem. Can you get over here?" I went over there. I think we were at the Vine Street Playhouse. I remember that cast. He handed me the script. I think it was in poetry and that was the problem. It was written that way, but Norman didn't want it played that way. He just wanted it played like dialogue and let the rhymes and meters just fall naturally, instead of striving for them and hitting them.

JASON: I have a copy of that script that Norman sent to me. His director's notes say just that. It may be written in couplets, but do not read it that way.

ELLIOTT: You know, the one he did on the Sears-CBS thing, was all in rhyme. He went through the same thing with that cast. It's very hard to do. When I was doing *Suspense*, producing and directing *Suspense*, I had a wonderful idea, I thought, and I pitched it to Guy Della-Cioppa. We were on our way to Chicago for our regular three-month meeting, where I would tell the advertising agency on the show and the Autolite Company rep, what we were planning to do in the next cycle of *Suspense* shows. On the plane, I told Del that I had a terrific idea. I said we would do *Othello*. We'd do it in two parts and we'd add some instruments to the orchestra and use Verdi's music from his opera to score it. He said, "If you say one word about that to these people in Chicago, I'll kill you. We cannot afford to lose this account." So I told him I wouldn't do it. So we got there, nice men, the guys we were meeting with. While we were talking about things, it seemed to me that they were open to any kind of idea and we were close enough so that, if I said something they thought was nutty, they'd tell me so. They wouldn't cancel the show. They'd just dismiss the notion. So I said what I had said to Del and they flipped. They said, "What a sensational idea. Great publicity! Who's going to cut the play down to time?" I told them I was going to do that with Tony Ellis. "Oh, fine, fine, who's going to play Othello?" I said that I thought that I would. They said, "Good, who will play Desdemona and who will be Iago?" I was married to Kathy at the time, so I told them she could do Desdemona and Dick Widmark is Iago. They said, "Gee, that's great. You go ahead and do it." So we did it. What started me on this was reading lines that are not written as dialogue. On the plane back, Del said, "I didn't know you knew that much about Shakespeare." I said, "I didn't." He said, "But you're going to cut the script, and you're going to direct the actors and you're going to play Othello." I said, "Yeah. I'll give it a shot, how bad can it be?" It didn't occur to me that the problem you have doing that kind of material is very tricky. It was what Norman was talking about. What you have to do is, do it the way I'm talking to you. Don't do it like it's etched in stone. If you do it that way, it's going to be pretty awful. We got a very good show out of Othello, as Norman gets excellent shows out of the stuff he does when everything is in rhyme. It takes awhile for the actors to catch on. It's kind of like, if you speak a lyric of a song that's been going around. Tony Bennett did one with a great lyric, *let's take the note that Mendelssohn wrote concerning the spring weather, let's sing it together.* That's just a splendid lyric. As a lyric, it just naturally falls into the rhythm it was written for. You don't have to emphasize or structuralize or do anything. If you speak it, just speak it. It says what it has to say and does it perfectly. It's like matching a performance to a person. There are actors and there are **actor-actors. Actor-actors** want you to know they're acting. Too much is declaimed. I don't like that kind of acting. I like the kind of acting where you are just talking to somebody. Something happens. You listen. You react. I like to write that way, act that way and I like to direct that way.

JASON: The problem I have with Norman's writing is the way he goes from blank verse, to couplets to straight prose and back to blank verse, with maybe a sonnet or a limerick thrown in, all in one script. You can never be certain what to expect next. I guess that is one of the things that make him so special.

ELLIOTT: That's true. We rehearsed *On a Note of Triumph.* We didn't know why we got called. We got to the studio and there was Lud Gluskin conducting an orchestra playing Bernie Herrmann's music. There was Martin Gabel who was flown out from New York, to be narrator. And there were the rest of us. I was in the army at the time. Norman Corwin called my commanding officer, Tom Lewis, for me on this highly secret thing. Nobody was to know what we were doing at CBS, rehearsing. Tom Lewis let me go for three days, most of them on a weekend. There were places where it was just speech and there were places where it was poetry. There were places where there were couplets. He had them all mixed in. There were places where a guy would be singing a song, "Round and round Hitler's grave. Round and round we go."

JASON: That was a recurring theme used over and over, each time with slightly different lyrics.

ELLIOTT: They had Marty Gabel in an airlock to keep him away from the rest of us. What did he say? "The rat is dead in back of Wilhelm Strasse. Free men have done it again."

JASON: Here's the speech you're referring to, powerful words.

****

So they've given up. They're finally done in and the rat is dead in alley in back of the Wilhelm Strasse. Take a bow, GI; take a bow little guy. The superman of tomorrow lies dead at the feet of the common man of this afternoon. This is it kids. This is the day. All the way from Newbury Port to Vladivostok, you had what it took and you gave it. Each of you has a hunk of rainbow round your helmet. Seems like free men have done it again.

****

ELLIOTT: Wow! He came up with some stuff. On that show, there was a submarine sunk on the bottom of the sea. Marty Gabel is trying to tell the people aboard the sub that the war in Germany is over. To get the effect of pounding on the sub, the soundman had a big empty gas tank, a huge one, brought into the studio. He pounded on it with a long steel rod. He got so excited doing it that when he did his back swing, the steel rod, went right through the wall. The hole in the wall may still be there. Anyway, the rhyme was, "You in there, rest assured..." I forgot the rest of it.

JASON: Let me help. Here's the bit.

****

You who are resting, rest assured of this. Over your heads above the sea, victory has risen like a sun and moves west as we tell these things to you. Your brothers going down to the sea, in ships sail towards the settling of a score. Here with you on this ocean bed lie fighting comrades, men of the Cisco and the Perch, the Yorktown, the Chicago and the Liscombe Bay. Each shall be vindicated in good time.

****

ELLIOTT: It made my hair stand up. There was Norman in the booth nodding, winking at people and doing his job as a radio director. He was just brilliant.

JASON: That whole broadcast could make your hair stand on end. It was a fantastic piece of work all the way through, one of his best.

ELLIOTT: After we talk, I'm going out to my garage and dig that one up. I don't even know what I did on it. I think I had four parts. We all did.

JASON: The most dominant part was that of Martin Gabel. He could deliver lines as well as Orson Welles.

ELLIOTT: Absolutely, and what strength. He sat on a high stool, in front of a ribbon mike with the script on a music stand in front of him and never stopped talking for three days. Anytime he picked up he went at it full volume. He wasn't saving his voice. He wasn't winging it because he didn't know when we would broadcast. We were going to do it when the announcement was made that the war in

Germany was over. The trick was, that the minute
the announcement came they would say, "And now
a special broadcast," and boom! This guy was
singing, "Round and round Hitler's Grave" and we
did this show that sounded on the air as if we were
making it up, that it just happened. No one knew
what we were doing there except the executives at
CBS. It was another of Paley's triumphs. I did so
much stuff with Norman. I love being identified
as having worked with him because he was and is
a genius.

JASON: Later on, the *Columbia Workshop* became the
CBS Radio Workshop and Norman was not involved
with some of them. I'm thinking of one you
wrote, produced, directed and starred in, called
"Nightmare."

ELLIOTT: Bill Paley called me and said, "We're doing the
Workshop. It's still on the air. I'd like to give you a
half hour." I asked him what he wanted me to do
and he told me to do whatever I wanted. I thought
if you're going to do it, do an entirely personal
experience with narration. Do internal stuff. So I
wrote "Nightmare," and asked him if it was OK.
He said, "Fine. If you're going to do that kind of
thing, there are so many flavors you want to get in
it. It's easier to do it yourself, from your own
script, than to write it and explain it to somebody
else, tell them what you were thinking." That was a
great experience. I enjoyed that show. Fred Steiner
did the music. We were able to change scenes on
radio, as they would be in a nightmare. I remember
one of them. He's at a football game. He's announcing
the game and one of the players on the field is
down. All of the other players start jumping on
him and hitting him. Ninety thousand people in
the stadium stand up and cheer, and as the cheer

hits its peak, it turns into a wave crashing on the bow of a ship on which he's a passenger, that sort of stuff.

JASON: And it segued from dream to dream.

ELLIOTT: Exactly. It turned out at the end that all the beatings and that kind of stuff you're listening to is a man having a heart attack. Something that had taken a half-hour had actually only taken ten seconds.

JASON: Let's switch gears. I spoke recently with Gale Gordon, who was one of many people who did the *Cinnamon Bear* series many years ago. I also had a brief chat with Frank Nelson, not long before he passed away. Gale couldn't remember the series, but I'm quite sure Frank would have if we had had more time to converse because according to my sources, he compiled the cast list that I have. It was twenty-six episodes that were aired every year from about Thanksgiving to just before Christmas. I think you were one of the players.

ELLIOTT: I remember a man named Glan Heisch. I believe he was involved as a producer, director and perhaps, writer for the *Cinnamon Bear*. The reason I remember him so well is that Mary Jane and I went to New Mexico for a vacation. When we got off the plane in Albuquerque, we were walking down one of those long tunnels and coming towards us was Glan. We stopped and greeted each other. He was leaving and we were arriving. He said, "Incidentally, the *Cinnamon Bear* is on locally." I didn't have the faintest idea what he was talking about.

JASON: It first ran in 1938, a long time ago.

ELLIOTT: A little later, I got a note from Glan.

JASON: He is the man who wrote it.

ELLIOTT: Anyway, I got a note from him with a check for eight dollars or something like that.

JASON: Royalties?

ELLIOTT: Yeah. It surprised me because nobody was paying royalties unless you sued them.

JASON: There weren't any in those days.

ELLIOTT: No, of course not. He said, and I'm paraphrasing, 'We've sold the series in such and such places and we're showing a profit. All of you should share, so here's your share.' That was very nice. He was a nice man.

****

Of all of the Hollywood, New York or wherever personalities I spoke with during the two year, six-station run of *Life in the Past Lane*, I will not hesitate to say that Elliott Lewis was the one I would most like to have gotten a chance to know better. He was so down to earth, so lacking in ego and just plain easy to communicate with. Normally, my interviews took anywhere from one to two hours. In Elliott's case, it was nearly four hours and could have been longer.

There were so many things left unsaid. We did not get into his involvement with Armed Forces Radio at all. His contributions to that organization were overwhelming and thereby, to the preservation of radio history. Along with Tom Lewis, Jerry Lawrence, Bob Lee, Howard Duff, True Boardman and a few others, Elliott helped to create the infrastructure of Armed Forces Radio. Throughout the fifties, he brought *Suspense* to a new level of quality despite ever shrinking budgets. Radio was on the wane, but he did his best not to allow the inevitable to happen. When it was over, he fell back to his first love, writing mystery books.

He passed away on May 26, 1990. He was never given enough credit for his huge body of work over five decades.

ACT VII:
SCENE TWO
IMPORTANCE

Pioneer; risk taker; innovator; experimenter; tactician? Those are appropriate words when describing this man, but hardly adequate. Was he a pioneer? Unquestionably! He and his family go back to the earliest days of broadcasting in his birthplace, Pittsburgh, Pennsylvania. He and that fledgling industry grew up in perfect harmony. Did he take risks? Indeed! If he wanted to make a point, nothing was beyond his realm of possibility. Could he innovate? Absolutely! He took new ideas and new equipment to levels unheard of before. He was undeniably an experimenter and a tactician. Someone had to nurture and develop radio in its infancy.

This piece is about a man who admirably fits in all of those categories and much more. His name was William N. Robson, Bill Robson. We had this discussion from his home in Virginia on September 7, 1986.

****

JASON: You've done so much for so long, Bill, I'm sure we're bound to miss a lot, but let's see if we can at least cover some of the high spots. I understand it all really got started at KHJ in Los Angeles.

BILL: That's correct. It began with an interview with Don Lee, who was looking for someone for his staff. That interview happened the day after the president, Mr. Roosevelt, closed the banks in March of 1933.

JASON: You're going back to within twelve years of when radio broadcasting began.

BILL: As a matter of fact, I have a little short cut statement about myself in that respect. I was born in Pittsburgh in nineteen hundred and six. Radio was born in Pittsburgh in nineteen hundred and twenty. We were married in Los Angeles in 1933 and it was a happy relationship until radio died of terminal illness, television.

JASON: Of course, you're referring to KDKA in Pittsburgh.

BILL: Yes, curiously enough, my father was involved in that very first broadcast. He was an exploitation man, which is a fancy way to say press agent, for Paramount Pictures, at that time in the Pittsburgh area. He read about the fact that Dr. Frank Conrad was going to broadcast the election returns. Being the smart cookie that he was, he thought of a way to tie this up with his job. He got a radio receiving set and put it backstage at the Olympic Theatre where Paramount was running a very important first run picture. During the time that KDKA was broadcasting the election returns, all afternoon and evening, dad was back of the screen with earphones, receiving the broadcasts and noting them down. Every few minutes he'd come out in front of the screen and give the up to date election returns to the audience. After that was over they estimated that more people heard the broadcast in the Olympic Theatre than throughout the whole of the Western Pennsylvania area, there being very few receiving sets in that day. That was my first connection with radio, so to speak. Almost three years later, another connection, a little closer to the microphone, happened. I had gone with the Allegheny High School team band, of which I was a member, to play at a very important football game over in Dayton, Ohio. We won and we were some kind of champion. I set up a system with my dad whereby I sent him, from the field, telegraph reports on the game. He placed copies of the telegrams in a retail store close to the high school for anyone interested to see how the game was progressing. When dad had gotten the message that we had won, he got in touch with me and said, "When the band gets in tomorrow have everybody dressed and ready to march." I didn't know what he was thinking about, so I told the bandleader and we did what dad asked. We marched off from the railroad station to an office building and up into a huge room that seemed to be decorated with commercialized Indian sign blankets. This was the broadcast studio for WCAE. There, in that barn, with blankets strewn about to cut the sound bounce, we played a little concert in celebration of the team's victory. That was the first time any of us had been near broadcasting, actual broadcasting. That was 1922.

JASON: You never got very far away from it after that.

BILL: Eleven years later, I was back in it for good.

JASON: There's always been a question in this part of the country, and it's backed up by several historians, as to whether KDKA or the forerunner to the public radio station here in Madison, WHA, was actually first on the air. It all comes down to the question of public service or for profit. Our station went on the air in 1919.

BILL: I don't know the answer to that. We Pittsburghers know that the first scheduled broadcast was Election Day in 1920. I don't think that was sponsored, unless you can call the Westinghouse label sponsorship. They identified KDKA as a Westinghouse station. I can't make any further claims for it.

JASON: But, in effect, it was a commercial station because it wasn't owned as a public station is, by the people.

BILL: I think you're right there. I think it was Dr. Conrad's experimental station coming out of his garage. Later it became the Westinghouse station.

JASON: Let's move on. You did your first big things in New York, but you were in Los Angeles in between. How did that all come about?

BILL: I started in Los Angeles and I did some pretty big things out there before I came back East. I had a show called *Calling All Cars*, which predated all other police shows on radio. I was tied up with the Los Angeles police department and with other police departments due to the fact that the sponsor, Rio Grande Oil Company, was out making gasoline contracts for police cars. That show was only heard in that area, Southern California and parts of Arizona; however, it was very successful in that area. Our opposition at that time was *Merton Barge*. We just killed them rating wise and that was a very popular national show.

JASON: What year would that have been?

BILL: *Calling All Cars* was '35 or '36.

JASON: That jibes with my data. Since it was a West Coast only show, I don't have much information. Then you moved on to New York at the request of William Lewis to do *Columbia Workshop*.

BILL: Yes, but it didn't happen quite that fast. Let me go back a minute. At that time, when I was doing *Calling All Cars*, there was only one organization out of California that went to network. That was a sustaining show on Sundays called *California Melodies*, which Ray Paige conducted. Otherwise, all of the shows that we originated on the West Coast were only for the West Coast and were not heard in the East.

JASON: A great deal of the radio that you did have out there came out of Chicago.

BILL: Right. It was the heyday of Chicago radio. Getting back to Bill Lewis, he came out in '36. He was a heck of a nice guy. He had just gotten the job of program director for CBS. He was scouting out the territory. They were on the edge of coming out and establishing themselves on the coast. He was also looking around for people. He met me or I met him. It wasn't very firm. He said, "If you're ever back East, look me up." That's all I needed. I wanted to get out of there. I wanted to get into the big time. I packed my typewriter and left for New York with no promise of a job. I was only in New York a few days when Bill Lewis said, "I want you to go out to Chicago and sit around out there as rain insurance." I said, "What the hell is that?" He said, "Well, this is a Sears Roebuck show and it's going to be agency produced. I heard one of their audition records and I think we're in trouble. Sears Roebuck may be in trouble. If it starts to rain, I want you to take care of the leaks." So I went to Chicago and was employed by Sears Roebuck. I sat around while they were putting the show together. The advertising manager and I and some other Sears Roebuck fellows heard the audition the agency had put together. We all went to lunch and I was with one of them in the men's room. I said, "You know, I think it's starting to rain." He said, "Rain? I think we've got a cloudburst on our hands!" With that, I was appointed producer of the show. A very smart man from the agency said, "I'll accept him, so long as I pay him." So I went to work for the agency and did six months of the show out of Chicago, then returned to New York to start my work for CBS. That eventually led to my being producer of *Columbia Workshop* when Irving Reis heard the siren song in Hollywood. Actually, I was the first guest director on *Columbia Workshop*, just about fifty years ago in 1936.

JASON: I think you're getting to something I was about to ask you about, *The Fall of the City*. You were one of several directors.

BILL: That's right. *The Fall of the City* came the following year in April.

JASON: It was a very interesting concept for that time or any time. It was done in an armory. It had three different directors, including yourself, and some big name stars. It was an Archibald MacLeish story with a different approach than people were accustomed to hearing. It worked very well.

BILL: It was the result of a great script. MacLeish was interested in radio as a potential medium. He was a great writer. He wrote the script and he wrote it so well for the medium of radio. And then a great director, Irving Reis, saw its possibilities, saw the necessity for the kind of production he gave it. The action took place in a timeless time, at a placeless place, in a city not identified by location or historical period. The action was in the open plaza of the

city. There was no place in New York where you
could get out and broadcast in the open, but Irving
wanted to get that sense of openness that was subtle,
but there. He wanted the largest enclosed area he
could find and that was the Seventh Regiment
Armory. Then he had some problems about the
crowd. The crowd was actually a character in the
action of the show. This meant the crowd had to,
sometimes with moans and groans, sometimes with
cheerful laughter or shouting, the crowd had to
have a director. He asked me to direct the crowd.
Also, the leading voices were very important so that
they weren't just reading words. There were all
kinds of subtleties. The job of dialogue direction
was required for this thing. There was also a
tremendous acoustical problem and the overall
problem of putting it together and making it work.
So Irving assigned Brewster Morgan to be dialogue
director. Irving himself threw the cues and paced it
and so forth.

JASON: Wasn't Earle McGill the director of sound effects?

BILL: No, Earle was sort of a company manager. He took
care of details. It was so complex we had to have
someone like that. He was the other staff director.
Every staff director was involved.

JASON: You had a cast of thousands.

BILL: Not quite, but almost. The crowd consisted of
over a hundred, one hundred and thirty or forty
students from the drama department at New York
University. They were with me. We had a hundred
seats in the control booth because Irving wanted to
segregate us as much as possible. He also, for the
first time, had a little booth built in which he put
Orson Welles, the narrator, so he could be picked

up without interference from the crowd or the dialogue that was going on. It was complete isolation and that became standard for radio production from that time on.

JASON: Wasn't Burgess Meredith there too?

BILL: Burgess was one of the stars.

JASON: Some big names of the future and some even then.

BILL: That's right. The political ramifications became quite interesting. A year or so later, Vienna, fell on a Thursday. I went in on Friday and said I wanted to do *Fall of the City* on Sunday night on the *Workshop*. This was what MacLeish was writing about. The conqueror had come. The people have met their oppressors. Lewis took the idea upstairs and came back with a flat "No." He had talked to a vice president. I don't remember his name right now. His reason was that it would give the Germans bad ideas of what we thought of them. So, that was that. We never did do it when we should have done it. There is another thing about it that just occurred to me within the last few years. Two great things happened out of the German attack, fighter attack on the little city of Guernica in Northeastern Spain. One of those was *Guernica*, the great painting by Picasso and the other was, I said to myself, *The Fall of the City*. That must have been what inspired Archie. Before he died, I got on the phone with him. Every now and then, we'd talk on the phone. I asked him directly if Guernica had inspired him to write *Fall of the City*. He said, "Yeah, I guess it did, come to think of it."

JASON: One of those scenes that's planted subliminally.

BILL:

I'd have to look back on my notes, but he seemed to be convinced that I was right.

JASON:

A little later on, while you were still doing *Columbia Workshop*, you had a bit of a problem after coming back from a Mexican vacation, with your boss at the time, Ed Klauber. Remember that?

BILL:

I'm not sure it was Klauber, but it might have been. I came back from Mexico with a lovely, full black beard at a time, when I assure you very few young men were wearing beards, very few old men either as far as that's concerned. I wasn't back more than a few days when I was called into Bill Lewis' office. He was only two or three years older than me, a hell of a guy. He said, "Bill, the beard's got to go." I asked him why and he said, "It just has to." I don't think he ever attributed it to upstairs. He said, "The feeling is that it's got to go." I said, "OK. By the way, Bill, why don't you and Sarah come over for dinner Thursday night?" This being Monday or Tuesday, he said, "Sure, I guess so. We're not doing anything." I invited ten or so other people, I don't know how many, all over to my place for dinner. After dinner, my wife brought out some shaving cream and a bowl and a razor. I said, "I've been ordered by the program director at CBS to shave off my beard. I think it's a violation of my privacy, so I've brought you all here to watch the program director of CBS shave off my beard as he requested. All right Bill, take it off." He did and we took pictures.

JASON:

Later you did a special called *Open Letter on Race Hatred*. It drew a lot of interest from a variety of people.

BILL: The summer of '43 was a very bad summer for race relations in this country. In May, there was a terrible race riot in Detroit, which was much more serious than reported. There was a great deal of tension around the country in various other centers. I won't get into all the reasons, but the basic reason goes back to the Civil War. Blacks were needed then to work in the war plants, so they were being recruited from the South to come into northern manufacturing centers to help make guns and stuff for the war. Detroit was one of the biggest. Roosevelt himself called it The Arsenal of Democracy. Along about sometime in June, Walter White, who was the secretary for the NAACP (National Association for the Advancement of Colored People), came to CBS with the man who was then the head of AFRA (American Federation of Radio Artists), with a request that we give time for a show dramatizing, recreating the Detroit race riots. Wendell Willkie was to come on at the end with a statement on the subject. It was a very touchy subject. CBS decided they would do it. Walter suggested that they assign it to Bill Robson. Walter and I were good friends and he knew my feelings about the whole problem. It became a matter of "Yes we'll do it, provided that Robson does it." So I set out to research it. When I wrote it, it went through Paley's desk, because this was a matter of high importance. We had to do it right without antagonizing the white population, but to do it fairly in the representation of the black population. We finally did the whole thing on a recorded disc for Paley and I got called by the head of the programming department. We listened to it and discussed it. I made certain changes, rewrote it and recorded it again. This was on a Friday afternoon. We were to be on, on Sunday. Again, changes had to be made. I took it back to the drawing board and made some more changes. That Friday the manager of WBT Charlotte was in New York and Paley played the disc for him. He said, "You can count us out. We know how to handle our blacks down there." As you can imagine, he didn't use the word blacks. So that was one station lost. To be sure, that everybody else knew what was coming; Paley scheduled it for release for the early part of the day on Saturday. With that production, we lost the whole Texas Network, whatever that was, several stations in Texas. Finally, we went on at seven o'clock on Sunday. The only repercussion from the broadcast was from a newspaper in Detroit, which was associated with our CBS outlet. They were carrying the program. They were furious when they heard the earlier broadcast. There was nothing they could do about it because the ads were already in the paper. Here's a simple side aspect of that story that I always like to tell. I had my program. We were on the air at, let's say seven o'clock. There was a three-hour difference, three hours to kill before we did the repeat for the West Coast. So I had a problem. I had Walter White, who was the guy who got me into this, and Wendell Willkie. Walter had white hair and blue eyes. He did not look black at all. He was married to a lovely woman who did look black and he had two lovely children who did look black. They were all there. Also, his assistant, who was named Thurgood Marshall was there and the other fellow who succeeded him.

JASON: Roy Wilkins? Was he around then?

BILL: Yes. Here was a group of people and here was Wendell Willkie. I wanted to keep them together because people can get lost in the studios. In mid-town Manhattan there was no place possible where I could take this group to a restaurant, have a meal and just sit around. I lived right around the corner from CBS, so I invited them to my house for cocktails. They came. We had a lovely time then went back to do the repeat for the coast. During the time, Mr. Willkie sat in one particular chair and never moved from it. A year or so later, I was doing a show involving Mrs. Roosevelt and Mrs. Morgenthau, the wife of the Treasury Secretary. We had to go over the idea and the script. Mrs. Roosevelt was coming to town, so where could I meet with her and Mrs. Morgenthau, where we could do a little work away from prying eyes? Can't go to a restaurant and can't go to my office. So I set it up in my apartment. Then, with the sense of history that I have, I said to myself, "I'm going to seat Mrs. Roosevelt in what I called the Willkie chair." Well, Mrs. Morgenthau arrived first and sat in the yellow chair. Mrs. Roosevelt came in and we had our meeting and at the very end, with her rising up I said, "I've got to tell you something, Mrs. Roosevelt. I had a historical moment all planned and Mrs. Morgenthau cheated me out of it." Then I told her the story. She asked, "Do you want me to sit in it now?" So she sat in the yellow chair and made my day.

JASON: In spite of all your work for better race relations and civil rights, you were victimized by a McCarthy spawn called *Red Channels*, along with one hundred and fifty other writers, producers, directors and actors.

BILL: That's right. In his book, *The Golden Web*, Erik Barnouw called it "The Radio Honor Role." That didn't really come from McCarthy, but it was part of that whole mind set.

JASON: Not directly, but the impetus did.

BILL: The problem started with the Hollywood Ten. The presumption was that, if there were all these 'Reds' in Hollywood, there had to be 'Reds' in radio. A man named Lawrence Johnson, in Rochester, New York, owned a small chain of supermarkets. He started the ball rolling, investigating people and their shows. He attacked through the sponsors, for instance, a cigarette company. If they didn't get so and so off their program, his stores would not carry their brand. The advertising agencies turned chicken, the networks turned chicken and heads rolled. If your name came up you were not renewed. In my case, I was out of Hollywood at the time and Harry Ackerman, the boss in New York, called me. He wanted me to come to New York to do a new television show. When I got there, Harry said to me, just in conversation, "All right, just be careful. You're such a dirty Communist." I said, "What the hell do you mean?" So he unlocked his desk drawer and pulled out this book. It was *Red Channels*. He showed me the citations. I told him I never saw anything so ridiculous in my life. He agreed. It had such things as I was a sponsor of Artists to Win the War. I said, "You know, among the sponsors at that particular rally were Mrs. Roosevelt, Bing Crosby and many other celebrities." But of course, that citation in *Red Channels* came from the *Daily Worker*. That increased the Communist connection because they quoted it from the *Daily Worker*. It was all nonsense, so I gave it no further thought. I set about putting together this one hour, every other week mystery show. About three shows in, I'm taken off it and no explanation was given. With the atmosphere being what it was at the time, I realized what was going on. I called Paley's office and was told that he was out of town. Then I called Frank Stanton. Stanton said, "Can you get down here at one o'clock and have lunch with me?" I said, "I'll be there before." I went down to his office and told him what happened. He said, "The theory is that you are a Communist." I said, "Of course I'm not a Communist." He told me not to worry about it. That was the last I ever heard from him. I sat in New York for the whole time until my contract ran out. They paid me six hundred a week, but I was never reassigned to anything. When the contract ran out, I came back to the coast and found that I was not acceptable. I thought, all right, I'll use a pseudonym. I used my two son's first names. I was Christopher Anthony. That lasted three weeks until they figured it out. I was out of work for three years.

JASON: I have a copy of *Red Channels*. The names on the list are incredible, people who were trying to help people. Norman Corwin was listed. Ireene Wicker, the lady responsible for *The Singing Lady*, a popular kid's show, Howard Duff, anyone with any connection to the University of California.

BILL: That was another one of my citations. My name was on the masthead of *Hollywood Magazine*, which was published by the University of California.

JASON: On a happier note, tell me about *Man Behind the Gun*.

BILL: That was a great series.

JASON: Some big names were on it. Frank Lovejoy and Jackson Beck did the narration.

BILL: Jackson did all of the narration. This was an idea of Ranald MacDougall's. When he came over to CBS from NBC, he was just a young guy. He first did a series called *The Twenty Second Letter*, which was the twenty-second letter of the alphabet, "**V**" for victory. The title was suggested by Mrs. Paley, so that became the title. It was a pretty good series about the resistance to the Hitler regime in various countries in Europe. Then he came up with this idea for *Man Behind the Gun*. It was a natural. I could see that it couldn't help but make it. Our first show was on the RAF, in defense of London. It worked pretty well. We were still feeling our way. I had some trouble with people in my own organization. First of all, my narrator was to be Everett Sloane. During the meeting he said, "Bill, you're rehearsing six, eight hours on this thing." I said, "Yeah, I've got to recreate the war here in the studio. We don't have any of the sound effects. We have to make them up." He said, "Yeah Bill, but I've got a lot of other things. I just don't need that much rehearsing." I said, "Everett, I'm sorry, but I do." We parted friends. I grabbed onto Jackson Beck, who had never worked for me. We used him the next week. There was nothing wrong with it. He was pretty good and he got better and better. We had him do first person singular, second person singular, which in itself, was one of the things that made the show so compelling because we grabbed the listener and made him participate in the action. Jackson was simply superb. We had him in an isolation booth. He had his own world in there. The other problem was Bernie Herrmann, who did the score for the first show. He came to me after the show and said, "What are you trying to do, win the war with music? You want to win the war with music, get Wagner. He's your man." I told him I understood how he felt and we parted friends. Van Cleave was available, but he had never done anything like that before. Van Cleave was an

arranger. He became a splendid composer and
conductor of this kind of music. I asked him once
to do the "Marine Corps Hymn," scored as
Stravinsky did "The Rites of Spring." He looked at
me with a Cheshire cat grin and said, "Boy, what
an experience." So we had Stravinsky writing the
"Marine Corps Hymn." He was that kind of guy.
He ended up as the head of the music department
at one of the studios. When we finally got it settled
down, we had a magnificent group of people. For
actors we had Lovejoy, Billy Quinn and Art
Carney. After he went in the Navy, Art was
assigned to Governors Island, so he'd come down
in his sailor suit and play in *Man Behind the Gun.*
A rather interesting thing in connection with all
this, all along, as I said before, I had problems
recreating the sounds that I had never heard.
MacDougall and I went everywhere. We went
where the money is in Kentucky, Fort Knox. We
went around in tanks. I went out on the East
River in a PT boat. We flew in pursuit planes, but
all of this was in this country. So it was a difficult
production. In the first three shows, I wasn't
getting the perspective I wanted. These guys were
reading their lines and the sound effects were
spinning off whatever phonograph discs, six or
eight feet away and there was no separation. It
didn't make any sense. It didn't sound real. Then I
remembered what happens at a cocktail party. The
louder other people talk the louder you talk. So I
got eighteen-inch loud speakers, one on each side
of the cast mike. Those mikes were bi-directional,
not universal directional, so the speakers were on
the dead side of the microphone. All of the sound
effects were sent through those speakers, so if you
were in the middle of a gun battle, a gun battle
was happening in your ears. The actor speaking his
lines has got to shout over the sound that's coming

into his ears. That made the picture. That completed the bare similitude of *Man Behind the Gun*. It won a Peabody Award, Best Radio Show of 1943. The things that to me were interesting, that I look back on with love and affection, were those projects or those scripts that offered a challenge. Ordinary run of the mill radio is something I'm not interested in doing. I did a lot of *Romance*, for instance, but it was dull, dull, dull, until you got some sort of slant that made it important. I wrote one *Fort Laramie*, which was a long running show. I got an idea that intrigued me. I had a young second lieutenant from the fort fall in love with an Indian girl and we did the story of *Romeo and Juliet*. The boy starts out with these savages and a trapper, a squaw man and they stay out there long enough to start to feel different about it all. So now, you're talking. You've got something to talk about. That kind of idea is fun. It's not just playing soldier on the radio.

JASON: In other words, taking a mundane subject and making it into a thought piece.

BILL: Not only that, but saying something that is important. What I was saying in that particular show was coming straight up against racism in terms of the American Indian.

JASON: A reinforcement of *Open Letter on Race Hatred*, in a slightly different direction.

BILL: Another aspect of the same thing.

JASON: Of your later radio work, what might you consider to some of the most important?

BILL: *Man Behind the Gun*. But there were other individual shows that stand out and never get any mention. I meet people and my name means nothing to them until somebody says *Suspense*, but I did some individuals that I think were outstanding. Nobody remembers them, but they were important to me. One that you haven't mentioned, because it isn't in any of the books is *No Help Wanted*, which was a dramatization of the panic. I did it for the BBC. CBS wouldn't handle it. They didn't want to touch anything that had to do with the New Deal. This was a great show about the WPA. It was done with the WPA orchestra and WPA actors. The only people from private industry were myself, as director and writer, and Lee Stevens as conductor of the orchestra. It was to go at seven o'clock London time. At ten o'clock in the morning, which was five o'clock London time, I was called from Washington by the head of the WPA project. He said, "You've got to cancel the show." When I asked why, he said, "We're afraid, down here, it will give Hitler the wrong idea of our financial situation." I said, "Well, all right. I'll have to get in touch with the New York head of the BBC. I'll get back to you." I called the fellow right away, Felix Greene, who was in charge of the New York office, a wonderful guy. I called him at his apartment and said, "Felix, get lost! Leave your apartment. Don't go to your office. Get lost for the next three hours." He said, "What's the matter?" I said, "I won't tell you what's the matter. Just get lost." So I sat there in my apartment and every thirty minutes the phone would ring. "Did you get him? Did you get him?" I said, "No, I can't find him. I don't know where he is." So the word never went out that the United States government wanted the British Broadcasting Corporation to cancel the show. *The London Times* called it the finest drama ever to come out of the United States. Nobody ever knew it here. It was finally broadcast by a local station in California at Christmas time in '37. It was a splendid show. It was a great show and it brought another Peabody. There were things that I did for the government that can't be broadcast. The last show that I did for the government was the recreation of the Battle of Lexington on the *Two Hundred Years Ago Tonight* series, during the Bicentennial. That show, a single broadcast, got a Peabody. It's very rare when a single show gets a Peabody. Series get Peabodys. The wall of my office here has six Peabodys on it. More, I've been told by the Peabody Award people, than any other individual. This stuff was for things that would never appear on a show called *Romance*, for instance, the bread and butter earners of radio broadcasting. Those never interested me very much. I like to get into a situation where I can say something and take a point of view. On American radio and television, you don't take a point of view. I managed to skip through that after fifteen years of service to the government. I still took a point of view.

JASON: I haven't mentioned many of those other shows like *Escape* and *Suspense* and *Big Town*, because I know you've done so much other good work. There are a lot of people who can do the routine shows. You don't consider them as high points in your career.

BILL: There's one thing, in connection with *Suspense* and that type of show that to me is very interesting. I was the last director of *Suspense* and the things that I did were completely different from the kind of thing that was done in the forties. They would take a story like H. G. Welles' *Country of the Blind* and give it a whopping good radio production. You were there. I was doing all kinds of things, you know, like "Don't Call Me Mother," a mother with an incestuous yen for her son, or my show, "Headshrinker," which had two characters and one sound effect, a psychiatrist and his lady patient, whose love has finally gotten directed toward him. She suddenly realizes that she's going to kill him. At the end of thirty minutes she throws the gun down, says, "I won't do this anymore," and walks out. It was unthinkable. We got into the father-daughter relationship. We got into all kinds of things in that thirty minutes that radio would never have touched twenty years earlier. That kind of thing was fun. The problem was, 'What will I do next that makes any sense.' All I can say is, don't hold out any hopes for radio. It ain't coming back!

****

A giant in his chosen field is what he was. His indelible footprint is in evidence wherever you look in radio history, from its earliest days, until it passed from the scene in the form that made it what it once was. He did so much to advance the medium that it would take volumes to expound on all of it. No challenge was too great or too small for him to take on and accomplish his intended goal. His insight was enormous, always knowing intrinsically what to do in any situation.

Bill Robson was, without a doubt, a risk taker, always sensing just how far he could push the envelope and still come out on top. His list of credits and awards may never be surpassed. Sad to say, some of them do not appear prominently in any reference sources.

He died at his Virginia home in 1995, where the Willkie chair still stands as a testament to his genius.

FINALE:
THE MASTER

There are not enough superlatives in the English language to adequately express the gratitude we all owe, for the work that is still being used every day, of this magnificent man of letters. Media writer, producer and director, award winning author of prose and poetry, university professor and lecturer, he was all of those and much, much more. When I first thought of contacting him, I was not sure I could do it. He had been my personal idol for many years. In spite of having spoken comfortably with many other big name celebrities, I was afraid my tongue would fail me. As it turned out, that initial chat was far from our last. We had been conversing with regularity ever since, with our last conversation just three days before his passing. He was my mentor. He was Norman Corwin. I am not alone in my admiration of his great talent. Here are several unsolicited comments from folks who have worked directly with him.

****

"He did beautiful, esoteric and meaningful programs. Corwin is really an unusual, and I think tremendously important kind of talent."
Burl Ives—balladeer and Academy Award-winning actor.

"Corwin is one of a kind."
Bill Robson—winner of six Peabody Awards.

"Norman Corwin is one of the really genuine geniuses of radio, a brilliant man."
Vincent Price–fine actor–master chef–art aficionado.

"A man who will never be replaced."
Arch Oboler—prize winning playwright.

"No matter what he does, it is just brilliant. I love to be identified as having worked with him."
Elliott Lewis—writer–producer–director–actor

"He is more than a peer to all of us, intellectually and creatively. A remarkable, wonderful man and a close friend."
True Boardman—silent movie actor–radio and television writer and producer.

****

In order to obtain some additional insight into the life of the man himself, I spoke with R. LeRoy Bannerman, professor emeritus of telecommunications at Indiana University.

Roy spent ten years researching and compiling a biography of Norman Corwin. The result was an admirable book, *On a Note of Triumph: Norman Corwin and the Golden Years of Radio*. The date of our conversation was March 28, 1987.

****

JASON:	"I cannot chide my inner soul, I must confide, I've set a goal." Those are words from *The Undecided Molecule*, written by Norman Corwin. I feel that he has met just about any goal he ever set for himself.
ROY:	His story deserves to be told because I think he is undoubtedly one of the high spots of American Broadcasting. He's best known for radio's highest moments of creativity. It can be said that he brought to the medium, a literacy and quality that was truly outstanding. When thinking about broadcasting, only rarely does the medium produce a sense of art equal to other avenues of expression that we tend to associate with the high moments

that came to him so often, stage and literature and so on. I guess it's because radio and television have to pander, for the most part, to a mass audience. When a person like Corwin comes along, he elevates the medium to a tremendous height, making it truly an art form. He did so much in that respect. He didn't do it alone. There were others as well who contributed, but I think he extended their work. He brought his own originality, making it a remarkable medium during those golden years.

JASON: Some of those people, who should be considered during that era, would have to be Archibald MacLeish, Irving Reis, Bill Robson and Arch Oboler. Ed Murrow was there and John Houseman was on the rise as well.

ROY: I think that is one of the remarkable things about the Golden Age of Radio that it attracted so many of the leading writers and poets of the day that we don't find today because the medium can't breathe. That kind of creativity today is found in different areas.

JASON: I don't think too many of the truly creative people of today are willing to contend with the commercialism of radio and television.

ROY: That's another aspect of the golden age that we're talking about, the latter part of the thirties and the forties. During that period, it wasn't such a heavily commercial medium. There was a lot of time to fill. As a result, it provided the opportunity for artists like Corwin, Robson, Oboler and others, to participate freely in creating original material, unique material for the medium. It attracted such artists as Carl Sandburg, Stephen Vincent Benet,

Maxwell Anderson, people with that quality of literary work.

JASON: A great deal of Corwin's work was done in print as well as for radio, television and motion pictures.

ROY: He did make contributions in that respect. Very notable contributions, I must say. For the film, *Lust for Life*, he got an Academy Award nomination for the scenario he wrote for that. Then of course, he's written a number of books. He's done a number of stage plays. Despite this work, even the notable aspects of this pursuit, I think he made such a tremendous name for himself in radio, that his fame during those years sort of overshadows his contributions in later years.

JASON: The point I was trying to make is, that Norman always was, and still is, a workaholic. At times, when he really had no time for writing books, he was doing exactly that. I'm thinking specifically of when he was doing his *26 by Corwin* series, which was a weekly show. He did everything on those. He did the writing, the production, the direction and he hired the talent. It was a Sunday show and sometimes he didn't have the foggiest idea for the next one until, at least, the following Tuesday or Wednesday.

ROY: That's true. He would boldly enter into those series with no backlog of scripts. Then he had to work his head off to keep going and keep the series on the air. When you consider that the broadcasts those days were live, it was an outstanding achievement to be able to write those shows and maintain the quality that they were able to achieve in all those facets, usually twice, once for the East Coast and a second time for the West Coast. On a week-

to-week basis, it was breath taking. Corwin himself
said he disliked doing the repeats. He'd work
himself up get the adrenalin flowing for the first
one. It was very difficult to get things moving
again for the second. It was hard for the cast and
the rest of the crew as well.

****

We will come back to Roy Bannerman, but first, it's time to hear
from Norman. This is from August 5, 1986.

****

JASON: With your background, it's hard to know where to
start. Maybe we can begin with your days at the
Springfield, Massachusetts *Republican*. I understand
you did a little sports reporting in verse.

NORM: Oh yes, that was a little aberration I did one day. I
got a little bored with straight reporting, so I broke
into verse. It was not a regular feature, the editor
was happy to note, and the public too, I should
think.

JASON: What took you from Springfield to WLW in
Cincinnati?

NORM: I was trapped in a job that seemed to be going
nowhere, so I cast about for opportunities to break
loose from a small town in Massachusetts. After
considerable trying, I was auditioned for an
announcer job at WLW. It was called "The Nation's
Station." It had 500,000 watts. They would send
recruiting missions to New York City. I went down
there and auditioned and they engaged me. They
hired me and I had a meteoric career at WLW that
lasted two weeks.

****

Now we return to professor Bannerman.

****

JASON: Maybe you could tell me about how Norman's brothers helped him and how he helped them and about growing up in Boston. It was quite a team, the Corwin family.

ROY: It really was. Emil is the oldest. Al was the second. Then came Norman and Beulah, his sister came last. It was a very close-knit family and they tended to help each other. I think one of the best stories about this assistance comes from the newspaper days. Emil was working at the *Springfield Republican*, which was an outstanding paper. Norman got his first job in Greenfield and then Emil left to go to a job with the National Editorial Association in Cleveland. When he left, he made sure Norman knew about the job and could take over. It was a big promotion for Norman. When Norman left, he told Al about his spot being vacated, so Al took over from there. When Emil ended up as publicist for NBC, he heard about an opening at Twentieth Century-Fox and he was able to let Norman know about it. He was insistent to have him come up to a conference he had arranged for him. It was because of Emil that Norman got the job as publicity writer at Fox and that placed him in the center of where he eventually got into broadcasting.

JASON: And their father is still active as we speak.

ROY: He's one hundred and ten years of age. As Norman says, he's a minor celebrity in his own right. He's getting a lot of publicity, on his own right, for his longevity. He's a remarkable man. I've met him and I know him. As you said, he's still active. He would surprise you if you saw him. Norman calls him every Tuesday. They have a short conversation and his father always asks him, "Norman, are you keeping busy?" He insists that his son and all people keep busy. You mentioned that Norman is a workaholic. It's rather ironic that his father should ask him, because Norman does indeed keep busy and he's seventy-six years of age himself.

****

Back to Norman.

****

JASON: When you began at CBS, were you in any way involved with some of those early classics? I'm referring to things like *The Ghost of Benjamin Sweet* and more importantly, *The Fall of the City*.

NORM: I was at the network when *The Fall of the City* was done, but I was not involved. I knew all of the people who were associated with it. I knew Archibald MacLeish. I knew Bill Robson and I knew Irving Reis. Reis and Robson were two of the directors on it. To this day, it is a landmark production. I have very high respect for that script and production.

JASON: Is that where you met Orson Welles?

NORM: I met him later. Orson was on some of my programs. It was a pleasure working with him. As a matter of fact, I was broadcasting from a studio at CBS on Madison Avenue, directly below the one he was on the night of the Mars show. My program followed his program and, I dare say, it must have been heard by cats and dogs, whose masters left their radios on when they fled. That was the infamous Mars panic when people thought they were actually being overrun by aliens from Mars.

JASON: In 1938, you did your first original work on *Words Without Music*. The title of that opus was "The Plot to Overthrow Christmas." You met someone who would be a long time friend, because of that one.

NORM: Yes. The morning after that program was on the air, there was a knock on the door of my little office at CBS. There stood this handsome man who introduced himself as Edward R. Murrow. He was in from London. He was, by then, world famous for his broadcasts out of London beginning with, "This is London." He said he and his wife had listened to the Christmas show the evening before and they liked it. He just wanted to meet the man who wrote and directed it.

JASON: Didn't he say that it was the nearest thing to W. S. Gilbert that he had ever heard?

NORM: He said it had a 'Gilbertian spirit.' While I was not conscious of it, it was not my deliberate aim. I guess he found in it a kind of sense of British humor. It is Gilbertian, I suppose, in its *soussiance* and general rhyming.

JASON: It was redone year after year after that first production. You did something very intriguing there. You had a narrator and also a secondary narrator called *Soto Voce*, who explained what the first was saying. You did another piece for the workshop called *Seems Like Radio Is Here to Stay*. Didn't that become a sort of promotional tool for CBS?

NORM: They liked it well enough to make a privately printed and distributed edition, of one thousand copies in color, with various type styles and with original engravings. They sent it out to people in broadcasting and in government and to agencies, that sort of readership. It was a piece that I do not count among those I'm happiest about. It was an okay piece, but I don't think it holds up, in my mind, to some of the others.

JASON: You had so many to compare it to. There are always several names listed as the backbone of radio in the thirties. Among them are Archibald MacLeish, Arch Oboler, Bill Robson, Ed Murrow and, of course, Norman Corwin. That's pretty good company.

NORM: That is very good company.

JASON: Three of my recent guests on *Life in the Past Lane* were Vincent Price, John Dehner and Parley Baer. They all referred to you as a genius. Each of them worked with you at different times, so I think they should know.

NORM: Well, thank you Jason. I don't know what identifies a genius or qualifies one to be called that. I never felt that I was other than fairly well equipped to do the work I was doing and lucky in the bargain because CBS was a great network and gave freedom to its writers, at least this writer. Whenever I did a series, it was a big commitment of network time. They never said, "Can we read the script? How's it coming? Can we see the first twenty pages? Give us the titles of the programs that you are going to do on *26 by Corwin*." The first they heard of those broadcasts was on the air. What kind of freedom can match that on today's radio?

JASON: I've seen conflicting references as to what was your first regular series. I suppose it could be a matter of what could be called, a series. There are two usually noted, *Words Without Music*, in '38 and *Pursuit of Happiness*, in '39. They were entirely different formats.

NORM: *Words Without Music* was in the latter part of '38. The one you talk about in '39, *Pursuit of Happiness*, was not my original writing. I wrote a few things for it, but mainly, I directed it. That was a variety show. It was a sustaining show. The network took advantage of the fact that Hollywood stars, people of the theatre and concert world, were constantly moving in and out of the city. We grabbed them while they were there, prepared something for them and put them on the air. It was a variety show with Burgess Meredith as the emcee. In that way, I got a lot of network experience in musical forms and other things and I met many good people who became lifelong friends. That included Fredric March and Walter Huston and Burgess himself, quite a number of stars.

JASON: There were a wide variety of people on that show. People like Woody Guthrie, Betty Comden, Adolph Green, and even Danny Kaye.

NORM: It was Betty and Adolph's first radio exposure, Danny Kaye's as well. It had some historic value. I was going over some memorabilia not long ago and I came across some of the fees paid to those stars. They were around two to three hundred dollars.

Incredible! In that day, two hundred was the equivalent of two thousand today, at least.

JASON: That was way above scale in the thirties.

NORM: It was. I bought a Buick, an eight-cylinder convertible Buick, the most beautiful car I have ever owned, f.o.b. Detroit, $1500. That puts it all in perspective.

JASON: You didn't touch on *Words Without Music.*

NORM: *Words Without Music* was a program in which I took poetry, poetry of poets, I hasten to say, other than myself and adapted it. I gave it sound and sometimes music. I gave it a kind of dramatic setting without violating the spirit of the poetry or even the letter. The effect was that poetry, which had been a neglected art in this country and still is, suddenly reached a lot more people than had ever dreamed of it, or been exposed to it. As a result, it was a favorite program of English teachers throughout the country. I would get a lot of mail from them. They would assign their students to listen to it. It was a great pleasure to work with that material because, as I said, poets are neglected people in our culture.

JASON: It must have been a successful effort because at about the same time, Alfred Kraneborg appeared on NBC with *Fables in Verse*, a similar format.

NORM: I believe he did. You know, Jason, I'm a little ashamed to say that, while I was a good friend of Kraneborg, I never had a chance to listen to his program. I was working at the same time on mine. There was no time for scouting the opposition, so I didn't know exactly what he did on that series. I know that independently, not on that series, he wrote for NBC, a program on the planets. I think he used the Gustav Holst music of *The Planets* as a sort of thematic background.

****

Here is how Roy Bannerman described the origins of *Words Without Music.*

****

ROY: The story, as related in my book, tells how he came to do this. He just simply volunteered to do it. It was really an outgrowth of an effort he did back in Springfield. He had his first taste of radio while he still worked at the newspaper back there. He did a poetry program for the local station. When he went to New York, he offered to do a similar program for *The New York Times* station there. He went to New York due to his brother Emil's interest in furthering his career. Emil knew a publicity writer named Ted Church. Through Ted, Norman was able to take one of the programs he did for WQXR and do it for NBC, which was the network feed for RCA. This was his first appearance on a network. Strangely, nothing came of it. Ted Church managed to get him in to see the secretary of William Lewis, the vice president for programming at CBS. He persuaded the secretary to get Lewis to listen to one of the broadcasts from WQXR. One night Lewis was home nursing a cold. He did listen and he heard what he thought to be a remarkable broadcast. He called Norman to appear for an interview. That's how he came to work for the Columbia Broadcasting System.

JASON: There were some memorable programs that came out of *Words Without Music*. One in particular was "The Plot to Overthrow Christmas," which became an annual tradition. He did something that became trademark Norman Corwin. He wrote in a style that was strange to the ear, but in the final analysis, it was fascinating. He used couplets and free verse all intertwined in the same script. It was difficult for the actors because he wanted to hear the words, not the meter. Not an easy thing to do. Other programs told many of the secrets about what was going on in the studio during the presentation.

ROY: He loved the medium of radio. He could talk about different techniques within the broadcast itself. He would call attention to them, but in a very interesting way.

JASON: One example that fits that mold was a program from *26 by Corwin*, called "Radio Primer." He went through the alphabet and used each letter to describe a facet of the business. Here is what he had to say for the letter C.

****

NARRATOR: C is for Crosley. What is Crosley?

2ND VOICE: Crosley is a system of measuring radio audiences. If a program is rated at thirty points, that is very good because it means that twenty-five million people are listening.

NARRATOR: Twenty-five million is very good. If only seven million people are listening, that's not so good. You tried your best. We know how you feel. Too bad. If one million people hear you, you're talking to yourself. Radio people take Crosley ratings very seriously. Let's make a scene by consulting the office of an advertising agency handling a big radio account.

R. M: J. P.!

J. P.: Yes, R. M.?

R. M: What is our Crosley this week?

J. P.: Twenty-six point two.

R. M: What was it last week?

J. P.: Twenty-six point three.

R. M: You mean we've dropped a tenth of a point?

J. P.: Yes, R.M.

R. M: And the report before that? We also dropped a tenth?

J. P.: Two tenths.

R. M: I can't stand it! (*Door slams—gun fires*)

****

JASON: Another series that Norman did early on that was quite notable was *Pursuit of Happiness.*

ROY: The initial idea for that was from Bill Lewis. Things were brewing over in Europe. Hitler was on a rampage. Bill Lewis felt that we should have something a little patriotic on the air, reinforcing the American ideals. His idea was to do it, not with a heavy discourse, but rather to do it in a variety show. He enlisted Corwin to do the directing. It was interesting in that he could do almost anything on those programs. While he tended to follow the theme of patriotism, it involved a number of things. The highlight was *Ballad for Americans*, which was done with Paul Robeson as singing narrator.

JASON: *Ballad for Americans* was a story unto itself. That was Earl Robinson's play that he did for the Federal Theatre with John Houseman. It was more or less a flop when it was done there, but Corwin had him make some changes before it went on radio. He had him shorten it quite a lot.

ROY: Earl Robinson brought it to Norman. He sat down and played it on the piano. Corwin was perceptive enough to suggest that changes, to better adapt it to the medium, and also to improve the overall flow, were in order.

JASON: He also changed the title.

ROY: It was originally called *Ballad for Uncle Sam*. There are so many parallels in Norman Corwin's career. We talked about *The Plot to Overthrow Christmas*. Later he did a similar program using the same technique, called *The Undecided Molecule*. He used it again for *Lonesome Train*, which Earl Robinson composed. He made certain suggested changes for that broadcast. In a sense, he is a true artisan who can create for a medium, but he is also very perceptive in seeing what needs to be changed in other people's work.

JASON: *Lonesome Train* was the story of Abe Lincoln's funeral train and featured Burl Ives. On *Pursuit of Happiness*, we got one of our first exposures to Burgess Meredith.

ROY: Yes indeed. One of Corwin's concerns was how Burgess was doing his part as emcee. I don't know if you could call it a character trait or not, but Norman is very aggressive when it comes to trying to achieve perfection.

****

And now, more from Mr. Corwin.

****

JASON: In 1941, you were contacted by Bill Lewis to do a special tribute to the 150th anniversary of the ratification of the Bill of Rights. It turned out to be a bellwether of your career. It was called *We Hold These Truths*. There were some problems along the way.

NORM: Only logistical problems, in the sense that there wasn't much research data available to me. The anniversary dealt with the ratification, the 150th anniversary of the ratification of the Bill of Rights. Ratification was a whole process that had inherent in it, a great deal of drama because there was a big fight about it. I remember getting permission from the Library of Congress to work in the lower stacks after the library was closed for the day. The program was done under tremendous pressure. This was winter and the library was not heated, certainly not for a researcher looking up stuff at midnight. I caught the flu. That was a problem of considerable size considering that I had to go to Hollywood to do the program. I had to write it to begin with and then cast it, produce and direct it. It was a big, big logistical problem. Also, the program was scheduled to air on December 15.

JASON: That was the problem I was getting at.

NORM: Ah, of course. Remember, the year was 1941 and it was scheduled for December 15. On December 7, I was on my way to Hollywood on board the Santa Fe Chief out of Chicago and there was news that the Japanese had bombed Pearl Harbor. There was such an uproar. It was so upsetting to everything, including the broadcasting schedule that I had a question as to whether the program would go on the air. I wasn't quite finished with it yet. I was still writing it on the train. At Kansas City, I got off and called Washington to find out if there had been any change of plans because the President, Mr. Roosevelt, was to be part of the program. He was to be the last member of the cast, so to speak. They said they would get back to me. They spoke to the President as to whether he was going to keep that date. Roosevelt's answer was that it was more important than ever, that it must go on as planned. So it was done. It was an all networks program. All four networks carried it simultaneously. It had never been done before on a dramatic program, or perhaps, anything else.

JASON: There was a young actor who introduced Mr. Roosevelt that night. I'm sure you recall who that was.

NORM: Jimmy Stewart. Jimmy was a corporal in the air force, having dropped out of movies to enlist. Jimmy was my narrator and a spanking good one he was. Yes, he had the distinction of introducing the president on the air.

JASON: In 1942, you did another program than ran into logistical problems. Ed Murrow produced it and you wrote and directed it. It was part of a series from London called *An American in England*, simulcast by CBS and the BBC. What happened on that first program?

NORM: There was a circuit open between New York and London, a telephone circuit between CBS and the BBC, which I used for those broadcasts. Prior to the broadcast, we would talk about technical things. We did that, but I neglected to mention what the opening routine would be. On that particular program, I decided to open it 'cold.' The term used was cold, that is to say, without an announcement and without a musical theme or anything of the kind. My approach there was to grab the attention of the listener because, after all, it was a competitive medium. If you don't grab him in the first ten or fifteen seconds, he's going to tune to a different wavelength. So I opened with an actor saying, "Hello, Hello!" Jiggling the hook and saying, "What's the matter with this line? Hello! Are you out there?" My theory was that a listener, hearing that, would think that he'd stumbled across some big goof-up, some mistake in broadcasting. There's nothing anybody enjoys more, than being in on some technical foul up. By nature, we all eavesdrop, not in any mean spirit. It's just that we catch strange bits of conversation or strange noises or strange something else, and this was strange. Well, master control in New York, heard the jiggling hook and a voice saying, "Hello! What's the matter with this line? Operator, are you there? Hello!" They assumed the same thing that a listener might assume, that something was wrong, so they pulled the plug. The program was off the air. It wasn't received in New York. By the time they discovered their mistake, so much had been lost, that they decided not to come back to it. This meant that we had to do the whole program live the next week, all over again.

JASON: So, it was all because of a missed cue?

NORM: A misinterpretation rather than a missed cue. After that, you can be sure I sent all of my opening cues to New York so they would not make the same mistake again. It was human error by one man.

JASON: That's funny. I'm sure it wasn't then, but it is now.

NORM: It was not at the time, especially because this was wartime and all of London was blacked out. For that program to be received in New York at ten p.m. Eastern time, we had to leave London very early in the morning to get it on at four a.m. London time. There was a big orchestra and a big cast plus all the soundmen and engineers, a whole caravan of buses. We went to the outskirts of London. There was a place called Main Avail where there was a big studio. Don't forget that London was being bombed in those days. The whole thing had to be done in a blackout. There were certain lights in the studio. If they went on that meant there was a raid and we would have to go down to the shelter, suspend the program. So, it was not a matter of putting a needle on a record and playing it again. We had to go through the whole physical production once more.

JASON: At the end of the War, you did a short piece that I found particularly gut-wrenching. It was called *14 August* and was read by Orson Welles as only he could do it. It contained many powerful lines, but one that still engenders much thought in retrospect was *God and uranium were on our side.*

NORM: That was, of course, the end of the War. It was the

surrender of Japan. The 14th of August was the day of the surrender. That ended the fighting. On the previous May 8, there had been the end of the war in Europe, V-E Day, Victory in Europe. For that, I had time to prepare. I had the benefit of some weeks of preparation for that. That was an hour broadcast called *On a Note of Triumph. 14 August* was a minor exercise compared to the breadth and width of *On a Note of Triumph*, both productionally and thematically. I prepared *14 August*, literally over night, because the surrender came so suddenly. The surrender was related to the second bomb, dropped on Nagasaki. Then the Japanese threw in the towel. It was only a fifteen-minute program. I wrote it and cast Orson Welles and Olivia de Havilland in it. While it is nice to know that it is remembered and to hear you allude to it, Jason, it really was a small production compared to *On a Note of Triumph*.

****

And now, some parting words from Professor Bannerman.

****

JASON: There were so many classic programs that Norman wrote and put together over the years. There is no way we can mention them all, but there were two that must rise to the peak of the mountain. Those two were *We Hold These Truths* and *On a Note of Triumph*.

ROY: Certainly, in my estimation, those are the two high spots of his career. I've always considered Archibald MacLeish's *The Fall of the City* a true American classic, but I think the next two have to be *We Hold These Truths* and *On a Note of Triumph*.

****

Since we have talked so much about *On a Note of Triumph*, here and elsewhere in this book, I think it is appropriate to offer the opening of that masterwork for your edification. It was read by a fine actor, Martin Gabel.

****

> *Close your eyes and concentrate and listen. If you don't mind, there are some things we guys would like to have. First of all, who did we beat? How much did it cost to beat him? What have we learned? What do we know that we didn't know before? What do we do now? Is it all going to happen again? Can it be? In the interim, between making a toast and the drinking of it? That's the question on the lips of fighting men tonight. Questions from the areas of truth, insistent, footnoting the armistice.*

****

JASON: That show was interesting from another aspect, something that could never be done in today's world. It was put together and rehearsed and rehearsed and rehearsed and reworked in total secrecy, so that when the big day of victory came, they could throw it on the air as if it was an impromptu event. It had a tremendous impact.

ROY: Because this was one of the few times that Corwin was truly prepared. So many of his works were done at the last minute. He did manage to complete this particular one, only because he didn't know exactly when V-E Day would come. It's interesting to note that while he was looking at the events in Europe and, seeing that the war was going to end because the allies were moving up against Germany, Hitler was going to cave in eventually and perhaps quickly, Corwin was worried that he would not be ready for this particular broadcast. Then the gods were with him, to the extent that the end of the war in Europe was delayed by the Battle of the Bulge. That gave him a number of weeks to reprieve. If you know Corwin, know him well, you know he's never quite satisfied with anything. If he has time, he's constantly reworking.

JASON: Normally he didn't have time. A case in point is the piece he did for the end of the war in the orient. That came rather suddenly. He put *14 August* together overnight. He doesn't count it as one of his better works.

ROY: That is one of the remarkable things about the man. He was able to work against horrendous deadlines and to come through with amazing quality.

JASON: And work better with deadlines than without them.

ROY: In a sense, he is a perfectionist.

****

Let's give equal time to *14 August*, written overnight. The reader is Orson Welles.

****

This day is the father of all anniversaries. Men and fate shall be mixed together on 14 August down more years than you or I shall see. So say it tonight with saluting guns. Say it with roses. Say it with a hand *clap. Say it any way you want, but **SAY IT!***

****

JASON: There is a great quote in your book attributed to
           Norman. He said that, of all the work he has done,
           some of it was brilliant, some was very good, but
           none of it was really bad. That means that he was
           never completely dissatisfied with what he had
           done. There was always room for honing, but then,
           that could apply to almost anything. When starting
           on his level, it would be very hard to rise much
           higher.

ROY: A remarkable thing about him is that he survived
           despite his immense talent and his tremendous
           contributions to broadcasting. It's amazing that he
           was able to survive in the way that he did survive
           throughout his career in radio, to the extent of his
           being as independent as he was in the things he
           did. When you consider that nearly all of the
           things he did were unsponsored, but rather,
           sustaining programs for the network. That would
           be unheard of today. Of course, there were hints
           all along the way that the hierarchy at CBS was
           not quite satisfied with having him. If you recall,
           Douglas Coulter, after the *26 by Corwin* series
           ended, actually fired Corwin. He dismissed Norman
           because he thought he was not contributing,
           even though he was an amazing talent. CBS just
           couldn't afford to have this artist performing as an
           artist.

JASON: We both know that the media can be a very fickle
           boss. Today's hero is tomorrow's goat. What was
           interesting, though, was that while they were
           watching him so closely, ninety percent of the work
           he was doing was aired without prior creative

approval. He put programs on the air before
anyone read his scripts.

ROY: That's why I say that it is so remarkable that he
was able to progress. I suppose his career could
have ended after *26 by Corwin* if he had not had
the opportunity to do *We Hold These Truths*,
which was a magnificent success.

****

There are reams of scripts and other materials available, written
by this erudite master of the printed and spoken word. It is an
avenue well worth pursuing for entertainment and educational
purposes. Of the many books he authored, I highly recommend
two. One is a lesser-known work titled *Overkill and Megalove*, which
comes to us in both poetic and prose forms. The other is a must
read, *Trivializing America*.

There are many titles that may be applied to this winner of two
Peabody Awards, an Emmy, a Dupont-Columbia Award, an Oscar
nomination for his screen play for *Lust for Life*, and finally, a much
deserved Oscar in 2005 for helping to promote and produce a
documentary short subject called *On a Note of Triumph: The Golden
Age of Norman Corwin*.

There is so much to learn from this man. In this brief tribute to a
master wordsmith, I've covered but a few of his many accomplishments
in order to trigger your curiosity. The rest is up to you. I doubt that
you will be disappointed by what you find.

Norman Corwin was many things to many folks. For me he had
two titles, first mentor and more important, my dear friend.

AFTERWORD

A terrible thing happened between the completion of this book and publication. On October 18, 2011 we all lost a giant talent and for me, a good friend. On that date, at the age of one hundred and one, Norman Corwin passed away peacefully at his home in California. Having had my last conversation with him just a few days prior to that, I was, as much as anyone, stunned to hear that news.

I will dearly miss him, as will the many others he helped during his long and fruitful life.

I can best express my feeling toward Norman with a short poem I call *On a Note of Triumph and Tears*

****

When twilight comes and shadows fall upon my day'
I think about a wondrous man who showed the way.
He showed the way by telling me to persevere
When I had doubts about the work I held so dear.
My work on radio was zilch compared to what he did.
I always was his biggest fan since I was but a kid.
He helped me with his letters and his conversations too.
Those chats went on for years and years, it wasn't just a few.
We talked about his writings and his programs on the air.
We talked about the history of radio so fair.
For years, he's been my mentor, my hero and my friend.
I don't know how to take it now that all of it must end.
One day I may get over this. I know that that is true,
But for the moment, like or not, my mood is very blue.
So now, I must say sadly, my fond farewell to Norm.
We'll never see his equal, no one in any form.

With love and respect,
JASON HILL

BIBLIOGRAPHY

Bannerman, R. Leroy. *On A Note of Triumph: Norman Corwin and Golden Age of Radio*, Tuscaloosa: University of Alabama Press, 1986

Barbera, Joe. *My Life in 'Toons, from Flatbush to Bedrock in Under a Century*, Nashville: Turner Publishing, Inc., 1994.

Barnouw, Erik. *The Golden Web: A History of Broadcasting in the United States: Vol. 2 1933-1953*, New York: Oxford University Press, 1968.

Blanc, Mel and Philip Bashe. *That's Not All Folks!*, New York: Warner Books, 1988.

Burns, George. *Gracie, A Love Story*, New York: G. P. Putman's Sons, 1988.

Dunning, John. *On the Air: The Encyclopedia of Old-Time Radio*, New York: Oxford University Press, 1998.

Fein, Irving, *Jack Benny, An Intimate Biography*, New York: G. P. Putman's Sons, 1976.

Houseman, John. *Unfinished Business, Memoirs, 1902-1988*, New York: Applause Theater Books, 1988.

Keyes, Evelyn. *Scarlett O'Hara's Younger Sister: My Lively Life In and Out of Hollywood*, New York: Lyle Stuart, 1977.

Peyser, Joan, *Bernstein: A Biography,* Sag Harbor, NY: Beech Tree Books, 1987.

Sackett, Susan and Cheryl Blythe. *Say Good Night, Gracie! The Story of Burns & Allen*, Boston: E. P. Dutton, 1986.

Simon, George T. (Frank Sinatra–Forward) *The Big Bands, Fourth Edition*, New York: Schirmer Books, 1981.

INDEX

AUTHOR BIO
OF JASON HILL

Jason Hill was born in Stuttgart, Germany, and his family moved to the USA when he was eleven years old. After attending college in Illinois and obtaining pilot, airframe, and engine licenses, he returned to Europe and worked for Royal Dutch airlines as a co-pilot and flight engineer. At age twenty-three, he returned to the USA and flew many of the WWI and WWII aircraft for movies and television, as well as doing contract work for the forestry service fighting forest fires.

His eyesight eventually became too imperfect to fly, so he reeducated himself in the field of audio engineering. That accomplished, he then joined a recording studio in the Chicago area and rose to the level of vice president and production manager. From there, he went on to form his own studio with an international clientele. In 1980, he sold that business and went into radio work in Wisconsin, first as an engineer and producer, then as a broadcaster. He took early retirement in 1993.

Jason had taken the advice of his friend Norman Corwin and had been honing his writing skills in ways that enhanced his work in each of these careers. Since the passing of his dear wife two years ago, Jason has been writing every day, having completed two novels and a three-volume series documenting his interviews with people from the golden years of radio, film, big bands, and even the world of cartoons.

www.ingramcontent.com/pod-product-compliance
Lightning Source LLC
Chambersburg PA
CBHW070542270326
41926CB00013B/2171